# A DEFENCE

OF THE

# AMERICAN POLICY,

# A DEFENCE

OF THE

# AMERICAN POLICY,

AS OPPOSED TO THE ENCROACHMENTS OF

# FOREIGN INFLUENCE,

AND ESPECIALLY TO THE

INTERFERENCE OF THE PAPACY

IN THE

POLITICAL INTERESTS AND AFFAIRS OF THE UNITED STATES.

BY THOMAS R. WHITNEY.

NEW YORK:
DE WITT & DAVENPORT, PUBLISHERS,
160 AND 162 NASSAU STREET.

W. H. Tinson, Stereotyper. R. Craighead, Printer. G. W. Alexander, Binder.

# PREFACE.

THIS volume is written for the People in the United States, whether Native or Foreign, Protestant or Catholic. It affords a review of the five prominent elements in the political atmosphere of the present day viz., AMERICANISM, FOREIGN INFLUENCE, PROTESTANTISM, ROMANISM, and STATE SOVEREIGNTY.

The discussion of these subjects necessarily involves an analysis of the several phases of Republicanism, and especially of American Republicanism; as, Human Equality, and the innate right to Life, Liberty, and the Pursuit of Happiness. Also, the qualification of citizenship; the philosophy, effects, and abuses of Naturalization; the character and results of immigration under our system; the nature, uses, and abuses of the Right of Suffrage; the influence of Religion on the affairs of State, or Politico-religious Government; the Right and Sovereignty of individual States, including the social, legal, and political aspects of Slavery, etc. etc.

As cognate subjects of interest, the volume will present a view of the efforts from time to time made in resisting the encroachments of foreign and papal influences in our national policy, embracing a history of the rise and progress of the great "American Party," and the secret societies from which it sprung into existence.

The policy, purpose, and character of the American Party have been so constantly assailed, and so generally misrepresented by men whose political aspirations were liable to suffer in its success, as to demand a clear and impartial exposition of the whole subject, which should serve as an antidote to the errors of opinion set on foot by its enemies.

The object of this volume is to present such exposition, and afford a candid view of the dangers to which our free institutions are exposed through the deleterious innovations of foreign influences, the encroachments of the Papacy, and the recklessness of demagogues.

In this effort to forward the great ONE IDEA which constitutes the basis of the American policy, I have endeavored, by comprehensiveness and interest, to adapt the volume to the tastes, circumstances, and wants of the great mass of the American public—to encourage and fortify the friends of that policy—to convert its enemies, and to convince the doubting.

THE AUTHOR.

# CONTENTS.

## CHAPTER I.



## CHAPTER II.



## CHAPTER III.



## CHAPTER IV.



## CHAPTER V.



## CHAPTER VI.

PAGE

## CHAPTER XVII.



## CHAPTER XVIII.



## CHAPTER XIX.



## CHAPTER XX.



## CHAPTER XXI.



## CHAPTER XXII.



## CHAPTER XXIII.



## CHAPTER XXIV.

PAGE

## CHAPTER XXV.



## CHAPTER XXVI.



## APPENDIX.

# DEFENCE OF THE AMERICAN POLICY.

## CHAPTER I.

POPULAR GOVERNMENT—EDUCATION IN THE SCHOOL OF SELF-RELIANCE—FRENCH NOTIONS OF LIBERTY—CHARLES X.—LOUIS PHILIPPE AND LAFAYETTE.

"If humanity shows to the God of this world
A sight for his fatherly eye;
'Tis that of a people with banner unfurled,
Resolved for their freedom to die.
'Tis a spark of the Deity bursting to light,
Through the darkness of human control,
That fires the bold war-arm in liberty's fight,
And flames from the patriot, burning and bright,
Through the eye of an heavenly soul."

PHILLIPS.

MANKIND are entitled to just such privileges, social and political, as they are capable of employing and enjoying rationally. American Republicanism comprises this theory, no more.

By *American* Republicanism, I mean the system of government in use in the United States of North America, as distinguished from all other systems, forms and theories of Republicanism heretofore, or now in use elsewhere. A republic may be an oligarchy, like that of Venice; or, it may be a democracy, like that of Athens. American Republicanism is neither the one nor the other. The Venetian and the Athenian exhibit the extremes of what is termed popular government; the American presents the just and rational medium. Republicanism in the form of an oligarchy, imparts to the people little more of political or social freedom than an absolute monarchy. It is, in fact, but one step removed from that form of government. In a monarchy, the prerogative of government is monopolized by a class, whose only claim is that of birth. An aristocratic republic presents a similar phase, and the greatest liberty enjoyed by the people is the privilege of choosing their rulers from that monopolizing class. And even this degree of liberty, when granted, is confined to a limited portion of the whole people, because the right of suffrage is so hedged in and restrained under "property qualifications" and other hindrances, that, comparatively speaking, but few of the people ever reach the standard of eligibility. It is apparent, that under such a system, a majority of the people might as well live under monarchical restraint—for in an aristocratic republic the poorer classes are regarded with no more favor or consideration than they are under a liberal monarchy; possibly they are regarded with even less consideration.

It does not follow, however, from this fact, that the people of the Venetian Republic were entitled to a greater degree of liberty than they possessed. We must not lose sight of the maxim that "mankind are entitled to just such privileges, political and social, as they are capable of employing and enjoying rationally," and we have no evidence that the Venetian republicans had attained to the intellectual qualifications necessary to fit them for the rational enjoyment of a larger liberty than they possessed. Communities and nations far more enlightened than were the republicans of Venice, have tried the system of popular liberty, and failed. They have overturned thrones, beheaded kings, and exiled or executed whole aristocracies, without avail. Rational liberty has, in every instance, fled like a phantom, or an *ignis fatuus* before them, constantly eluding their grasp, and eventually leading them with headlong and fanatic speed, through avenues of horror and torrents of human blood, to disappointment, ruin, and disgrace. The Robespierrian republic, and the Cromwellian commonwealth, are terrible proofs in support of our theory.

But we have a later and fortunately a less fanatical, and less bloody witness, in the efforts of the French people to throw off the monarchical shackle. The first fruit of this popular revulsion was the overthrow of the Bourbon dynasty, and the expulsion of Charles X., and the entire royal family. The headstrong leaders of that revolution were eager to declare a republican form of government, but they were confronted by the Marquis de Lafayette, who silenced their clamors with the bold declaration that the people of France were not in a condition to enjoy and employ in a rational manner the delicate responsibility of self-government. Lafayette had been a pupil of George Washington, the Father and founder of the American Republic. He had devoted the energies of his youth and the fortune of his inheritance to the completion of American independence, during its struggle against the oppressive exactions of the British crown. He had shared the inmost confidence of the great champion of liberty; he had listened to his counsels, and imbibed his spirit. He had studied the history of the colonists, he had analyzed their spirit, and he had witnessed the establishment of their republic. He had seen Washington in the presidential chair, directing the tottering steps of the new-born nation, and his comprehensive intellect realized the great secret of its success.

Lafayette saw and realized the fact that the American republicans, so far from emerging by a sudden and violent step from the serf-like condition of monarchical subjects, had been prepared for the transition by the training of a century and a half in the school of self-reliance, and that, although nominally the subjects of Great Britain, they were, in the principal essentials of their character, free men, long before the blow was struck for national independence.

Their sovereigns rather encouraged than restrained the spirit of self-reliance, in the early settlement of the colonies, with the view to encourage emigration, and thus people the new territories. Even the first successful colony of Europeans, which, in the year 1607, settled in Virginia, under a grant from James I., of England, was vested with a local legislature, chosen by the people, and it also enjoyed the right of trial by jury. I say the first *successful* colony, because the colony established by French Huguenots at St. Augustine, Florida, in 1562, was broken up, and the colonists—nine hundred in number, murdered in cold blood by the Roman Catholic expedition under the monster Melendez.

For generations the whole lives of our ancestors had been the initiative of republicanism. Their remoteness from the parent government, whose authority was exercised more by tacit consent than by absolute dictation, so far at least as its effects were felt by the hardy populace; their exemption from the constraint of aristocratic intercourse; the local dangers by which they were surrounded and exposed, forcing upon them a community and equality of interest for mutual protection; their wild and romantic habits of life, tempered with an uniform reliance on Divine Providence; together with an innate spirit of resistance to despotic authority, inherited from their Puritan ancestors; all contributed to qualify the people of the United Colonies for a system of self-government, at the very moment which saw their national independence consummated. In their local affairs, each community of Anglo-Saxon pioneers, constituted within itself a limited miniature republic, and not a man among them had been taught to rely for protection upon any government, other than that primitive police which he had himself assisted in creating; and for personal protection his reliance was in the quick eye, the sure weapon, and the strong arm. These were among the important elements which qualified the early patriots of America, for the grand experiment of a popular government.

With these truths impressed upon his mind, Lafayette could not be blind to the disparaging contrast presented by his own countrymen at the close of the French Revolution in 1830. In a contest of only three days, the Parisians, inhabitants of a single city, had overturned one of the ancient dynasties of their own powerful nation. They had driven their monarch into precipitate exile; burned the throne of state in the public street, before the doors of the Royal Palace; dissolved the legislative department, annulled the judiciary, and left themselves without a government. The whole affair was "French," from first to last. It was an act of impulse performed by an impulsive people, without any immediate necessity, or any definite object.

The greatest and most immediate act of despotism of which Charles X. had been guilty, was the suppression of public sentiment by muzzling the public press; an offence of sufficient magnitude to arouse the popular indignation it is true, but one which in all human probability might have been corrected without bloodshed or revolution. The parties most aggrieved, however, were the editors and the higher classes, whereas the brunt of the fight fell on the workingmen. France is not like America, and the people of France are not like the people of the United States. In France, the papers are read, comparatively, by very few of what we call "the people," the masses, the men who give bone, muscle, and nerve to any nation. In the United States it is different. Here everybody reads the newspapers; the news of the day forms a very large part in the economy of the life of the American workingman, and the freer and bolder the press, the better he likes it. It would be safer to stop his bread and butter, than to stop his newspaper, or what is quite as important, deprive it of that interesting spice which the free discussion of political topics and public men imparts to the diurnal publication. To silence or muzzle the public press of the United States, would consequently come home with telling effect to the very hearts and bosoms of the working classes of the country. Abolitionism, the Fugitive Slave Law, and even the Maine Liquor Law would sink into insignificance in comparison with this, and it is questionable whether the known respect of our citizens for the laws and authorities of the land, would be sufficient to restrain the just and overwhelming indignation that would grow out of so arbitrary an act.

But, as I have said, it is not so in France, and it was not so at the time of the revolution in 1830. Editors and politicians were the parties most directly aggrieved by the act of their sovereign, and as the editors and politicians were not alone sufficient to cope with the government, they found it necessary to enlist the sympathies of the populace. This was easily done by careful conversations in the *cafés* of Paris; and by reiterating and recalling other instances of real or imaginary wrong, it was quite as easy to make the lower classes believe that their bread and wine, the two staves of a Frenchman's life, depended upon the overthrow of the Bourbons. Matters having been arranged on this basis, the populace took it into their heads to get up a revolution, and they had it; but when the work was consummated, and the excitement over, they were at a loss to know what to do with themselves. They had built barricades, sung the Marseillaise, and massacred the government troops to their hearts' content, and when the thing was done, and the lassitude of satiety had taken the place of enthusiasm, they were quite willing to settle down again under a monarchy. But the inspiring words "*Vive la République!*" uttered by a *sans culotte*, was the suggestion of a new idea. It sent a thrill like an electric shock through the whole Parisian heart, and the cry was echoed and re-echoed through the thronged streets of the insane city. It was at this turn in the tide of Parisian impulse, that Lafayette stepped forth upon the balcony of the *Hôtel de Ville*, above the heads of the excited multitude, leading by the hand a scion of the House of Orleans. A motion of his honored hand was the signal for universal silence, but again arose the cry "*Vive la République!*"—"*Vive Lafayette, le President Premier!*" Silence was again restored, and the aged patriot—the Father of *his* people, waving aside the proferred honor, in paternal tones addressed the impulsive populace. He told them it was too soon for the Republic; that the transition by a single step from a known policy to one unknown and untried, would be fatal alike to public peace and private happiness, and, in a word, that France was unprepared to enter upon the experiment of popular sovereignty. Under such circumstances, Lafayette, wisely temporizing with the inflammable element by which he was surrounded, ventured to recommend a medium course. He advised that a sovereign should be chosen by the popular will, and with a firm voice nominated on the spot, the man who stood at his side, Louis Philippe, Duke of Orleans!

This nomination was received with a shout of approval which shook the old palace to its foundation, and Louis Philippe was there chosen by acclamation, to be the "citizen king of the French!" Thus ended the revolution of 1830, begun and finished within three days in the city of Paris, and with this *dénouement* the people went back to their workshops and sour wine, fully satisfied that they had accomplished a glorious triumph over despotism! *

But time wore on. The good Lafayette had been gathered to his fathers, and the "citizen king" proved in the end to be anything but a republican. In admitting Louis Philippe to the sovereignty of France, the people, if they had any definite object in view at all, aimed at the establishment of a new principle in their government. They sought to do away with the old idea of "legitimacy," and to introduce in its stead the elective system. They were willing to be governed by a king, but that king must be one of their own choosing; they were willing to live under a monarchy, but the monarch must be one of their own creation. This did not meet the approbation of Louis Philippe. He had a large family of the blood royal to provide for, and although he made the most of his time in amassing a stupendous fortune during his reign, he had no idea of allowing the Orleans dynasty to expire at his death, if he could find it in his power to prevent such a catastrophe.

It was quite natural under the circumstances, therefore, that he should shape his course with a view to a legitimate succession, and in doing so, as a matter of course, he ran bolt against the most sensitive chord of popular sentiment. The press, in the most delicate manner, reminded his majesty of the events of July, 1830, and his majesty retorted by

* In derision of "legitimacy" Louis Philippe was denominated, with more of terseness than piety, "*Roi de France, par la voix du peuple et non par la grâce de Dieu!*"

restricting the privilege of the printer. Like the exiled king who, but a few years before, had fled from French territory leaving his crown behind him—but too happy in the reflection that his head was not in it—Louis Philippe committed the fatal error. He placed the press under censorship, and put a muzzle on the types. The corps editorial and the republican aristocracy again had recourse to the *cafés*, the suburbs, and the *vin* haunts of the metropolis; another revolution was gotten up, and in a brief space of time the "citizen king" found it convenient to follow in the footsteps of his illustrious predecessor and take up his abode in England. On the 26th day of February, 1848, Louis Philippe was dethroned, and Monsieur Lamartine, amidst the shouts of the whole people, declared France to be a *Republic!*

# CHAPTER II.

NATIONAL BEVERAGES—THE FRENCH REPUBLIC—LOUIS NAPOLEON BONAPARTE.

> "They were red-hot with drinking;
> So full of valor that they smote the air
> For breathing in their faces."
>
> SHAKSPEARE.

THE cheap wines of France have much to answer for. They have a marvellous effect upon the political temper of the people, and hence, upon the government itself. They have done more to foment revolution than all other causes combined. They exhilarate without intoxicating. They send a genial glow through the veins, and make men at once valiant, voluble and saucy; they produce a momentary chivalric enthusiasm, bold, daring, and uncompromising; and as the French populace drink these wines as freely as the Americans drink water, we should not be surprised when we witness the effects in *émeutes*, insubordination, and revolution. How different the national beverage of old England. ALE—strong, dreamy, and stupefying. Ale—"pale," or "nutbrown," "double X," "old," "new," or "half-and-half;" it is all the same in its results. As the Frenchman partakes of the character of his light wines, gay, buoyant, and sprightly, so the Englishman personifies *his* beverage in his rotund, sluggish, and contented habits. Give your Englishman, after a day's labor, his mug of ale with a bit of cheese, a pipe of tobacco, and a companion or two at the ale-house table, and he will care little who is prime minister or sovereign. Of all the beverages in the world to keep people quiet, I would recommend the ale of old England. In fact, the study of the subject of national beverages might form a profitable theme in the political economy of all nations, and especially of despotic dynasties. Cheap wines should never be allowed. Louis Napoleon may profit by this hint, and perhaps, all things else being propitious, secure a succession.

Every nation has its beverage and its drinking customs, as distinctly marked as its language, or its general habits. The French, English, and German, will sit the night out in social carouse, at a single table. The Irishman takes his "poteen" at random, or wherever he can get it. The Portuguese sips his port, with an elegant and courteous grace. The true Castilian demands the best of the vintage, and will utter his "*Gracia Dios*" over every bumper. He seldom usurps the prerogative of the low priesthood, by getting intoxicated. In spite of the prohibitary law of the Koran, the Turk drinks his sherbet. The Chinese are tea-drinkers, and for intoxication they resort to opium. In the Argentine *maté* is the national beverage. And in the United States water is the staple thirst-quencher, though we do partake of the good things of every clime, from the finest cogniac down to rye whisky of home manufacture.

Your German, now, will dispose of his wishy-washy *lager-*

*bier*, by the gallon, with little more than a physical effect for which he finds a ready antidote. Men of certain temperaments will get intoxicated on lager-bier; but most men, accustomed to it, will absorb a keg of the article in twenty-four hours, with no other effect than the inconvenience of repletion. The petty kings and princes of the Germanic confederation would have little to fear from popular ebullition if they would confine their subjects to the distinct national beverage—*lager-bier*. But the people, although they like it, are not satisfied with it alone. It is neither one thing nor the other. A man must drink an uncomfortable quantity to become either exhilarated or stupefied, and so they qualify it with an alternation of French wine. This may afford a key to the whole secret of the late Germanic revolutions. Had Louis Philippe contrived to change the beverage of France, from buoyant and exhilarating wines to plain English ale, and let the printers alone, he might have reigned to the day of his death, and left his son, the Duke of Orleans, a king instead of a refugee. But Louis Philippe was more of a man than a philosopher, and as a consequence he lost his crown, and his heirs their succession.

In February, 1848, France was again without a government.

There was now but one sentiment animating the French heart, and that sentiment demanded the establishment of a republic. Lamartine, the purest and soundest Frenchman of the day, took the lead in the formation of a provisional council, and immediately became associated with a few of the leading spirits of the revolution, including some of the best, and some of the worst men of the time. They declared the republic, and having constituted themselves a government *pro tempore*, proceeded to make arrangements for the election of a president.

Mr. Louis Napoleon Bonaparte was at that time a refugee, in England. In the year 1841, he had attempted, at an obscure town, to get up a revolution, under the prestige of his uncle's memory, on his own account, and failed. He was laughed at for his silly *faux pas*, and in order to restrain his youthful impetuosity, Louis Philippe shut him up in the Château of Ham, under a sentence of *perpetual imprisonment.* From this confinement he managed to escape in the garb of a laborer, made good his retreat across the frontiers, and took refuge in Belgium. Thence he made his way to England, where he remained until the overthrow of Louis Philippe. This personage now presented himself to the provisional government, and in polite terms, tendered his congratulations and his services. The congratulations were received, but the services were declined; and he was very plainly given to understand, that his presence in French ground was unnecessary, and perhaps, injurious, at a period so critical.

With all his follies and vagaries, Louis Napoleon had in his composition a spice of the old stock, and not relishing the cavalier reception he had met with at the hands of the "provisional government," he resolved to trim his sails to the popular breeze, and try his fortune under the new *régime.*

He had been a prince, an exile, a refugee, a revolutionist, a prisoner for life, and a roystering b'hoy in the purlieus of

Church street, in the city of New York, and he doubtless deemed it strange if out of all these vicissitudes and transitions he had not picked up enough of experience to make a statesman.

Proud of his imperial name, he was an aristocrat in every vein; but he *talked* republicanism as volubly as the most ultra "Red," and had sufficient tact to secure first a seat in the National Assembly, and finally, his election to the presidential chair of the republic. His term of office was to extend during four years, deducting the interregnum between the declaring of the republic, and the time of his inauguration. The election for president took place on the 10th and 11th days of December, 1848, and he was inaugurated president in the early part of 1849. The following was the vote rendered on this occasion.

For Louis Napoleon, 5,524,520. For General Cavaignac, 1,448,302. For Ledru Rollin, 371,431. For all others, 71,999.

France had now attained the topmost round in the ladder of her ambition. She was a republic, in the enjoyment of *universal suffrage!* She had a president and legislature chosen by the ballots of the entire people.

This state of things was not the result of an impulsive tumult. It was the calm deliberate act of reflection (if Frenchmen do reflect), and every man, when he voted for president, knew, or ought to have known, what he was about. There was Lamartine, and other good men, it is true, who would have been, either of them, as a father to the people, but the people chose *Louis Napoleon.* This was their first act in the republican drama—their *début* in the character of freemen, and if they erred the world looked on with indulgence.

The whole event was one of deep interest to the people of the United States of America. For the Americans, although determined to stand on their own ground, and to enter upon no "entangling alliances" with other powers, feel a direct sympathy in the efforts of any and every people who make the struggle for freedom, and popular sovereignty. When France threw away her crown, and burned her throne, in 1830, America rejoiced. She gave vent to her gratification, by public demonstrations, illuminations, processions, and addresses. The *fleur-de-lis* had been cast aside, and the tri-color mingled its folds with the stripes and stars of our own blessed Union. When, in 1848, France abolished the monarchy, and declared for the republic, the people of the United States renewed their congratulations, but when they elected Louis Napoleon as president, they saw plainly the forecast shadow of coming events, and were silent.

But France was content with her own act—she was gay, frivolous, and happy—she thought she had secured the boon of civil liberty. Alas! what a mistake. With a republican government, and the right to choose their rulers, the people imagined that nothing was left them to do but to enjoy themselves! Well, France *is* France, and it would be difficult, with all her enlightenment, to make her rational.

With all the glories of science which illustrate her name; with all the magnificence of her works of art, and the genius of her artists; with all her triumphs in literature and in arms, France is still frivolous, fantastic, and unreflecting. She has within her all the elements of grandeur and power, but not of rational freedom. England *may* sustain a republic—France never! *Subjects* cannot become good *citizens* in a moment. Men must be *educated* to freedom. The early republicans of the United States of America had more than a century of practical training in the theory of self-government, before they ventured on the bold experiment, and when they set about it, they did so with a will—a calm, fixed resolution, and they maintained that resolution through a tedious, unequal, and bloody war of seven years, against one of the most powerful nations of the earth! France fought *three days* in the city of Paris, in 1830, against her oppressor! Would she have maintained that fight *seven days*, had it been necessary to accomplish the object? Doubtful. When the people of France have the nerve to sustain a seven years' war with despotism, they will deserve a popular government, and be prepared to sustain and enjoy it. Till then their *émeutes* and revolutions are nothing but *fillagree*—the mere effervescence of the wine-cellar!

Under the circumstances in which France was placed in 1848, the election of Mr. Louis Napoleon Bonaparte, for president, was an appropriate choice, because the people having had their periodical amusement, gave little thought to the future. The new president knew the calibre and temper of Frenchmen better than they knew themselves, and as the title of president was but secondary in his ambitious fancy, he was not long in preparing to reach the primary object. The imperial diadem of his uncle, Napoleon the Great, glittered in his view, and he determined to seize it. He flattered the vanity of the populace, fêted the army, and restrained the legislature and the press, and just before the completion of his presidential term, he accomplished his notorious *coup d'état* of December 2nd, 1851, and in a single night *reduced the Republic to an Empire!* During that eventful night, those statesmen and general officers who were known to be attached to the republic from principle, were each aroused from their slumbers by a corporal's guard, arrested in their beds, and thrown forthwith into prison, from which they were soon after banished, by the imperial order, and sent to terminate their existence under tropical rigor at Cayenne. The public press was instantly silenced, or compelled, on pain of banishment or death, to sustain the despotic act. A few executions took place, and then the work was accomplished. No revolt occurred, but little resistance was made, no expression of popular indignation was heard. To those who have studied the peculiarities of that nation, this circumstance created no surprise. France had attained the acme of despotism, yet her people tamely and disgracefully acquiesced. The men who had so recently built barricades and poured the blood of their innocent countrymen through the streets of Paris, for no other purpose than to depose a king of their own choosing, and build up a republic, calmly looked on, saw that republic wrested from them to gratify the ambitious will of a single man, and had not, seemingly, the courage, or the disposition to prevent it.

Still, with all his audacity, Mr. President Bonaparte assumed an extraordinary virtue. He graciously announced that he would submit his right to the title of emperor to the sovereign will of the people, and that, *ad interim*, or until an election could be held to determine whether he should be permitted to wear the imperial diadem or not, he would exercise the prerogative of emperor *pro formâ* only. This course was rendered the more necessary, perhaps, from the fact that one or more of the leading powers of Europe refused to recognize the empire until the people of France had sanctioned it with their votes.

Preparations for an election were accordingly made. The right of universal suffrage was still left to the people, and they were now called upon to say, of their own accord, whether they would retain that august privilege, or cast it from them. The result proved that they were incapable of self-government. *The people of France voted away their own liberty.* That Republic, for the attainment of which they had fought so valorously when under a transient excitement, was now deliberately abandoned. The empire was sustained, and the *coup d'état* endorsed by an immense majority of the popular vote, and Louis Napoleon was accordingly crowned, and ascended the throne of his uncle with the title of Napoleon III.

Here we find the external and the internal evidence of the fact that the people of France possessed under the Republic of 1848, more liberty than they were capable of employing and enjoying rationally, and yet these very people, who could not govern themselves, when they come to the United States, assume to improve upon our system of government! They who could not maintain their own liberty when they had it, seek to instruct us in maintaining and improving ours! They offer us Red-republicanism, and talk of universal suffrage, as though France had been the cradle of liberty, and the United States no more than a novice in the science of free government. It is not unlikely, if we should give them what they demand, universal suffrage, they would, aided by the impulsive and irrational Germans, vote away *our* liberties as cheaply as they did their own! No, no; if Frenchmen prefer a despotic empire to a republican government, this is not the country of their desires, and before they seek to instruct us in the appliances of civil liberty, let them show us that they themselves understand the *rationale* of those appliances.

## CHAPTER III.

HUMAN EQUALITY—TAXATION AND REPRESENTATION.

"All men are created equal."
DECLARATION OF AMERICAN INDEPENDENCE.

AMERICAN REPUBLICANISM implies popular sovereignty. But when it says the people shall govern, it means that they shall govern to the extent of their intellectual and moral capacity. The spirit of our institution does not presuppose that every man is competent to govern or to take a part in the government. It does not presuppose that all are qualified to choose their rulers—or if it does admit this principle as a general rule, it reserves the right to determine the exceptions to the rule. Under this reservation three classes of citizens, native born or otherwise, are especially prohibited from taking any part in public affairs—even from the right to vote. This settles the question, that however, all men may be created equal in the language of the Declaration, they are not equal under the law of the land, and that inequality is the result of their personal incapacity to perform the responsible duties of free, honest, and intelligent citizens. The law declares them incompetent on account of either a moral or a mental inability.

To declare *equality* in the contracted, strict sense of the term would be to declare that mind and matter are identical. What is equality but stagnation? Equality is not found, and cannot be attained in the moral, social, physical, or elemental universe. Inequality is the source of action; action is the source of life, thought, fruition. It is attraction and repulsion that cause the electric particles to vibrate, and the needle to point the north. Equalize the attractive power, and the compass becomes inert, the chemistry of vegetation is no more, and the principle of life ceases to act. It is on the unequal ground that the pure stream meanders, or rushes onward in the full vigor of vitality; but in the equilibrium of the stagnant pool the waters become fetid and repulsive.

If the earth were an even plain, how the eye would weary over it! Draw the misty vapors for ever from the sky, and it would lose its grandeur. Let the hues of the flowers be equalized into a single tint, and there would be no attraction to please the sense of the optic nerves. So is it in the moral and social world. It is the inequality in desires, necessities, taste, genius, station, talent, power, and mind, that calls forth the energy of man, and causes him to invent, achieve, amass, adorn, aspire, or toil, and so gives zest to life, and impetus to the on-rolling car of progress.

Establish equality in these things, and a moral paralysis would pervade the earth. The perfection of the universal system is the result of superior and subordinate inequalities, the attractive power of the superior orbs controlling the motion of the inferior, thus consummating the harmonious equilibrium of the great whole, and evincing the omnipotent and perfect wisdom of Almighty God.

To argue, therefore, that the founders of the Republic asserted a contrary theory, or that they meant to be understood as declaring all men "equal" in intelligence, genius, or morals; that all men are equally competent for self government or even self protection, were but to insult *their* intelligence and degrade them in the eyes of the world.

The classes to which I have alluded as forbidded to participate in the government, are the idiots, the insane, and the convicted felons. The first two classes are declared to be *non compos mentis*, or mentally incompetent; the last is declared to be morally incompetent; and here we find the great principle laid down, and universally recognized, that in order to exercise the full functions of a free citizen, the individual must be both mentally and morally competent to exercise those functions honestly and intelligently. I say *both*, because the law of restraint applies to those in whom *either* of these disqualifications may be found. The felon may be a man of superior mental ability and refinement of education, yet he is disqualified in consequence of moral imperfections. On the other hand, the idiot or the lunatic may possess the highest moral qualities, yet they are disqualified on account of their mental imbecility.

It is clear, therefore, that the letter and the spirit of our institutions both require, that in order to exercise the full political prerogatives of a citizen, the individual must be of sufficient intelligence, and of a mind sufficiently well-balanced, to understand clearly the nature and effect of his political acts; and he must, *also* possess a moral sentiment, sound enough to ensure the exercise of his prerogative to honest purposes.

Thus far the law performs its duty to the community, and no honest and sane man will question the wisdom of such a course of policy. If an idiot were permitted to vote, and should be told to attend the poll at an election, and vote for governor, or legislator, or town officers, he would answer with a vacant stare, and, utterly unable to comprehend the meaning of the direction, would turn aside and walk away. He would not vote, for the simple reason that he could not understand either the process of voting, the motive of the vote, or the effect that it would produce. But he may be induced to vote, notwithstanding the darkness that encompasses his mind. The act of voting is a mere physical act, and the idiot may be led, or persuaded, step by step, by some person known to him, to perform that physical act, and with his own hand present a ballot to the inspector of the election, and that ballot placed in the box, may turn the scale of an entire canvass, and thus an intelligent expression of the voice of the people would be lost, and the object of the election, which is to get that intelligent expression, defeated. In this case the idiot is but an automaton, a machine wrought upon by the person who led him to the poll, and who placed the ballot in his hand—a passive instrument in the hand of the demagogue.

An insane man brought forth to exercise this delicate privilege, would, on the other hand, be governed by the opinions of no man—no set of men. He would have a policy of his own. His visionary imaginings would frame a new theory of government. He would see, in the old, time-honored system of the republic, a thousand errors, and his oblique fancy would suggest as many reforms, adapted to the vagaries of his own distempered organs. He would select his own candidates, make out his own ticket, and vote for men, who, first of all, would pledge themselves to throw open the doors of all lunatic asylums, and set their inmates free. He would be, *par excellence*, your advocate of universal liberty. What glowing speeches he would make from the rostrum against the despotism of society! What tropes, what metaphors, what thrilling eloquence he would employ to sway the souls of an impulsive multitude!

The convicted felon, the man void of moral sentiment, one who is impatient of all legal restraint, and the foe of social government; one whose selfish propensities absorb the respect due to wholesome authority—such an one would employ his political privileges in attempts to overthrow law and order. If an unprincipled candidate should, by any possibility, be presented for the suffrages of the people, that candidate would be his choice; and inasmuch as that society demands the enactment of laws, he would seek the attainment of such laws as would best suit his nefarious plans. If in his power, he would punish virtue, and reward vice. His policy would be a return to first principles, where might takes the place of right, and the weak have no protection against the strong.

These three several classes are in the spirit and the letter of our laws, declared incompetent for the performance of any public duties, and are denied the privilege of political suffrage; yet they are all citizens in the common acceptance of the term, and it is not improbable that all of them pay direct taxes to the government. The idiot, the lunatic, and even the felon, may be all men of property, and if so, their property is placed under taxation precisely the same as the property of those who exercise the highest and the freest political privileges. It does not follow, however, that they are taxed without representation, merely because they are not permitted to choose their representatives. If they were taxed as individuals, or as classes, apart from the community at large: if the idiots were taxed as idiots, the lunatics as lunatics, and the felons as felons, this objection would hold good against the law. But it is not so. Taxation in this country is made equal. The men who impose the taxes are among those who pay the taxes, and they are compelled to tax themselves in the same ratio that they tax others, so that the party who does not vote for representative is protected through the interest of the representative himself. No man will impose on himself a severe tax merely for the sake of being severe on other men, but, on the contrary, out of respect for his own purse, he will make the burden of taxation as light as may be consistent with the public necessities. Thus, the party who does not vote, is protected against oppression, and thus his property and his interests are as perfectly represented and guarded, as the property and interests of any individual in the community. If the party who does not vote is by any inadvertence subjected to unjust exaction on the part of the government, the men who do vote, and the men who make the laws are subjected to the same exactions in every respect. This fact should be a source of consolation to those strong-minded women, who claim that their sex should be permitted to vote because those of them who are so fortunate as to possess property, are required to pay taxes to the local government.

Thus the broad principle, that taxation is entitled to representation, is fully carried out by the American Republican system. It is the property, not the person, that is taxed; and all property is represented in legislation. Besides, every dollar of tax paid into the public treasury, is appropriated, directly or indirectly, to the protection, development, or improvement of the property itself; the improvement of harbors, and the protection of commerce generally:—the building and maintenance of public roads, the removal of obstructions from navigable streams; the making, repairing, cleaning, and lighting of streets; the support of a police, the guardianship of public health, the support of a judiciary, the removal of criminals, the maintenance of the poor, and the education of the young, are all the fruits of our healthy and equable system of taxation. These are tangible and profitable results, which every man can witness, and which all must appreciate. Their beneficial effects fall alike upon the voter and the non-voter. They are the fruits of taxation in a legitimate sense, and the idiot, or the insane contributor, though he may not realize the fact, is pecuniarily as much the recipient of those fruits, as he who chooses the lawgiver.

How different the character and objects of that species of

taxation against which the fathers of our Republic rebelled! In that case, neither the person nor the property were represented. The money demanded by the parent government, instead of being appropriated to the necessities of the communities who paid the taxes, was carried off to a distant continent, and employed in the support of a regal tyrant, and a voluptuous and profligate aristocracy. They who paid the taxes reaped no benefit therefrom, either directly or indirectly, and those who imposed them, bore no share of the burden. There was taxation not only without representation, but without a visible motive or necessity. The infliction was purely mercenary, and at length the oppressed colonists justly and manfully resisted and overcame it.

Our system of government then, while it recognizes and sustains the principle that taxation is entitled to representation, also recognizes the principle that representation does not involve, invariably, the right of suffrage; or, in other words, that property may and must be represented, even though the owner of the property, under certain circumstances, is not permitted to choose the representative.

Having recognized and established the principle, that there does exist in the human family a mental and moral inequality, and that owing to this inequality, certain classes of citizens are unfranchised, it follows, as a necessary consequence, and as due to consistency and sound justice, that *all* who are mentally or morally incompetent, should occupy the same ground, without regard to the causes of their incompetency. As the idiot is held disqualified from exercising the right of suffrage, because he cannot comprehend the full force, responsibility, and extent of the vote, so any man of like incapacity should be debarred from voting, whether he be an idiot, or only an ignoramus. The latter is, in fact, of the two, most likely to make a mischievous use of the suffrage; because, with all his ignorance, he possesses all the passions of humanity, which the idiot does not possess to any practical degree. These passions may be inflamed by designing men, to a pitch bordering on insanity, and thus whole classes of frantic enthusiasts may be marshalled by thousands to the polls, and with their unreflecting votes bear back the calmer judgment of the nation. An appeal to a single prejudice, like a spark of fire in a magazine, is alone sufficient to produce the direst results. It produces a flame more easily kindled than subdued, and the demagogue who fans it into life, may deem himself happy if he burns not in the general conflagration. Especially does this view of our subject apply to the millions of illiterate foreigners, who come to us with their home prejudices (both religious and secular), so sternly fixed, that neither time nor association can ever efface them.

# CHAPTER IV.

## LIFE, LIBERTY, AND THE PURSUIT OF HAPPINESS.

"We hold these truths to be self-evident: That all men are created equal: That they are endowed by their Creator with certain inalienable rights, among which are Life, Liberty, and the pursuit of happiness."

DECLARATION OF INDEPENDENCE.

AMERICAN REPUBLICANISM recognizes the principle that all men are *created* on a moral, political, and social equality; but it does not recognize the principle that all men reach the condition of manhood, having within them the same moral, political, and social capacities. To declare that would be to declare a palpable absurdity. It would be to declare that the man whose intellectual faculties had been expended on the mixing of mortar, or the carrying of a hod, is competent to administer the affairs of a nation, or superintend the classic studies of Cambrige or Yale. It would be no less than saying that the idiot is fit for a statesman, the rogue for a preacher, or the ignorant man for a preceptor.

Again, it recognizes the principle that all men are endowed by their Creator with certain inalienable rights, among which are "life, liberty, and the pursuit of happiness." But is there no qualification to this recognition? Are we to construe the sentiment literally, and be governed in our intercourse with mankind by the simple letter of the text? If so, it is apparent that many of our most wholesome laws, laws enacted for the protection of society, and of individuals from violence and outrage, are in themselves a violation of the inalienable rights of man. Among those rights is the right to live; now, if that right is unqualified, by what authority does society take away the life of the murderer? How are individuals justified in taking the life of a fellow-being in self-defence? Both of these acts are held justifiable by the laws of Christendom and by public sentiment everywhere, and yet the right to live is inherent, and, in a general sense, inalienable with all God's creatures, including the whole animal kingdom of which man is the chief member. But this right may be forfeited, and therein we find the exception to the general rule. This forfeiture of the right to live may be voluntary or it may be involuntary. With man under the influences of civilization it is at all times a *voluntary* act; because the law does not demand his life until he has voluntarily committed an act, the penalty of which he knows to be a forfeiture of the right to live. The *involuntary* forfeiture is where life is given up to serve some useful or necessary purposes to the living. All things are created for some object beyond the mere enjoyment of life. If this be not so, why is it that we find in every human breast the innate sense of a future state? There is not a barbarian on the face of the globe, nor a civilized man living, who has not (coupled with the possession of the natural faculties of his species), an indistinct but positive idea of a spiritual existence, and the realization of an overruling, superhuman power; and this instinctive impression, apart from the testimony of revealed religion, is, in itself, sufficient evidence of a preordained purpose in human existence beyond the mere necessities of physical life. But besides this spiritual purpose, the mere instincts of animal existence bear almost conclusive testimony that one of the purposes of animal life is the sustenance of life in other bodies. For example: the animalcula supplies food to the insect, the insect to the subordinate classes of birds and beasts, the subordinate birds and beasts to the superior animals, and all affording nourishment to man, who, by the supremacy of his reasoning faculties, is enabled to bring all other animals into subjection to his appetite and his will. The law of nature, and of nature's God, seems to have ordained this as a living principle of the universe, and where a life is given up under this law, it may be designated as the involuntary forfeiture of the right to live, because the right is alienated; it ceases when the necesities of others demand its sacrifice.

But throughout the entire economy of this principle it is perceivable that the inferior in power and intelligence always become the prey of the superior—the inherent, inalienable right continues only until the creature has reached a condition to fulfill the object of its existence, whether that object be to afford food for others, or otherwise. The silkworm weaves her cocoon about her, and afterwards becomes a butterfly. In the butterfly transition she lays her eggs for a future family of worms, and then dies. The right to live extends only to this object, and when it is accomplished the involuntary forfeiture takes place. So is it with man. The physical creature is but the embodiment of a spiritual existence. It is placed on earth for a double purpose; the first of which is the preparation of the spirit for a future existence, and the second is the propagation of new creatures for like purposes; and when these objects have been accomplished, or when the physical machine is worn out with age, the involuntary forfeiture occurs, and the creature passes out of its earthly existence.

But this inherent right to live may be violated. Life may be taken and destroyed without any useful or necessary demand, and when this occurs among civilized men, it is met with the Almighty law of retributive justice. "An eye for an eye, and a tooth for a tooth." "Whoso sheddeth man's blood, by the hand of man shall his blood also be shed."

This is the Divine law, and it cannot be supposed that the framers of the Declaration of American Independence intended to ignore or abrogate it, when they declared that the right to exist is inalienable in the human race. The philosophy of American Republicanism, therefore, while it recognizes "life" as one of the inalienable rights of man, admits also the exception, and takes the life of man under the voluntary forfeiture, whenever the good of society demands it.

Personal Liberty is another "inalienable right," which in the language of the Declaration of Independence pertains to all men. By this, I assume, is meant the liberty of conscience, the liberty of opinion on all subjects, and the free exercise thereof, together with the unabridged right to speak, proclaim, write, and publish whatever sentiments the individual may entertain, whether in politics, religion, or ethics ; the responsibility of an improper and unjustifiable use, or *abuse* resting on the party who enjoys it. The word was employed by the framers of the " Declaration," in a *political* sense, and as the antipodes of popular submission to a tyrannical government. It is a reiteration of the *vox populi, vox Dei*, or, in other words, that by divine authority the voice of the people should be made paramount in the government.

Liberty may be rational, or it may be licentious ; and it must not be denied that the broad use and interpretation of the word has led thousands to misconstrue its legitimate intent as applied by the fathers of the Republic to civil and religious freedom. It can never be supposed that in proclaiming Liberty as one of the inalienable rights of all men, the Continental Congress meant to promulgate the idea that all men possess the irrefragable right to do as they please at all times, and under all circumstances. A construction like that would imply the absence of a necessity of all legal restraint, and the consequent disjointure of the whole framework of society. Under such a theory there would be neither public nor private safety. Chaos would usurp the place of order, and mankind, from the very instinct of self-preservation, would be compelled to return to the feudal custom, each man holding his possessions and his life by the sword. Liberty to this extent would be irrational, and would lead to the most extravagant licentiousness. It is apparent, therefore, that this feature of our organic structure must be construed with such qualification as will render it consistent with propriety and common sense. It must be construed in its most dignified aspect, precisely as they intended to present it—as affording to mankind the enjoyment of intellectual freedom, and political and social equality to the extent of the capacity and adaptedness or fitness of the individual. In this aspect, Liberty secures to all men the noblest and most precious boon that human wisdom and benevolence can bestow upon the human race. It is the liberty of the soul. It affords to man an unrestrained opportunity to exercise the inalienable right of a rational, thinking, responsible being, without accountability to any politico-religious despotism, whether monarchical, or hierarchical. His conscience is unfettered. He is at liberty to embrace the theology of nature, or the theology of revelation, according to his ability, his instinct, or his judgment, holding himself responsible for his opinions to God and his conscience alone. This is one of the great fruits of Liberty as enunciated through the medium of American Republicanism.

But as the right of existence may be forfeited to the good of society, so it is with the *natural* right to personal liberty which God has conferred on all his creatures. If this clause in our national Bill of Rights were construed literally, society would possess no moral or acknowledged power to restrain the personal freedom of any man. The thief, the burglar, and the felon would go at large and commit their depredations with impunity; the relations of master and servant would cease, and all wholesome authority would be at an end. A strict construction of this clause would cripple the resources of human intellect and enterprise. It would reverse the maxim that "knowledge is power," because knowledge, in its true extent, is acquired by the comparative few, and without legal restraint, the intelligent few would be overcome and held under subjection to the obtuse and ignorant many.

One of the most impressive lessons in nature is found in that undeviating law which gives to mind the supremacy over matter, and every violation of that law disturbs the harmony and equilibrium of the intellectual world. Man is but one in the great family of animal creation, and being superior in intelligence, he brings all others into subjection. The horse, the ox, the dog, and even the physically powerful and sagacious elephant, are all made subservient to the superior intelligence of man, and he compels them all to contribute their material resources to his convenience, comfort and safety. Yet all these are endowed by their Creator, intrinsically, with as perfect right to life and liberty as man himself.

Who gave to *man* authority to lasso the noble steed as he bounds with the speed of the wind and the grace of the antelope, over the fertile prairies and broad pampas, and bind him down to a life of toil? Who authorized *man* to entrap and enslave the majestic elephant? Who commissioned *man* to place the galling yoke upon the neck of the patient ox, and chain him to the drudging plough? Who, but the Almighty dispenser of intelligences? Who, but God himself? And does the prerogative of intelligence end here? Is the animal, man, exempt from the operation of the universal law of nature? By no means. We see it demonstrated in every phase of society—superior intelligences controlling the inferior. We witness it in the relation of parent and child, master and laborer, the officer and his soldiers, the captain and his crew; the master and his slave. It is visible in the mere existence of the social classes, and palpable in the diversified races of the human family. The higher the intelligence, the nearer is the approach to civilization, and the further from civilization, the less do we find developed the faculty for self protection. The "Bushmen" of Southern Africa, for example, approach so near the brute in the scale of intelligence as to be incapable of erecting even the rudest shelter from the torrid sun. In the language of Governor Janssens "the burning sky is their canopy and the scorching sand their bed."

This characteristic argues not merely the want of education, but even an inferior *instinct*, to say nothing of *reason*, because, with the possession of hands, the readiest instruments of construction, the simple law of self preservation would suggest the erection of artificial shelter. One of these men might, it is true, by coercion, be taught to erect a hovel, precisely as a dog may be taught to dance, but it does not follow from this that either the man or the dog could be brought to understand the principles of civilized social government. We are constrained, in our reflection on these truths, enunciated by divine authority, to confess, that the framers of the Declaration of Independence never intended to utter an absurdity so glaring as that which a strict literal construction of their words would imply. Men are created equal in all natural, social and political rights, and those rights are to be enjoyed and exercised in proportion to the natural social and political faculties of the individual. This is the inalienable right to liberty as set forth in the organic charter of American Republicanism.

"THE PURSUIT OF HAPPINESS," in the words of the Declaration of Independence, is among the "inalienable" rights of man. This sentiment may be construed literally, although happiness, like knowledge, is sometimes pursued under difficulties—and it cannot be denied that it often outruns its pursuers. Still the right of pursuit is inalienable—it cannot be taken away, and the exercise of that right is universal. The miser seeks it in his accumulating hoard—the bride sees it in the perspective of domestic felicity—the prisoner in his cell pursues it in the prospect of release, and the dying hope for it in a future existence. But the declaration of this right as here set forth, carries with it a broader, deeper and more ennobling construction. It would be no less than a barbarous mockery to deprive a human being of all the elements of happiness, and then say to him, "You have *the right* to seek for happiness." It would be like binding a starving man, placing a loaf of bread in full view, but beyond his reach, and then saying to him, "Eat and be satisfied." The spirit of our institutions recognizes not only the right to eat of the loaf, but also the right to *obtain* it; the right to possess, and the power of consummating that right. It implies that all men possess the right of employing their talents, their energies, their judgment, and in fine, all their natural powers, in the rational and legitimate pursuit of happiness, and that government can possess no innate right to shackle or restrain those functions in the individual. Hence the pursuit of Happiness, in the full and intrinsic meaning of the expression, is a cardinal feature of American Republicanism, and it is so declared in contradistinction with any system of government which restrains by arbitrary and despotic acts, the individual resources of happiness in its subjects or citizens.

# CHAPTER V.

THE CHURCH AND THE STATE—THE SCIENCE OF RELIGION, AND THE SCIENCE OF GOVERNMENT.

"I'll teach you how you shall arraign your conscience."

SHAKSPEARE.

THE first article of the amendments to the Constitution of the United States, provides as follows:—

"Congress shall make no law respecting the establishment of religion, or abridging the freedom of speech, or of the press; or the right of the people peaceably to assemble, and to petition the government for a redress of grievances."

This clause of the organic law of the United States, comprises within itself a limited charter of civil and religious liberty. The rights of conscience, the right of free speech, the right of petition and an unshackled press. A *free press*, guided by patriotism and without licentiousness, is alone and unaided, the most powerful and effectual auxiliary of popular freedom, and when coupled with the popular right to to read and discuss, it becomes *invincible*. Even despotism itself fears to encounter the intellectual illumination of an unfettered press. The natural instincts of man are freedom of thought and action, and when those instincts are fed with the nutricious aliment of intelligence, they are irrepressible. They assert their prerogative, and woe to the tyrant who stands in the way of their development! The despots of the old world understand this truth, and hence the press is forbidden to publish, and the people are forbidden to read.

But the purpose of this chapter is not to deal with printing presses or publishers. Our present theme is Religion and Politics, the State and the Church.

Christianity, which we regard as the foundation of all true religion, was in its original perfection a simple principle, embracing the spiritual duties of man to his Creator, and to himself. Christ himself paid complete deference to the State, and commanded his disciples to observe implicit obedience to the civil law, and its authors, notwithstanding the fact that the law of that period, being in the main mythological, were "*repugnant to the laws of God.*" This is not precisely consistent with the opinions expressed recently by Mr. Orestes A. Brownson, editor of the Roman Catholic "Review," in his letter to a gentleman in Warrenton, N. C., but nevertheless it is the doctrine of the founder of Christianity. In his letter Mr. Brownson says:—

> "The temporal order, or civil government, is not supreme and independent, but in the very nature of things, subordinate to the spiritual," and he adds, "the Pope is the proper authority to decide for me whether the Constitution of this country is, or is not repugnant to the laws of God."

As a matter of course, if the Pope decides that it is repugnant to the laws of God, he, Mr. Brownson, and all good

Roman Catholics, would disobey them from a sense of religious duty.

It is a little singular that this gentleman, in the same letter, makes use of the following language :—

"In matters purely *temporal*, I, as a Catholic, owe no obedience to the Pope, because he has received from Jesus Christ, no authority as a temporal sovereign over me."

The Constitution of the United States is purely a *temporal* law, and being temporal, why then does Mr. Brownson allow the Pope to decide for him upon its merits ?

I say the Founder of Christianity taught us a different lesson. When the chief priests and the scribes, jealous of his growing popularity, resolved if possible to get him out of the way, they sought to ensnare him by eliciting from him, some treasonable expression, like that of Mr. Brownson.

"And they watched him, and sent forth spies, which should feign themselves just men, that they might deliver him into the power and authority of the governor. And they asked him, saying, Master, we know that thou sayest and teachest rightly, neither acceptest thou the person of any, but teachest the way of God truly. Is it lawful for us to give tribute unto Cæsar or no ?"

"But he perceived their craftiness, and said unto them, 'Why tempt ye me ? Shew me a penny. Whose image and superscription has it?' They answered and said, 'Cæsar's.' And he said unto them, 'Render, therefore, unto Cæsar the things which be Cæsar's, and unto God the things which be God's.' " *

It is apparent from this, that Christ himself regarded the temporal order supreme in temporal affairs, and that even

* St. Luke, chap. xx., verses 20, 21, 22, 23, 24, and 25.

the Church must yield to the State. This was the primitive views of the Christian Church. But Mr. Brownson makes it a question of opinion between the founder of that Church and himself. The issue is direct and positive. Let the world decide between them.

So far from the original Christian Church holding, or assuming to hold, supremacy over the temporal affairs of nations, it was the subject of Jewish and imperial persecution, during more than three centuries after the death of Christ, and it was not until the fourth century, that Christianity was even recognized by the civil government. It remained for the papacy, after the conversion of Constantine, to declare its own infallibility, and to usurp the temporalities of men and nations.

The pretension asserted by Mr. Brownson in his letter, which I have quoted above, is but a stereotyped edition of the pretensions of the Church of which he is a member, from the time of the first Gregory to the present. But the pretension is one of human origin, and as such is entitled to no consideration, especially since we find it refuted by the direct teachings of Jesus Christ himself.

It is not the purpose of these remarks to question the superior *interests* involved in the spiritual over the temporal affairs of mankind, but rather to elevate, in the estimation of men, the order of holiness above the turbid torrents of political turpitude. As the mental character of man is superior over his physical nature, so is pure religion above the affairs of earthly estate.

But the elements of religion and the elements of national

policy, comprise distinct natures and distinct attributes. The one is purely spiritual; the other is half sordid, and every attempt to combine the two elements into one, is certain to lessen the spirituality of the one, without increasing that of the other. Religion is reduced by this process, to a baser standard, while the secular character remains umimproved, and both the spiritual and the temporal interests of mankind are jeopardized. The first effect of a combination of the affairs of religion with the affairs of State policy, is to restrain the consciences of men, on the one hand, and to encourage, on the other, a spirit of temporal aggrandizement in the Church itself. All attempts at this unnatural and irreligious fusion have tended to the degredation of the church, at the same time that they have imposed additional and unnecessary restraints upon the people. Against these restraints the natural instincts of man have rebelled; and at each revulsion, the Church has fallen in its dignity, and in its power over the humun heart. Religion itself has been the sufferer from first to last, and atheism, deism, and infidelity, of every grade, have increased at a proportionate ratio.

These facts present a living, and incontrovertible argument in favor of the principles laid down in the Constitution of the United States, prohibiting the establishment of a national religion, and compelling the complete alienation of the Church and the State. By this wise provision, the State stands aloof from sectarian controversy, and is free to exercise its temporal functions with calm and impartial deliberation; while at the same time the Church and the individual are left to the untrammelled exercise of religious conscience.

Politics, or the science of government, is a progressive science. Theology, or the science of religion, is not so. From the hour that first echoed the voice of Jesus of Nazareth in the synagogues of Galilee to the present, the opinions of men on the subject of the "true faith," have been as various as the temperaments, and the shades of temperaments, in the human mind. Schisms, dogmas, creeds, and sects have risen, both before and since the establishment of the papacy, and each as indefinite as the other, each as unsatisfactory in solution as the forms, canons, and ceremonies of the (so called) mother Church. All that is known of religion in its intrinsic character, is written and revealed in the great Book of Life, and the most erudite commentators have failed to add a ray of light to its pages, or a ray of intelligence to the benighted mind. Speculation may wander through the interminable labyrinths of theology, and end only in rendering the obscurity more obscure—the labyrinth more intricate. The science of theology, I repeat, with all its humanizing and civilizing influences, with all its religious tendencies, with all its benefits to society, has developed no definite, or satisfactory rule of faith to mankind, beyond the revelations found in Holy Writ, and the human mind is left as completely the prey to speculative reason as in the era of the Gnostics and their contemporaneous heresies.

With all our scientific research in matters of religion, the demonologist, he who believes in spiritual appearances as an appendage of his religous faith, still claims a place for his dogma, and theology with all her erudition, has never yet annulled his claim, or satisfactorily refuted his theory. How forcibly is this truth exemplified in the tenacious hold which "spiritualism," so called, has recently taken upon the minds of many of our most learned, and conscientious people! Alas, how little has the mere *science* of religion accomplished when an Edmonds, or a Talmadge can be alienated in a moment, as it were, from the religious teachings of a life-time, and brought to believe in the tangibility of spectral illusions, or the manifestation of a spiritual presence by rappings upon a table! How little has that science acccomplished towards the establishment of an universal rule of faith, when thousands of intelligent men and women can be led by the mere arithmetic of a visionary, crack-brained theorist, to dress themselves in "ascension robes," and await, in religious confidence, the moment when they shall float in their corporeal realities, away from a consuming and a condemned world, into the regions of eternal glory! How little has theology accomplished in its mission, when an audacious journeyman carpenter, like Matthias, can palm himself off as "The Messiah," or an ignorant and besotted imposter, like Joe Smith, can raise up, even in the very heart of Christendom, a whole nation of believers in his absurd and impious doctrines!

Herein is the great secret of sustenance in the Romish Church, and the influence which it exercises over its people. Superstition is inherent in the human breast, and that superstition is the basis of man's religion, if not the religion itself. Thus it is that theology, in its mission of holiness, fails to accomplish its final purpose; thus it is that a mere fallacy, when adapted to the superstitious predilections of the soul, and adorned with mystery, sweeps away, in an instant, all the calmer attributes of reason and true religion, and leads the heart of man captive, a very slave to the dominion of fanaticism.

That theology is speculative, is proven in the diversity of dogmas that exist; most of them claiming to be emanations from the same fountain of light, the Old and the New Testament, and yet as opposite in their theories as the equator from the poles. Religion itself is a simple principle, and its science, theology, deals entirely with the attributes of divinity, and the *future* of the individual man. But it has failed to establish a fixed and perfect plan upon which the simple principle may be concentrated.

Politics, or the science of secular government, is also founded upon a simple principle; but instead of applying to divinity or the future, it applies solely to the *present* interests of man. This also has been a speculative science, but it is so no longer. The experiment of the American Republic in its intrinsic character, has abolished all doubt, and settled all speculation. It has been proven, by this experiment, that the American system is the true, and the only true system of civil government on earth, and the solution of the problem is accepted and acknowledged by every civilized people on the face of the globe. The fact that they have not all adopted it, is only an evidence of their present inability to do so. The theory once settled, the problem once solved and admitted, its universal adoption, is only a question of time and opportunity.

While theology has been searching in vain for a universal rule of religious faith, the fruits of progressive improvement in the science of civil government have been revealed on every hand, from the rude days of Romulus, with his augers, and his canine foster-mother, down to the adoption of the Constitution of the United States. Politics, aided by Christianity, each operating in its respective sphere, and each exerting its appropriate influence on the mental and moral faculties, has done that for civilization, which religion alone could never have accomplished. Religion, in its primitive character, is found wherever man makes his habitation. It is not so with the science of civil government, and where the latter is not studied, barbarism still holds its sway.

There are instances, as with the Chinese, for example, where the science of civil government has been in constant warfare with the local religion, yet in despite of the obstacles thrown in its way by the barbarous tendencies of the latter, the land of Confucius has maintained its onward march towards civilization. What can be more degrading and stupefying to the intellect of man, than the Pagan idolatry of the Chinese. In religion, they have not advanced a single step beyond the most primitive ideas, and with all their boasted antiquity, they are still on a par with the *fetichi* of Africa. Yet, from the inherent force and rigor of a judicious civil government, China surpasses, in many of the arts of civilization, all other nations of the earth. Literature and the physical sciences are cultivated and enforced, and industry, law, and order prevail among her idolatrous people. Her religion alone has been the great barrier to her progress. With the light of Christianity, and freedom of conscience among her people, China would, at almost any period of her history, have stood in the front rank of civilized nations, and wielded an influence second to none.

The language of the Constitution of the United States implies, and the practical experience of the nation proves, that religion, however essential as a regulator of the public morals, is not a necessary adjunct to the success of civil government. On the contrary, we have seen that religion, intrinsically understood, *may* retard the progress of knowledge and civilization, and when made a component of the government, through the instrumentality of the Church, it becomes the absolute foe of civil liberty. Witness Galileo in his cell, and the hostility of religious dogmas to the discoveries of Copernicus! Wisely, then, I repeat, the founders of the American Republic devoted their government to the secular necesities of the people, leaving to the Church and to individual judgment and conscience the guardianship of the spiritual interests. This is one of the prominent peculiarities of American Republicanism, as it is undoubtedly the most conservative element of the popular liberty.

If religion was to form a feature of authority in the government, we should have innumerable creeds, sects, and dogmas contesting for the prerogative, and the intellect of the nation would be occupied in disputes over the pretensions of the various claimants, each of which would assume to represent the "true faith." There would be the Roman Catholic, arguing the antiquity of his church, the infallibility of the popes, the doctrine of transubstantiation, mass, auricular confession, purgatory, winking Madonnas, and the miraculous conception; the Episcopalian, with his three orders of the ministry; the Puseyite, who hangs suspended like the coffin of Mohammed, between Episcopacy and Papacy; the Presbyterian, with his republican system, and no bishop; the Methodist, with his enthusiasm in the cause of religion; the Baptist, with his doctrine of immersion, his close communion, and his improved Bible; the Mormon, with his polygamy, and his golden Bible; the Universalist, disputing the doctrine of future torment; the Unitarian, with his single godhead; the Calvinist, the Lutheran, Old lights and New lights; the Jew, and even the Pagan, whose followers are now peopling the western coast of the Union, from the "Celestial Empire," each and all demanding precedence—each avowing for itself the sanction of divine approval, and each alike zealous in preferring his claim to the prerogative of controlling the affairs of the nation.

Who would decide a question so intricate? Since the days of Roger Williams, we have recognized the principle that man is accountable only to God and his conscience, for his religious opinions, so that if he act up to his conscience, we have no right to question the correctness of his faith. Congress cannot interfere in the matter, and if we leave it to the people to decide by their votes, the platform of our friends, the Methodists, would undoubtedly carry a plurality over that of any other sect. It is undeniable that the Methodists, as a class, are as intelligent, liberal, law-abiding, and patriotic as any other class of citizens, yet which of the remaining churches would consent to become the subjects of the Wesleyan system?

Or we may suppose the democratic plan to be adopted,

and a majority of votes made necessary to a choice of the national religion. What a warring of sects we should witness! What mining and countermining! What "pipe-laying!" What fusion of opposing elements! What un-Christian bitterness and rancor — tearing and *perhaps* swearing among the professions!—the alb, the surplice, and the broadbrim in open war! The hostility of political parties would sink into insignificance in comparison with this battle of the creeds. The satellites of the Pope, instead of making instruments of our political demagogues to accomplish their ends, would take the field in person, and fight under their own flag, and your Sewards and Weeds, your Greeleys and Van Burens, would be supplanted and overwhelmed by the dogmatic armies of a Hughes, a Beecher, or a Tyng. And these men would show no quarter, because, from the nature of the elements involved, no contests are so vindictive as those founded on religious sentiment—no foe so unsparing as the sectarian who fights for his faith.

Thank Heaven no such contest can occur in our land, so long as our institutions of civil and religious freedom are maintained intact, pure and uncontaminated, as they came to us from the far-seeing minds of the fathers of the Republic. And those institutions can be kept inviolate only by a total alienation of religion from politics—the Church from the State.

## CHAPTER VI.

ROMISH PRIESTS AND AMERICAN POLITICIANS—THE CHURCH POLITICAL.

"But then I sigh, and, with a piece of scripture,
Tell them, that God bids us do good for evil.
And thus I clothe my naked villany
With old odd ends, stol'n forth of holy writ;
And seem a saint, when most I play the devil."

SHAKSPEARE.

"The power which Christ has granted to the Church, is twofold; being *spiritual* and *temporal*."

POPE BONIFACE VIII.

IF we analyze this subject closely, we may discover a peculiar force and point in the phraseology of the Constitution, as quoted in the preceding chapter. It will be perceived that the Constitution forbids Congress to pass any laws for the establishment of *religion*. This phrase covers the ground intended more completely than if it had used the words *a national Church*, instead of the simple and comprehensive word *religion*, because, whatever may be the association of ideas in this connection, the *Church* is one thing, and *religion* another. Religion sometimes, has but little to do with the Church, and it frequently occurs that the Church has less to do with religion. I mean the religion of Christ. What is the

Church of Rome, for example, but a budget of mechanical and ostentatious forms and ceremonies, and a promoter of ignorance and low superstition? I find nothing of religion in the jugglery that first stifles intelligence, and then *compels* its illiterate dupes to believe that the figure of a woman painted on canvas, can, and does exhibit signs of physical life, as the so-called "Winking Virgin," or that a dry thorn will emit drops of blood, on the anniversary of the crucifixion. These are a part of the machinery of the Roman Catholic *Church*, and they are but two instances in a catalogue of thousands of like absurdity. And what are they but *villainous* inventions, by which a few men hope to control the political interests, and temporal destinies of the whole earth? The intellect of man, when permitted to have full play, revolts at them, spurns them, despises them. When the mind is sufficiently enlightened to see through their web, it finds in them not only the vilest hypocrisy, but an absolute sacrilege, and an insult to the natural intelligence of the human race. And this is the *Church* which Mr. Orestes A Brownson tells us, is to decide whether the Constitution of the United States is to be obeyed by him, or not; whether it is "in conformity with the laws of God!"

This doctrine may have answered before the Reformation, and it may answer now in such of the papal States as have not yet opened their eyes, or even in Brazil, Portugal, Spain, Mexico, or South America, where priestcraft still holds sway over reason, but it will not answer in the United States of North America. It cannot serve their purposes here, where free schools, schools free from sectarianism or bigotry, send forth their streams of intelligence through millions of channels, without money, and without price. This Church thrives best, too, with men of inferior minds. The bold and vigorous intellect of the Anglo Saxon race, though it has, from the force of circumstances, been compelled, at times, to recognize its present supremacy, has never, in heart, endorsed its pretensions, or its dogmas. And thus it has been, and is now, with the more perfect intellects of every people, who have received its hypocritical trusts. I can realize no spectacle more humiliating than that of the Anglo Saxon who permits himself to become its dupe, and its instrument.

The open and virulent attacks made by the Romish Church upon our free school system, affords a living evidence of the fact, that the Church fears the influence of education among the masses of the people, and the partial success which has attended those attacks, attests the venality of those political leaders who have yielded to its pretensions and demands. Such men are unworthy to hold and direct the destinies of the American people. They are like the general who, for a temporary policy, would yield to his enemy a point of vantage, which, at the next engagement, would command the field. They are either bad managers or traitors, but in either case, unworthy the confidence of the people, and they should be so regarded and so treated. The popular suffrage should never be squandered a second time on any man, who, for the purpose of his party or his person, or for any purpose whatever, has encouraged influences hostile to our institutions, or detrimental to the future welfare of the Republic. Such men as William H. Seward, who, when governor of the State of

New York, attempted to prostitute our system of public education to the behests of Bishop Hughes and the Roman Catholic Church, and who would have taken away the moneys contributed by *Protestants* for literary purposes solely, and given those moneys for the support of schools in which anti-republican and sectarian sentiments were to be inculcated, and foreign languages spoken and taught.* Such men as Thurlow Weed, who aided and abetted the schemes of Mr. Seward; such men as Horace Greeley, who delights only in metaphysics and abstractions—a man of theory without judgment—a child of impulse, who lives in dream-land, and knows no realities, no people, no country. Such men as Stephen A. Douglas, who, through the force of his political position, in a mistaken effort to attain popularity, plunges the nation in discord; these, and many others that could be enumerated, are alike unworthy the confidence and support of a free and enlightened people. Whatever may be their professions or pretensions; whatever their political creed, whether Democrat, Whig, or Native American; whatever their school of philosophy, or their talents and powers of sophistical reasoning, never trust them again. Never should they be made the keepers of either our conscience, our political opinions, or

* Governor Seward, in his message to the Legislature of New York, dated January 7, 1840, made the following recommendation:

"I do not hesitate, therefore, to recommend the establishment of schools in which they (the children of foreigners) *may be instructed by teachers speaking the same language with themselves, and professing the same faith.*"

And in a letter to Bishop Hughes, dated at Albany, May 18th, 1841, he adds the following declaration:

"I *reaffirm* all I have before promulgated concerning the policy of this country in regard to foreigners, and the education of their children."

our national destinies. Let them be repudiated from Maine to California, *via* Texas and New Mexico, and back again from Oregon through Kansas and Minnesota to the place of beginning.

But I am rambling. As one of the people, I write for the people. I am one of the millions who have too long allowed a few men to do their political thinking for them. I have determined to think for myself, read for myself, and, as far as I can, to understand for myself, free from the dictation of any party or faction, and I believe it would be better for civil and religious liberty if all my countrymen would "go and do likewise." We have all been too long harnessed in the party traces of a few designing men, and we have allowed them to rule over us until our union and our free institutions have been brought to the very verge of annihilation—another step, and we plunge into the abyss of anarchy and national chaos! Too long we have worshipped "hickory poles" and "hard cider"—too long have the ambitious leaders of party thrown in our eyes the dust of "tariff" and "free trade," "bank" or "no bank," "slavery" or "anti-slavery," till we have been blinded to the trust which our honest old grandfathers left to us, and our dearest interests have been made the subjects of bargain and sale. The patriarchs of the nation left us the inheritance of temporal and spiritual freedom, with the Holy Bible and the Constitution for our guides. The one is now sacrilegiously desecrated, and the other is trampled under foot; the Bible is thrown from our schools at the dictation of Romish priests, and the Constitution is violated and ignored by the public enactment of fanatical legislation.

One of the surest guarantees of permanent nationality is the perfect homogeneousness of the people. It is, therefore, an important duty on the part of the statesman, to encourage all that pertains to unity of character and custom, and to discountenance every influence that tends to produce the opposite result. This duty is the more imperative in the United States, where the conflict of individual character and custom is kept so constantly active by an unceasing and multifarious emigration. The course recommended by Governor Seward, instead of lessening, would increase this heterogeneous element by encouraging foreign languages and customs among the emigrants. Instead of forcing them into our body politic, and enforcing a unity of interest and feeling by instruction in the language and customs of America, Mr. Seward would encourage social antagonisms and multiplied nationalities within the American circle. A stronger evidence of his incapacity as a statesman could not exist.

Again, in the same paragraph of his message, he recommends that in schools supported at the public expense, the children of foreigners *should be taught by persons of the same religious faith.* This would be neither more nor less than the establishment of sectarian schools at the expense of the people. In this Mr. Seward distinctly violates two well understood principles of the American Republican system, thus again proving his unfitness for the responsible trusts reposed in him by his party. The first principle violated is, that the State shall not interpose in matters of religion among the people, or give encouragement to sectarians; and the second is, that no one religious sect shall be required to pay tribute to others—both of which would occur if Mr. Seward's recommendation was carried into effect.

Mr. Seward passes for a man of talent; he is regarded by some of his worshippers as an American Talleyrand. Yet among all his public acts it is difficult to find one that bears the mark of utility either to the nation or to his native State, or that would elevate his standard of statesmanship above that of a scheming partisan. He has achieved, in his public career, a *notoriety*, but no fame, and the future will look back upon his history only as upon a disagreeable reminiscence. But to return again.

The masses of those who are "born Catholics," and reared in its despotic faith, are scrupulously religious, so far as the teachings of their Church is capable of imparting religious sentiments—in other words, they are what is generally denominated "good Catholics." They sincerely believe in transubstantiation, so far as they are able to understand it, but generally without understanding it all. They sincerely believe that auricular confession is necessary for salvation, and that their priests have power to save them from damnation, and *vice versâ*. They sincerely believe that all who are not of their Church are heretics, and that heresy and damnation are identical; hence, when opportunity offers, they believe it would be a righteous act, and doing God service, to exterminate the disbelievers from the face of the earth. They sincerely believe all the jugglery of pretended miracles, palmed upon them by a crafty priesthood, as real evidences of the divine presence. They sincerely believe that learning is a prerogative of the clergy, and that ignorant, passive submission to clerical commands is the first duty of the laity. These things the masses believe, because they are trained in fear to believe nothing to the contrary, and thus far they are scrupulously religious. But in the hierarchy itself we find, at the best, only a hybrid, a politico-religious institution, with a large preponderance of the politica element in its composition.

At this day, in the States under the direct control of the papacy, it is a capital offence against *the State* to read the Scriptures, or discuss the topics of religion. Either of these offences are characterized, not as a heresy merely, not only as an offence against religion, but as *treason to the government*, a violation of the civil law, and as such it is punished. Yet this Church, relying on the "profligacy of our politicians," has freely declared its intention (being an alien), to substitute the mitre for our liberty cap, and blend the crozier with the stripes and stars! "*The jewels of Isabella the Catholic*,"said Bishop Hughes, "*would be an appropriate ornament for the sword of Washington!*"

It is not the purpose of this volume to recapitulate the historical proofs of the political character of the Romish Church, nor to review in detail the evidences of its despotic nature. They are to be found in a thousand authentic works already within reach of every reader. It is sufficient for us to know:

I. That the Church is a political government, claiming temporal authority over every nation and people of the earth.

II. That it is now striving directly, to establish its temporal or political power in these United States, and

III. That its form of government is diametrically opposed to the genius of American Republicanism.

In proof of the first, very brief quotations from the authorities of the Church itself will suffice, and, doubtless, be more satisfactory than any other evidence that can be produced Setting aside the political and despotic *acts* of the Church, which, of themselves, comprise incontestible proofs of its political character, I shall confine myself to extracts from the decrees of her councils, and the declarations of her writers. As early as the tenth century, during the reign of Pope John XII., the Council of Bishops decreed as follows:

"Whoever shall venture to maintain that our Lord the Pope cannot decree *what he pleases*, let him be accurst!"

This is a declaration of universal authority in the head of the Church. It has no limit. It comprehends no legal, social, intellectual or moral restraint. It makes no allowance for human frailty. It sweeps away all the forms and amenities of social life. It invades all the elements of life. It strikes alike at the individual, the community, and the nation, in all their relations, moral and political, and converts a *man* into a *god*. In connection with this decree, we have the declaration of one of the soundest of Romish authors, the Cardinal Zeba, who informs us that;

"The Pope can do all things which he wishes, and is empowered by God to do many things which he (God) himself cannot perform!"

It is apparent that if we adopt this infatuated view, there is little necessity of a god in controlling the affairs of earth. If the Pope can do what God cannot do, the supreme character and attributes of deity are no better than a fifth wheel to a stage coach. Protestants are educated to the belief that God is supreme, and that no mere man is fit to be his legate. When he found it necessary to send a representative to curb the waywardness of erring man, and point out the way to salvation, he sent not *a Pope*, but his only begotten son, the Lord and Saviour, Jesus Christ, whose counsel and example have been so sadly forgotten and ignored by those who are impiously styled his "vicegerents on earth," the Popes of Rome.

Next we have a decree issued by the Council of Bishops, during the reign of Pope Gregory VII., as early as the eleventh century, in which it is declared that

> "The Pope alone ought to wear the tokens of imperial dignity; all princes ought to kiss his feet; he has power to depose emperors and kings, and is to be judged by none."

The bloody pages of history attest the fact that he not only *had* the power to depose emperors and kings, but that he also exercised that power. Let us beware that he does not get the power to depose *presidents* as well as emperors and kings. The passage here quoted relates not in any shape to *religion*—it claims solely temporal qualifications—political authority. It invests him with earthly gewgaws—the "tokens of *imperial* dignity." It places him in a political aspect, above all governments, all social forms, and finally, it declares that he is to be judged by no tribunal. His earthly character and person are alike above the law, and exempt from the verdicts of human opinion. His acts are made supreme, and his commands are to be the guides for all men, all communities, all governments. American Republicanism inculcates the opposite notion. It is opposed to the one-man power.

But let us continue our quotations a little further on this head. Thomas Aquinas, another of the oft-quoted authorities of this *Church*, tells us that "The Pope, as *supreme king of the world*, may impose taxes, and destroy towns and castles," &c., &c.

Add to this the decree of the celebrated Council of Trent, and we have sufficient of ancient authority to establish the political character of the Church of Rome. In that council, whose ordinances have ever since been held as the complete rule of Romish faith, it was decreed that "The Pope is *prince over all nations* and kingdoms, having power to pluck up, destroy, scatter, ruin, plant and build!"

After these authorities, it remains only to show that the same views are entertained at the present day. And to do this I will quote a single paragraph from a paper called the *Freeman's Journal*, the avowed organ of the Church in the State of New York, and edited by a Mr. McMasters, a native of New York, born of Protestant parents, but *converted* to the Romish theory of government. In one of his numbers, published in 1853, he says:

"The Pope of Rome has supreme authority over every diocese, and over *every square foot of surface on this globe*. His rights are circumscribed only by the ends of the earth and the consummation of ages."

This, it is true, is a mere echo—a parrot-like reiteration of the sayings and doings of wiser men; but inasmuch as its authenticity is not denied by the heads of the Church, we must regard it as official, therefore, as the doctrine of the Church at the present day.

The "Church" claims through its hierachy to be infallible; that it is the same in all time; and hence, what it was in the eighth century, when the the emperor of the Greeks, Philippicus Bardanes, was excommunicated and deposed for refusing to sanction the worship of images, it is now. Pope Pius IX., the present pontiff, reigning in the 19th century, claims the same attributes, by *divine right*, that were claimed by, and conceded to, the first Gregory, and by every intermediate occupant of the papal chair. In proof of this, I quote a passage from the coronation address, delivered on his receiving the triple crown. It is in the following words:

"Receive the tiara of three crowns, and remember that thou art the father of princes, and guide of kings upon the earth, the Vicar of our Saviour Jesus Christ, to whom be honor, and glory, for ever and ever, amen."

Under this authority, Henry IV., Emperor of Germany, was excommunicated, persecuted, and finally driven from his throne. Leo, the Isandrian, was excommunicated, his empire dismembered, and his Italian subjects absolved of their allegiance, and the same treatment was suffered by his son, the Emperor Constantine. Leo IV. was incapacitated by poison, and his edicts against image worship annulled. Childric, of France, was deposed by an order from the Pope, and Pepin, an usurper, placed upon his throne. Basilaus II., king of Poland, was deposed and excommunicated. Alphonso X., king of Gallicia and Leon was excommunicated and anathematized, for marrying without the papal consent. John, king of England, was interdicted by Innocent III., for refusing certain concessions demanded by the Pope. All places of worship in his kingdom were closed for three years, and the dead were buried in the highways like brutes. Still refusing concession, he was excommunicated, his subjects absolved of their allegiance, and he deposed. Philip, duke of Suabia, was excommunicated, and the claims of Otho, his antagonist, preferred by the Pope. Otho, who became emperor of Germany, was subsequently himself deposed by the same hand, and Frederic II., his pupil, placed on his throne. Frederic II. was also in turn persecuted, and finally driven from the throne. Philip, king of France, for refusing to recognize the assumed *temporal* power of the Pope, was excommunicated, but by firmness and force of arms, maintained his throne. Henry III., of England, was excommunicated, and an edict issued by the Pope, absolving his subjects, and deposing him from the throne. Elizabeth, of England, was the subject of the papal anathema, on account of her Protestant faith, and a bull, deposing her from the throne, was issued by Pope Pius V. Henry III., of France, was assassinated by order of the Pope, on account of his Protestant faith. His successor, Henry IV., met a similar fate for the like reason. Prior to the accession of James I. of England, he being a Protestant, Pope Clement IX. issued a bull commanding all Romanists in the kingdom to use their utmost to keep him from the throne. It was during the reign of this monarch that the celebrated "gunpowder plot" was detected. The treaties made by Charles VI., emperor of Germany, with the Protestant princes of his empire, were annulled by an edict from Pope Clement XI., and his subjects absolved from obedience of them.

These are some of the prominent acts of the papacy in its exercise of the temporal or *political* power *by divine* authority. It will be seen that they extend over a period of a thousand years, and they have been withheld during the present, and a portion of the past century, only in consequence of the increased power of Protestantism, and the relative decrease of the papal power. In the papal States, and all countries avowedly Roman Catholic, the same authority in temporal affairs is held, and in some of them, still conceded. Even in the United States, a nuncio of the present Pope has dared to declare invalid a sovereign State statute, and commanded his people to disobey that statute! I allude to the papal edict against the trustees of the "St. Louis congregation" at Buffalo. Not long since, the Congress of New Granada, in South America, were anathematized on account of one of their political acts, and at this moment the Spanish Cortes and sovereign are the subjects of papal denunciation, in consequence of a law, recently passed, in relation to the tenure of Church property. Thus much, I have deemed it necessary and proper to mention in illustration of the political character of the papal Church.

## CHAPTER VII.

### Papal Aspirations in the United States.

"You shall see anon; 'tis a knavish piece of work."

Shakspeare.

"While you here do snoring lie
Open ey'd conspiracy
His time doth take;
If of life you keep a care,
Shake off slumber, and beware:
Awake! Awake!"

Ibid.

I pass now to the second feature, viz., that the Church "is striving, directly, to establish its temporal or political power in these United States." The evidence on this head must, of necessity, be mainly presumptive, or circumstantial. Jesuitism, the principal working element of the Church, especially in the department of the propagandi, does not openly declare, or make known its projects and purposes, until it is morally certain that all the rudiments of success have been perfected, and that a consummation is sure. The presumptive evidence is, however, in overt acts, which amount nearly to absolute proof, and in the occasional, or casual expressions of their authorized speakers and writers. When those acts and expressions are of such a nature as to bring conviction to the general mind, or to the observant spectator, we have a right to presume an intent. For example: when a bishop of the Church declares, that it is the intention of the papacy to *convert* the President of the United States, the Senate, and House of Representatives, the Judiciary, the Legislatures of the several States, the officers of the Army and the Navy, and in fact the whole people of the United States, to the Roman Catholic Church, his meaning becomes too apparent to be misunderstood. It is the same as if he should say, "It is the intention of the papacy to secure the government of this country," or "It is the intention of the papacy to bring this country under the Roman Catholic dictation," because, nobody will be foolish enough to believe that when Bishop Hughes made that declaration, he intended to be understood as saying that the persons named would become converts to the Roman Catholic *faith*. His meaning was plainly this: It is the intention, and the expectation of the papacy, to obtain by immigration and annexation, and by its influence over the demagogues of the country, sufficient political power and influence to control its laws, and shape them to the purposes of the Roman Catholic party; thus *converting* it into a papal nation and government.

This purpose was so plain thirty years ago, that it did not escape the observation of the Duke of Richmond, at that time Governor of the Canadas, and the duke did not hesitate to express his views on the subject, from which I make a single brief extract. Speaking of the probable subversion of the institutions of the United States, the duke used the following language:

"The Church of Rome has a design upon that country, and it will in time be the established religion, and will aid in the destruction of that Republic. I have conversed with many of the sovereigns and princes of Europe, particularly with George III, and Louis XVIII., and they have unanimously expressed these opinions relative to the government of the United States."

The course of Jesuitism is so subtle and insidious; it performs its work by such slow, and almost imperceptible degrees, that the people most directly interested, the Americans, are the last to take the alarm. Each change that is made in our old Protestant system and customs, towards the papal intention is so slight as to attract no particular notice, the more especially as the changes are made ostensibly under the sanction of one or the other of the political parties; and as each party has vied with its opponent in efforts to secure the Roman Catholic vote, neither has ventured to expose the encroachment when it has been made by the other; hence we have not realized the amount of progress actually made. But if we look back, and contemplate the aggregate of those changes, and draw a comparison of the past with the present, the extent of Roman Catholic encroachments become palpable and startling.

When the Republic was established, Romanism could scarcely be said to have had an existence in the land. Certainly, it had no influence—it made no pretensions—it was modest, humble, solicitous. As a religion, it took its place side by side with Protestent creeds, scarce visible in the preponderating numbers of surrounding churches. A Romish priest could not be recognized by his attire and demeanor, from his Protestant neighbor. The external forms and ceremonies of the Church were humbly kept from view, and the whole demeanor of priest and laymen was that of unostentatious Christianity.

But what a change has taken place in the demeanor, and the numerical power of that Church, since the foundation of the Republic!* Its humility has been changed to defiant audacity; a bold, commanding ostentation has taken the place of its retiring simplicity. It builds its nunneries, its Jesuit colleges, its churches, in every nook and corner of the land, and it consecrates them in all the pomp and formulæ of its ancient pride, surrounded by the drawn swords and bayonets of its martial legions, who are organized, commissioned and armed *as a part of the militia of the State.* It *baptizes* its *bells* amid superstitious trappings and ceremonies adapted to the palmiest days of its benumbing power. It holds its councils of bishops who issue their edicts in conformity with the despotic character of its government. It sends its nuncio to decide a controversy between a bishop and his congregation, and the nuncio decides *against* the people, and in violation of the law of the land, and the principles of Republicanism. It tampers with our public men and our public policy, and has already, in most of the States, erased from their constitutions, that conservative feature which prevented clerical interference in political affairs. It has perverted legitimate and authentic history whenever that history portrayed its own enormities. It has driven the Word of God from many of our public and district schools. It has obtained the control of our post-

* See Chapter X. of this work.

office department, and secured the chief-justice of the United States. It has increased numerically, from comparatively nothing, to about four millions, and now, self-confident, it claims to possess a controlling political influence in the affairs of the country.

These are the presumptive evidences of its intention to establish its political power in the United States. But we have more than presumptive evidence. We have the proof positive in the declaration of its own writers. In the month of July, 1852, before the public mind had been awakened to the Romish encroachments, and when the hierarchy was flushed with success, and confident of accomplishing a full and speedy triumph, the *Freeman's Journal*, a Roman Catholic publication, to which I have before alluded, was permitted, by its censors, to utter the following declaration:

"Our country has started forth with a beautiful fabric of institutions, and political framework. We have lived to see the existence of these threatened, and to hear grave men predict their speedy fall. We have lived to see desperate corruption in our leading statesmen, and heedless, fickle passion swaying the crowds that give statesmen their popularity. *But it is at this moment that the Catholic Church,* not only in the view of the prescient and philosophers, but to the consciousness of all who have eyes, *stands forth,* as we have said, *the only living organization,* which, *professing* to guide men from a principle above the interests of the hour, *holds millions of souls in her grasp, and fearlessly directs them,* and with *unerring aim,* to the course that high duty and *the true good of the country demands.*

* * * * * *

"The great conservative and living principles of our *civil and political institutions* ARE HENCEFORTH TO BE IDENTIFIED PECULIARLY

WITH THE CATHOLIC CHURCH AND ITS FRIENDS. Every year that rolls by will make this fact more clear, and will develop its consequences more fully."

In this we find more than a declaration of the intentions of the Church; it is the self-confident boast of an adversary who imagines that he has at length inflicted the death-blow, from the effects of which his opponent must speedily yield up the ghost. He believes the plans of the Jesuits have been so far successful, as to give his party an actual, preponderating influence from which it is impossible for the country to escape, and then he triumphantly proclaims that *henceforth* the civil and political institutions of the United States are to be controlled by the policy of the Roman Catholic Church!

He is ready to exclaim, in the words of Hotspur: "By the Lord, our plot is a good plot as ever was laid; our friends are true and constant; a good plot, good friends, and full of expectation."

In this case, Mr. McMasters "whistled before he was out of the wood." Romanism is not yet at the helm of American affairs. At the time when he wrote the paragraph quoted above, the condition of our public affairs certainly seemed to favor his opinion, and had the old party organizations held their respective positions and influence, it is difficult to conjecture how far the declaration might have been carried out. But it was ordained otherwise. At the very moment when this boastful shout of papal triumph was uttered, there was a patriotic influence at work, as subtle and invisible as his own nefarious enginery. It knocked at the *hearts* of the people when the partisan demagogues were asleep, and those hearts were opened to it. It spoke to them in the language of *home* and *country*, and they listened. It pointed out the encroachments of the papal power, the corruptions of public men, the dangers that beset their free institutions, and they were convinced. Their eyes were opened. It called on them in the name of LIBERTY, and they sprang up to the rescue. They came forth like an army with banners; they tore the faithless and corrupt political parties to pieces, and scattered the fragments to the four winds of heaven. They met the Jesuit in his subterranean mine, and under the starry folds of their country's banner, they swore to be no longer the slave of the demagogue! With a single purpose, and with hearts sternly resolute, they gathered around the altars of Liberty, rekindled the expiring embers of patriotism, and with one voice, resolved that the insidious power of the Jesuit should be no more in the land; that the stranger within their gates should not become their master, and that AMERICANS ALONE SHOULD BE THE RULERS OF AMERICA.

But I have yet another and more absolute avowal of the views of the Romish Church, in regard to our institutions, and its aspirations in this country. It is from the pen of Mr. Brownson, and appears in his Review. I am fully aware that Mr. Brownson, owing to the freedom of his expressions, the plain, straight-forward manner in which he lays bare the character and intentions of his Church, and also to the fact that he has exhibited an extraordinary versatility of political and religious talent, has come to be regarded as of little or no authority on these subjects; and many reject his declarations in toto, as the offsprings of a diseased mind. These circumstances would have as great weight with me as with the most skeptical of his disclaimers, and I should be as ready as any to denounce him as a fool, a fanatic, or a madman, were it not for the fact that among those who characterize his writings as the ravings of a lunatic, we do not find one of the lights of the Church, and the further and more important fact, that his most ultra and "insane" sayings are in strict conformity with the ancient canons, and the invariable practice of the Church. If his writings were not orthodox, the bishops, in whose hands are entrusted the interest and character of the Church itself, would undoubtedly be, as they should, the first to rebuke his misstatements, and silence his pen. But this is not done. On the contrary, his statements his speculations, his arguments in favor of the temporal authority of the Church, his anti-republican notions, his asseverations that it is the intention of the papacy to control the destinies of this country, in a word, his whole course, is *officially endorsed* by the whole council of Romish bishops in America, and every number that he has published during the past six years has borne that official announcement on the cover, over the signatures of the following prelates, and in the following words:

"BALTIMORE, *May* 13, 1849.

"DEAR SIR:

"After the close of our Council, I suggested to our venerable Metropolitan the propriety of encouraging you by our approbation and influence to continue your literary labors in defence of the faith of which you have proved an able and intrepid advocate. He received the suggestion most readily, and I take the liberty of communicating the fact to you, as a mark of my sincere esteem, and of the deep interest I feel in your excellent Review. I shall beg of him and of the other prelates, who entertain the same views, to subscribe their names in confirmation of my statement.

"Your devoted friend,

"† FRANCIS PATRICK KENRICK,

"*Bishop of Philadelphia.*

"O. A. BROWNSON, Esq."

† SAMUEL, Archbishop of Baltimore.

† PETER RICHARD, Archbishop of St. Louis.

† MICHAEL, Bishop of Mobile.

† ANTHONY, Bishop of New Orleans.

† JOHN JOSEPH, Bishop of Natchez.

† JOHN, Bishop of Buffalo.

† M. O'CONNOR, Bishop of Pittsburgh.

† MATHIAS, Bishop of Dubuque.

† JOHN M. ODIN, Bishop of Galveston.

† MARTIN JOHN, Bishop of Lingone and Coadjutor of Louisville.

† M. D. ST. PALAIS, Bishop of Vincennes.

† WILLIAM TYLER, Bishop of Hartford.

† J. B. FITZPATRICK, Bishop of Boston.

† RICHARD PIUS, Bishop of Nashville.

† JOHN BAPTIST, Bishop of Cincinnati.

† JOHN HUGHES, Bishop of New York.

† RICHARD VINCENT, Bishop of Wheeling.

† JAMES OLIVER, Bishop of Chicago.

† JOHN M. HENNI, Bishop of Milwaukee.

† JOHN, Bishop of Albany.

† AMEDEUS, Bishop of Cleveland.

† PETER PAUL, Bishop of Zela, Coadjutor and administrator of Detroit.

† IGNATIUS AL. REYNOLDS, Bishop of Charleston.

† ANDREW BYRNE, Bishop of Little Rock.

With this fact staring us in the face it is idle to talk of

Mr. Brownson's vagaries, or to deny the authenticity of his opinions. He has the avowed sanction of the whole Church, in the course he is pursuing. He is their oracle, their mouthpiece, their agent, and so long as they acknowledge him as such, we, who are not in the secrets of the papal star-chamber, assume a voluntary responsibility in saying, "Mr. Brownson does not speak the views and sentiments of the Roman Catholics." To do so is to act with an absurd criminality; and I find it difficult to hold patience with Protestant Americans, who are so excessively chivalric and courteous as to enter the lists on the side of Romish assumption, and volunteer argument to disprove for the Church what the Church itself has never denied. To say the least, it implies a vast stretch of *confidence*. It is like the fly who argued himself into the web of the spider, under the confident belief that so modest a gentleman could not mean to harm him. The difference, if any, is in favor of the good sense of the fly, because, in his case, the spider did not give notice of an intention to suck out his life's blood, whereas the voluntary Protestant champions of Romanism, are plainly and unequivocally forewarned of its intention. If the fly had been so informed, he would have had too much good sense to have gone into the web.

Under these circumstances, we have no right to question the veracity or the authenticity of Brownson's statements. His employers are the best and only *qualified* judges of his workmanship, and so long as they approve and endorse him, we do but put a bandage over our own eyes if we deny or attempt to palliate his positions. Well, this man, thus endorsed by the leading prelates of the Romish Church in America, used the following language as long ago as the year 1845, which being prior to the date of the certificate above quoted, is of course included in that certificate as being a part of his "labors in defence of the faith." We find it in the April number of the year 1845, in the following words:

"In point of fact, democracy is a mischievous dream, wherever the Catholic Church does not predominate, to inspire the people with reverence, and to teach and accustom them to obedience to authority. The first lesson for all to learn, the last that should be forgotten, is to obey. You can have no government where there is no obedience; and obedience to law, as it is called, will not be long enforced where the FALLIBILITY of law is clearly seen and freely admitted. *But is it the intention of the Pope to possess this country?* UNDOUBTEDLY. *In this intention is he aided by the Jesuits, and all the Catholic prelates and priests?* UNDOUBTEDLY, IF THEY ARE FAITHFUL TO THEIR RELIGION."

Here we have the naked assurance of the highest authority in the land; not the authority of Mr. Orestes A. Brownson, merely, *but of the twenty-five Roman Catholic bishops*, who, at their council at Baltimore in 1849, endorsed and ratified the declaration over their hands and crosses. Under their sanction we have assurance of the undoubted "intention of the Pope to possess this country," and that in that intention he is "aided by the Jesuits, and all the Catholic prelates and priests." Talk as much as you may of Mr. Brownson's obliquity of principle, or mental aberration, it is impossible to talk this fact out of sight or existence. For a

Protestant American to deny it is folly—to attempt its palliation is venal.

In justification of this intent, these twenty-five bishops assert the following doctrine in the same number and the same article from which I have just quoted.

> "If the papacy be founded in *divine right* it is *supreme over* whatever be founded in human right, and then *your institutions should be made to harmonize with it, and not it with your institutions*. The real question then is, not the compatibility or incompatibility of the Catholic Church with democratic institutions, but is the Catholic Church the Church of God?"

These prelates claim that our Republican institutions should be made to harmonize with the papacy, without regard to their incompatibility, and in order to bring about that *celestial* harmony on earth, it is necessary that the papacy should take charge of the Republic! The logic is certainly good, and the premises are clearly set forth, and as I have no means of knowing that they do not mean what they say, I do not feel at liberty, as some of my countrymen have done, to assert that they do not so mean. Our wisest course is to believe them sincere, and act accordingly.

It is a circumstance to be regretted that many Americans, sensible and discreet persons too, listen to these statements with an ear of indifference, or, perhaps, of actual disbelief. They cannot realize either the truth of the statement, or the feasibility of the popish plan, if contemplated; and they turn aside with a shrug of cold incredulity, or, with a self-satisfied air, express the philosophical opinion, "There is no danger."

These men read history to little purpose, and are generally poor judges of weak human nature. They would make most excellent subjects for that adroit genius known as "the Confidence man." Guileless and simple themselves, they judge all men by their own standard. Reared and educated under influences remote from papal despotism, and never having felt its tortures, they are willing to believe the massacre of St. Bartholomew a romance, and the skinning of Ugo Bassi a myth, though the one occurred during the 16th century and the other during the 19th.

If the warnings daily given, of the antagonistic nature and purposes of the Romish corporation towards the institutions of American Republicanism, were the inventions of those who utter them, there would appear to be more sensible ground for this marked indifference and disbelief. We might, in that case, set them down as the coinage of a distempered brain, or the fancies of a fanatical bigot. But this opportnnity is not afforded. *The Church itself is our authority*, and it cannot, if it would, deny the accusation. Protestant Americans, there, fore, who volunteer to become her champions, or who sneer at the more watchful zeal of their own countrymen, are the *dupes*, not of the Romish Church, but of their own simplicity. The Church is honest enough to have declared her own despotic character through all time. She has as frankly declared her intention to subvert, and crush the institutions of civil and religious liberty; the first of which she declares to be a horrible, and fatal license, and the last a damnable heresy! Now, as civil and religious liberty are the great components of our system of government, it follows (even without the recent avowals of her council of bishops), that the Church of Rome is the natural foe of our system, and that the two cannot exist where her power predominates. It requires no great logic to arrive at this conclusion.

Another class of insipid philanthropists suggest meekly that "it will not do to interfere with the *religious* opinions of men. Liberty of conscience is a sacred right, and must not be infringed," &c. Very true, but when religion and conscience are made the mere subterfuge of despotism are we still bound to give them license? Conscience, in its simple character, is an innate sentiment, but the direction of conscience is entirely the result of training or education. The conscience of a child is an unwritten tablet, and the impressions which it is to convey through life are placed there by the hand of the moral or religious tutor. The Quaker teaches his child the theory that it is sinful to take the life of a fellow being under any circumstances, and he grows up under a *concientious* belief in that precept; he refuses to bear arms, on behalf of his country, against an invading foe, or to strike a blow in defence of his own life when assailed. On the other hand, his next door neighbor teaches his child that it is not only his right, but his duty, to slay his fellow man either in defence of his country, the public peace or his own person; and that child grows up with a *conscientious* belief in all that has been taught, and he does not hesitate to make it a governing principle in his intercourse with mankind.

Now let us suppose that the *consciences* of a few millions of men and women within the United States are trained from childhood to believe that it is their religious duty to exterminate heresy and heretics, and to overturn governments hostile to their conscience whenever the opportunity is presented, are we required to tolerate that conscience? Is it our duty to nourish and tolerate the elements of treason and assassination because the traitor and the assassin are sheltered under the ægis of a religious conscience? The poor, starving wretch, pressed with a sense of self-preservation, *conscientiously* takes from the baker a loaf of bread, to keep body and soul together; yet we do not hesitate to send the poor creature to jail for the offence. His conscience will not avail in the presence of austere Justice.

But in the case of the Romanist, we do not attack his conscience, or his religion. He has avowed himself the political foe of our free institutions, and he has assailed those institutions. We but defend them against his assaults. So long as he is content to worship God after the fashion of his own mystical religion, I will be the champion of his right to do so without hindrance or interruption. Let him but keep his religious conscience out of the American ballot-box, and he will find no foe on the American soil. He will not need, then, to make his appeals to the overshadowing protection of the Constitution. The public sentiment will be his shield and his buckler.

But there is yet a third class of American citizens, who affect to despise our admonitions against papal aggression. They are the wire-pulling politicians, the demagogues of the land; they want voters, and they avail themselves of the amiable unsusceptibility of the two classes just described, to keep their parties together. Men who never had any definite religion, cry the loudest for religious tolerance and the rights of conscience, but *especially* the Roman Catholic conscience. In their vocabulary, the Romanist is a persecuted saint, and the American Protestant, an intolerant bigot. But it is a trade with them. They have offices and honors at stake. Most of them know better, but so long as they can win at the election, they care little for the future of their country.

## CHAPTER VIII.

### American Republicanism and Romanism—the Contrast.

"They are natural foes; they will not lie
In the same burrow. Their hostility
Is in the bones—in the very marrow—
Do what you will, they will not live on terms."

Anon.

Here are two *isms* that deserve the consideration of all men of all parties, but they are not the isms of *the* day, nor of *a* day—they are for all time. They are vital principles, venerable, pervading; and they will, doubtless, live and be discussed when Mr. Greeley's ephemera of isms will have gone the way of all fallacies, and been forgotten. What a pity it is that so fine a genius as that of Mr. Greeley, should have lost its balance, and been whelmed in the maelstrom of misty theories! I knew him when he was the oracle of a great and powerful national party—a man of clear judgment, and one of the best political statisticians (except the late Edwin Williams) in the United States. As an editor, he was persevering, zealous, and reliable; as an opponent, frank and honorable; and as a man, though never social, always civil and ingenuous. His paper was dignified, high-minded, and courteous, free from all vulgarity, slang, and low epithets. It was read far and wide, and commanded the respect of friends and foes, as much for its honest drift and manly force, as for its superior claims as a newspaper. That such a man should prostitute his talents, his genius, and respectability to low uses, is deplorable. But with *Fourierism* began the hallucination which has resulted in converting both the man and the paper into the antipodes of their former selves.

But we set out to show that Romanism is diametrically opposed to Republicanism, this being the *third* feature of this subject which I deem it necessary to review. It would seem almost unnecessary to add a word to what has been already written, in order to show that the Romish Church, in its whole character and spirit, is hostile to the character and spirit of our free institutions. The simple fact that one is an *absolute* government, and the other a *popular* government, establishes the antipodal. These are the extremes of social organism, and when extremes meet, decomposition of one or the other must ensue, unless the repulsive power is sufficient in the one or the other to prevent an actual contact.

American Republicanism cultivates intelligence among the people. Romanism suppresses intelligence.

American Republicanism recognizes and secures to all men the right of trial by jury. Romanism adjudicates in the sombre dungeon of the inquisition, or through the will of a single prelate, who may be at once the accuser, the judge, and the executioner.

American Republicanism ensures the freedom of the press, and the right of free speech. Romanism silences, or else muzzles the press and forbids discussion; it puts a bridle on the lips of its subjects, as we do on the lips of our state-prison convicts.

American Republicanism secures to its citizens the right of suffrage in the choice of their rulers, with the power to impeach and remove. Romanism chooses its executive officer or sovereign, by a vote of the college of cardinals; that sovereign holds his authority, which is absolute, for life, and the cardinals are appointed by him. The people have no voice.

American Republicanism secures the full liberty of conscience to all its people, and to the stranger within its gates. Romanism pronounces liberty of conscience to be a wicked heresy.

American Republicanism permits every human creature to read and study the Word of God. Romanism forbids it. In a word, American Republicanism is FREEDOM; Romanism is *slavery.*

In a late encyclical letter, issued by the present sovereign of Rome, he announces his views of the liberty of conscience, in the following unequivocal terms:

> "Liberty of conscience," he says, "is an absurd and dangerous maxim, or rather the ravings of delirium.'

It would, indeed, be a dangerous maxim in one who hopes to rule as a despot; but in our Republic it is regarded as essential to the welfare of religion, and as one of the inalienable rights of man. Where the rights of conscience are thus fettered, or rather *crushed out*, the men who apply the torture may well fortify their act by other despotic measures—

the suppression of the right of speech and discussion, or the spread of intelligence through the channel of an unfettered press. The opinion of the present Pope on the subject of a free press is given in the following words, which I quote from the same encyclical letter:

> "The liberty of the press is that fatal license of which we cannot entertain too great a horror."

In this, "His Holiness" coincides precisely with all despots, past and present. It is not a new feature, nor one peculiar to his office, yet if he rules in America, as a matter of course, the lightning presses, would "click" no more, and the people would have more time to labor for lack of anything to read. Moreover, as the privilege of discussion would be at an end, nobody would lose time in complaining. The Bible societies, especially, would be permitted to cease their labors, and wind up their concerns. There would be no room for their wares under a papal "father." It is contrary to the Romish "conscience" to allow people to read Bibles, and many a poor fellow has suffered for daring, even in secret, to violate the *state law*, which forbade his reading that Holy Book. The persecution of the Madia family, is fresh in the minds of my readers, as well as the still later case of the poor shoemaker, Cechetti, who was sentenced to a year's imprisonment, by the Grand Duke of Tuscany, for reading the Bible to his own family.

This reminds me that I saw, a few days since, an account of the release of Cechetti, from prison, on condition that he would submit to perpetual banishment from his native land. Well, let the poor Italian shoemaker come to the United States. He may follow his honest calling without interruption; read the Bible to his heart's content, and say what he likes of the Grand Duke, without fear of arrest or imprisonment.

We could very well afford to set aside the secular and political features of the Romish Church, and still it would remain, in its religious character alone, the antagonist of American Republicanism. Throughout its whole construction, there is not a single element in sympathy with our free, energetic, and soul-inspiring institutions. The hierarchy in the United States, *professes* attachment to the government, and her children from the Emerald Isle (made desolate and repulsive through priestcraft), avail themselves of the liberty *we* give to them, and weave the harp of oppressed, down-trodden Erin, in the folds of the unsullied ensign of American Liberty. What a mockery of their own vassalage! What a contrast! The relic of national degradation blended with the emblem of national glory and might!

But the hierarchy admires our institutions only for the facilities which they afford for the propagation of its power in the land. It will rear the stripes and stars on the topmost spire of its houses of worship during the ceremony of consecration. It will wave them over the heads of its listless votaries, and command them to fight under them and for them. It will struggle to maintain the name and the insignia of the Republic, but *the institutions of civil and religious liberty* cannot exist where the hierarchy presides. It matters little to the papacy, what form of government ostensibly prevails, or what colors are on the national bunting. The Austrian eagle, or the stars and stripes are the same to it, and the latter, even though shorn of its prestige, and its genius, and compelled to blazon to the world its own infamy, would float as gracefully from the turrets of a papal palace as over the capitol of a free people.

Like all other monarchical and despotical governments, the papacy demands a *hereditary* allegiance. The child born of papal parents is a papal subject at its birth, in whatever clime or country it is born. This is in accordance with the claim set up, that "the Pope is prince of all nations." It partakes in nothing of a religious character, but is a part of that system of regal authority, employed by monarchists, which stands, in its very nature, opposed to republicanism. Nothing can be more incompatible than the two systems are in this respect. In the one, the individual is held to be a free agent, social and religious; in the other, the individual possesses not freedom either of conscience or allegiance, and when, after the the conviction which age and reason afford, he revolts against the unnatural authority, he is proscribed as an apostate, a renegade and a heretic.

But there is another peculiarity of contrast between the two forms of government, which stands forth a tangible and visible embodiment, a living evidence of the incompatibility of the two systems, one with the other.

American Republicanism is the parent of progress; it encourages the development of human energy, and gives free play to the faculties. It expands the intellect, invigorates the soul, and elevates the standard of the individual man. It builds locomotives, erects manufactories, disembowels the earth, causing her to yield up her treasures to the uses of man. It encourages commerce, and sends its smoking steamships to the far ends of the earth. It strikes out into the wilderness, talks with the savage without enslaving his soul, and develops the resources of the earth. Romanism gives to the red man a cross and a rosary; American Republicanism places in his hands a Bible and a hoe. It builds a school-house for his children, and teaches him that sowing and reaping are more manly and more profitable than hunting and fishing. American Republicanism cultivates the sciences, arts and literature, as well as the soil, and puts in every bosom the heart and impulses of a *man*. It is honest, ingenuous, and courageous. It pays its debts, speaks its mind, keeps a clear conscience, and looks the world in the face without quailing or winking. How is it with Romanism?

Romanism is the open foe of progress.* It stifles the energies of its subjects, stultifies the intellect, and wraps the soul in a mantle of superstitions, prostrating all self-respect in the individual. It makes no advances towards civilization, and if it encourages art, it is only for the purpose of multiplying its own weapons against human freedom. It gives no incentive to industry, and by claiming to itself supreme sovereignty, neutralizes every sentiment of patriotism and nationality—it

* An officer of the American army in Mexico, noticing that the farmers of the country used that most primitive instrument, a knotted stick, instead of a plough, for turning up the earth, inquired the reason for doing so. He was informed that *the priests forbade the use of the plough*, and compelled the people to use the rude implement which he saw.

is cosmopolitan. Romanism denies the necessity of literature beyond what is required as an instrument of control over the souls and bodies of mankind. It is selfish, dishonest, double-dealing, and cowardly. Instead of openly combating the opinions and intelligence of the human race, and striving manfully, and by frank, overt means, to convert men to its own dogmas, it moves mysteriously, skulkingly, in dark corners, and by covert and insidious courses, and false pretences, Jesuitically seeks to entrap rather than to convert or convince.

Where Romanism prevails, there is stagnation and public lethargy. Where American Republicanism prevails, there is industry, intelligence, energy, and public prosperity. This assertion is too broad to be made without accompanying proofs, and I am not unmindful of the responsibility under which it is made. The evidences in its support are, however, so palpable, so plainly written on the moral and political aspect of the present moment, that there is no room for hesitation, and no need of elaborate argument. Look where we may, we find those evidences written in characters of living light. Whether it be in the immediate dominion of the Pope himself, the papal States of Italy, or in the despotic sovereignty of Austria; whether we look upon Spain in her emasculation, Portugal in her imbecility, or upon the *republics* of South America, the picture is the same; stagnation and superstition go hand in hand—ignorance and anarchy follow in the footsteps of the Jesuit and the priesthood. I need not point to the United States—she speaks for herself. Let her proud name and resources, contrasted with those under the papal rule, stand as my argument, as a living and incontestible proof that Romanism is incompatible with American Republicanism and liberty.

The Romish Church in the United States is, even now, violaing one of the elementary principles of the national government; one of the cardinal features of American Republicanism. It seeks to unite the Church and the State, it forbids the free exercise of religion, and thereby casts itself out of the pale of that code of protection which the Constitution extends over the conscience of individuals, and the free enjoyment of creeds and religious faith.

The spirit and intent of the Constitution of the United States covers the same ground as that more expressly recited passage which we find in the original Constitution, and in the present Bill of Rights, in the State of New York. It says, Art. 1, § 3:

"The free exercise and enjoyment of religious profession and worship, without discrimination or preference, shall for ever be allowed in this State to all mankind; *but the liberty of conscience hereby secured, shall not be so construed as to excuse acts of licentiousness, or justify practises inconsistent with the peace or safety of this State.*"

Hence, anything, or any person or persons who, under the *pretence* of religion, or even the sanction of religion, encourage licentiousness, or commit acts inconsistent with the peace or safety of the State, are not regarded as being under the ægis of the Constitution. Our institutions would not tolerate the practises of the Fetich, with his human sacrifices, nor the Mormon, with his libidinous licentiousness, and the Romish Church, when it violates, or seeks to violate any of the principles embodied in those institutions, either by a denial of the rights of conscience; the suppression or trammelling of the public press; by placing obstacles in the way of popular education; by alienating the minds of the young from parental authority; by restraining the liberty of individuals, or by exerting its influence, directly or indirectly, over the established policy of the state or country, violates the sanctity of good faith, and forfeits the protection which the Constitution affords to its *religious* professions. It places itself in an attitude *offensive* towards the best interests, the peace and safety of the nation, and the people of the nation would be recreant to every sense of patriotic duty, if they did not place themselves on the *defensive* against *it.*

## CHAPTER IX.

### CAN A PAPIST BE A CITIZEN OF THE AMERICAN REPUBLIC.

"'Tis not the many oaths that make the truth?"

SHAKESPEARE.

THE Roman Catholic Church being, to all intents and purposes, a temporal or civil government, we are brought to the grave inquiry:

CAN THE SUBJECTS OF THAT GOVERNMENT BE, AT THE SAME TIME, CITIZENS OF THE AMERICAN REPUBLIC?

The quality of a subject or citizen is found, not in the mere *profession* of fealty, but in *fealty itself*. The subjects of that government are denominated "papists," as distinguishable from the mere professors of the Roman Catholic religion. That such a distinction does exist is palpable. It is evidenced in the recent rebellion of the Roman Catholics of Italy against the temporal authority of the Pope; and it is demonstrated in this country, generally, among the Catholics who were born on the soil, and who have been reared under the institutions of the United States. This feature is distinctly visible with the descendants of the Roman Catholic settlers of Louisiana, embracing several generations, all of whom, while they retain the *religion* of their fathers, have no more respect for the papal character than is entertained for it by their Protestant neighbors. Whether this alienation of temporal submission is sufficiently positive to resist the mandatory authority of a papal bull, or a command in any shape, from "his holiness," is uncertain; but that a fixed hostility against the temporal assumptions of the papacy exists among those people, *is* certain.

In the genius of American institutions is found the quintessence of religious toleration. It allows the utmost freedom of conscience, and the Constitution distinctly forbids any interference that would impair the free exercise of religious opinion. It provides further, that when an individual assumes the duties and trust of a public office, no religious test shall be required of him; thus throwing open the door of promotion in civil affairs, to every citizen, without regard to his *religious* tenets. By these wise provisions, a complete alienation of religion and politics is contemplated, because where all sects unite in conducting the affairs of government, it was naturally supposed, that no particular sect would be able to gain an ascendency.

But while the Constitution is thus tolerant of religion, it certainly does not give political rights to the subjects of other powers. The laws, and principle of naturalization contemplate a total renunciation of *all former allegiance* to foreign authority, and an entire abandonment of the mind and person to the laws and goverment which the individual adopts as his future guide and authority. In this it is evident there must be no mental reservation, no division of the soul between two gods, no equivocation in the terms of the new allegiance, but a full, complete, and total renunciation of all past allegiance, and all foreign sovereignties whatever.

I have shown, in a preceding chapter, that the Pope of Rome is a temporal, or *civil sovereign*, and also, that the character of his sovereignty is of the most inflexible nature, and the question before us is, *Can a subject of that sovereign be, at the same time, a citizen of the United States?* The mere interrogatory, I confess, is little short of an absurdity in its intrinsic merits, but the practical construction of the subject, by custom, renders it necessary that it should be put and answered. No man will say that an individual can be a subject of two distinct, and opposite sovereignties at the same time, because it is plain, that whatever his pretensions may be, the predominant attachments, and sense of duty in the individual, must lean towards one or the other, and, in case of a disagreement between the two sovereignties, the individual will cast his influence in the direction that his sense of duty points out. Therefore, in the issue before us, if a papist realizes within himself a sense of duty to the papal sovereign over his duty to the sovereignty of the United States, he will throw his influence, heart, soul, and body upon the side of the papacy, and *against* the United States. Any oath of allegiance that he may have taken towards the latter will not deter him in his choice, firstly, because his sympathies are antagonistic to the spirit of the oath, and secondly, because he fully believes that he will receive absolution from any oath of that nature. The authority for this belief is found in the highest papal authority. *Lessius*, Lib. 2, cap, 42, dub. 12, page 632, says: "The Pope can annul and cancel every possible obligation arising from an oath."

And the priesthood do not hesitate to promulgate this idea among their people. The oath of allegiance, therefore, is of no moment to the papist. It has with him no binding force whatever. He will make it, listlessly, as a matter of form, and break it as a matter of conscience and duty, whenever he is bidden to do so by his priest, who, in his estimation, is superior in authority to any Protestant government on earth. With these living truths before us, I do not hesitate to aver, that no papist ever took or can take an oath of allegiance to the government of the United States, *in its letter and spirit*, and hence, no papist can become a citizen of the United States by the process of naturalization.

Convinced of this truth, the framers of the first constitution of the State of New York, in providing for the naturalization of aliens, before the states had relinquished that power to Congress, declared that the person naturalized should renounce allegiance to all foreign powers, "both civil and *ecclesiastical*." But even this would not make citizens of them *in fact*, because the oath is null and void under any and every form, whenever the Pope chooses to cancel it.

But the argument used against this view of the subject is, that the sovereignty of the Pope is only spiritual; that it does not conflict with the duties of the individual in his civil allegiance. If this be so, how is it that Mr. Brownson declares, in the letter which I have quoted, that the Pope is the proper authority to decide for him as to the merits of the Constitution of the United States? But we have a higher authority than Mr. Brownson in proof of the same theory, for in the instructions given to the Jesuits, *Bellarmin*, controvers, lib. 5, chap. 6, page 1090, we are told:

> "The spiritual power must rule over the temporal, *by all sorts of means and expedients*, when necessary. Christians should not tolerate a heretic king."

By *Christians* is meant Roman Catholics, because, say they, "that is the only religion that God has founded upon earth," and all others are pronounced *heretics*. Now, if Roman Catholics should not tolerate a heretic king, the same rule applies, of course, to a heretic *president*, or to any heretic government whatever, and they are in duty, conscience, and allegiance, bound to abate such governments whenever it is in their power to do so, "by all sorts of means and expedients," not excepting perjury, treason, or even murder!

Roman Catholics are also told by the *Sanctarel*, Tract de Hæres., cap. 30, page 296, that

> "The Pope can depose negligent rulers, and deprive them of their authority."

They are also taught by the *Emmanuel Sa*, Aphor., page 41, that

> "The rebellion of priests is not treason, because they are not subject to the civil government."

With theories of this nature wrought continually and perseveringly into the minds of the papal laity, coupled as they are with a superstitious sense of abject submission, it is morally impossible that those men can shake off their allegiance to the Pope, and become, in full heart, citizens of a government, whose every precept is hostile to all their preconceived opinions, both temporal and spiritual.

But as it is difficult to test the claim of superior allegiance with the masses of papists in this country, under any circumstances, less than a direct issue between our government and the papal sovereignty, and as the Pope has not yet ventured to arraign his authority against our government, we are left to present such external evidences of our theory as have been thrown in our way. Thus, The *Boston Pilot*, the editor of which is a thorough partisan under the banner of Pio Nino, and a thorough hater of everything American, except the liberty which America affords him to vilify her best men and her noblest institutions, in 1852 uttered the following declaration in connection with the presidential election, then just at hand:

> "Show the Catholic that his Church is likely to suffer by the election of a certain candidate, and *you can easily divine whither his vote will go.*"

In other words, make the Roman Catholic *believe* there is an issue between his Church and the interests of the country, and he will vote on the side of his Church—the latter claiming and receiving his superior allegiance. The hierarchy has only to declare to the people that the papal interest will be subserved by the election of certain men, and its people will vote for those men, because what may be required of one, may be required of all, being all alike subject to the political control of the Church. Besides, the same editor says, in the same article:

'Where Catholic interests are concerned, we present the spectacle, extraordinary in this age of the world, of a vast body, moving without any visible force to impel them, *as one man*."

Thus we see that in its political interest the entire papacy moves with a single impulse, and that *invisible* impulse is ever directed to the supposed interests of the Church. Oaths of allegiance are forgotten when the Church issues her secret command, partisan affiliations, individual judgment, personal interests, the laws of the land, nay, even the integrity of the nation itself, must be sacrificed and laid aside whenever *the Church* issues its edict to the papal subject.

The American people have seen this declaration of the *Boston Pilot*, practically illustrated in a small way, at our elections, a thousand times, and the only inference that can be drawn from the facts herein presented, is that a Romanist cannot renounce his allegiance to the papal authority, and yet remain a Romanist. He may swear allegiance, it is true, to forty different governments, with a quiet conscience, because the Pope stands ready to cancel his oath, but he is commanded by the Church, to "use all sorts of means and expedients" to make the civil power subordinate to the spiritual, by which is meant that all civil authority must yield to Roman Catholic supremacy, whenever the physical, moral, or political power of its subjects is sufficient to sustain the authority of the sovereign at the Vatican.

In this chapter, I have quoted certain ancient authorities

of the Church, to show that the obligation of an oath made by a papist, of whatever character or importance, may be rendered void and entirely nugatory, upon the simple fiat of a single man. I design now, to show that, at the present day, the oath of allegiance to this government is regarded by the officers of the Church, as absolutely *void in fact.* The public authority which I find, sustaining this view, is a statement made in the *Harrisburg Herald*, of Pennsylvania, in the month of November, 1855. The statement is in the following words:

"It is related of Dr. De Barth, the Jesuit priest and vicar-general of Pennsylvania, that when told by a brother that he could not take the oath of naturalization to America without violating the oath of ordination to the Roman Pontiff, he pronounced it a mistake, and promptly remarked that, *any part of the oath of allegiance to this country, which may be incompatible with the first and greater allegiance to the Pontiff, is of no obligation.*"

As this statement has never been contradicted, the public are justified in entertaining the opinion that it is truly made.

The *morale* of the declaration is just this, to wit: that the Romish priest or Jesuit may take the oath of allegiance to the United States without hesitation or scruple, because, in whatever it conflicts with his *superior allegiance to the Pontiff*, it is of no effect—a mere empty formula—in fact, a mockery, and intended as such. Now as the allegiance claimed by the Pontiff is superior in all things, temporal and spiritual, to that due to any heretical government, it follows, as a matter of course, that the entire oath is in conflict with the superior allegiance, and consequently the entire oath is null and void.

The editor of the paper in which this statement appeared, accompanied it with the following appropriate comments:

> "This is the true higher law doctrine of the papacy. It leads to perjury against the priest, or to treason and rebellion against the State. But what if it does? Perjury, treason, and rebellion can easily be pardoned for the good of the Church, and a temporal penalty can be better borne than eternal perdition. The pardoning power of the President of the United States does not compare with the pardoning power of the Pontiff and his priests. It is humiliating that three millions of the American people should be under the authority of two distinct sovereigns. Professing attachment to the constitution of their country, their hearts are corded spiritually to the throne of a foreign potentate."

These remarks apply with equal force to ecclesiastics and laity, or at least to that portion of the laity which surrenders its entire conscience to the priesthood, because the claims of the hierarchy, extending alike over the spiritual and the temporal—or, in other words, the *spiritual* authority being superior to the *temporal*—the latter is required to submit in all things to the former. This has been repeatedly declared by the modern as well as the ancient authorities of the Church, as has been already shown in this volume.

In connection with this subject, the following statement exhibits the deep-seated and absorbing servility of the adherents of the papacy to their regal master, the sovereign Pontiff.

In the year 1849, during that critical interregnum in which the present Pontiff was an exile, or rather a refugee from Rome, a rumor was circulated to the effect that it was the intention of the Pope to take refuge in the United States. This intention was urgently and prayerfully resisted by the Roman Catholic press in both hemispheres. The American people are certainly prepared to witness, at any time, and at all times, a devotional attachment, to the fullest extent, towards the Pope, on the part of his religious followers in this country, but it may be safely affirmed that they were not prepared for that utter humiliation, that prostration of manhood, that wholesale abnegation of patriotism, and that unblushing public avowal of servile prostration, which is embodied in the following extract from the *Freeman's Journal.* Alluding to the rumored intention of the Pope to make this country his place of exile, that journal uses the following extraordinary language :

"Sooner than that impracticable absurdity should occur, sooner than the consecrated foot of *the Vicar of Christ* should bear him to a soil where more than half of the public press would insult him, and more than half of the remainder exhaust themselves in efforts to make political capital out of him—sooner than he should come to a land *where more than one half the Catholic population, ignorant of the etiquette that so distinguishes even the poorest peasantry of a Catholic land,* would gape at him with their hats on, or sit in his presence with their heels up in the air—we would exclaim, with the *Cercle Catholique* of France—'Rather will we go to you—*our arms, our wealth, our lives, are at your service ;* yes, *we love you far more than we love our country or our homes*—we are ready, at a sign from you, to chase out those robbers from the patrimony of St. Peter, and to reëstablish your throne in the Vatican—but, Holy Father, do not afflict our Catholic hearts by seeing you in *a land which is so unworthy of you*, and which is *too little advanced in the race of the Christian civilization* to know how to receive you becomingly'"

Here is one, recognized as an American citizen, who does not hesitate to declare that he "loves the Pope of Rome far more than he loves his country or his home." What allegiance can such a man give to the government of the United States? It can be at the best but a negative allegiance, and therefore is void, without the formal intervention of pontificial authority.

# CHAPTER X.

The Past and Present Condition of the Papal Church in the United States—the Seven Provinces—the Hierarchy—Comparative view of Ireland, England, Scotland, and the United States.

The advocates and partakers of civil and religious liberty, while they recognize the antagonistic character and tendencies of Romanism, are unwilling to realize the possibility that an element so hostile to their welfare can by any possibility gain a foothold strong enough, or a political influence sufficiently pervading in this land of light and intelligence, to produce any perceptible adulteration of their darling institutions. I have already shown that through the corruption of demagogues, Romanism has made itself heard and felt in the public policy of the several States, as well as of the General Government. It remains for me to exhibit (what few persons have as yet realized), the rapid increase of the Romish influence in the United States, and the means which it possesses, of exerting a dangerous power over the public servants of the people.

Prior to the year 1808, we have no official data of the extent of Romanism in the United States, because it was not until about that time that the hierarchy of the country assumed a tangible and effective form. In that year, the number of Roman Catholics was so insignificant as to warrant the establishment of but *one diocese*, and that embraced the whole territory of the United States, including the Indian missions. In 1855, there are no less than *forty-one dioceses* and two apostolic Vicaries.

In 1808 there were but two bishops; in 1855 there are *forty bishops.*

In 1808 there were *no archbishops*; in 1855 there are *seven archbishops.*

In 1808 there were but sixty-eight priests; in 1855 there are *one thousand, seven hundred and four priests.*

In 1808 they were but eighty churches; in 1855 there are *one thousand, eight hundred and twenty-four churches.*

In 1808 there were no missionary stations; in 1855 there are six hundred and seventy-eight missionary stations.

In 1808 there were but two ecclesiastical institutions, and but one college; in 1855 there are *thirty-seven ecclesiastical institutions*, and *twenty-one colleges*, all of which are employed in the education of priests and Jesuits. The laity have no such means of instruction provided for them.

In 1808, there were but two Female Academies (so called); in 1855, there are *one hundred and seventeen* Female Academies. The object of these seminaries, which are all under the management of Jesuitical nuns, superintended by priests and Jesuits, is to obtain Protestant young ladies as scholars, and it is a singular circumstance that they are almost entirely supported by Protestants, notwithstanding that a large proportion of the conversions to Romanism are effected through these "Female Academies." Without the material aid afforded by Protestant pupils, the hierarchy could not sustain ten of these propagandist institutions in the United States.

The Roman Catholic population I have no means of ascertaining. It is evidently kept out of view from some sinister motive. In 1851, the *Catholic Almanac* gave what purported to be a nearly correct census, derived from the reports of the bishops, and at that time the Romish population was set down at a little over two millions and a half, evidently far short of the actual number. In 1855 the reports exhibit only 1,844,500! presenting an unaccountable decrease in four years. This matter is explained, however, in the following paragraph, which accompanies the official summary, as published in the *Catholic Almanac* for 1855, page 290:

"The figures of population in the table, are those returned by the most Rev. and Right Rev. Bishops, but as they are not complete, we forbear any hypothetical estimate of the total number of Catholics in the United States, *in regard to which there exists so vast a difference of opinion.*"

It may be deemed good policy, on the part of the bishops, to create this "vast difference of opinion" on the subject; and we are compelled to the belief that there is a motive in thus concealing their actual numbers. Certainly, no class of people possess the facilities for a correct census in so great a degree as the Roman Catholics, and to suppose that the bishops of the several dioceses do not possess a true record of their number would be no less than a reflection upon their proverbial accuracy in what relates to the interests of "the

Church." Whether the "very reverends," and the "right reverends" apprehend a panic in the United States, by an exposure of their real numbers, or whether they are ashamed to exhibit their actual weakness, after such self-confident declarations as they have put forth, remains a matter of conjecture. In either case, we are left to draw our inference of population from their ecclesiastical statistics, which I continue to quote.

In the year 1808, there were no *papal provinces* in the United States; in 1855, there are *seven papal provinces*, viz:

| | | | | | |
|---|---|---|---|---|---|
| The Province of | | BALTIMORE, | The Province of | | ST. LOUIS, |
| " | " | NEW ORLEANS, | " | " | OREGON CITY, |
| " | " | NEW YORK, | " | " | SAN FRANCISCO. |
| " | " | CINCINNATI, | | | |

Besides, the "Apostolic vicariates" of the Indian Territory, and of Upper Michigan. Thus it is to be seen that the "prince temporal and spiritual," whose throne is at the city of the seven Hills, whose possessions are the nations of the earth, has not hesitated to parcel and stake out the territory of "Uncle Sam" into *provinces*, over each of which he has appointed a *vice-roi*, or archbishop, with subordinate officials to manage the minor subdivisions. All that is now wanting to centralize this immense papal authority in the United States, and to give an absolute direction to its political influence through the right of suffrage, is the appointment of a cardinal, with supreme authority. Such an event will undoubtedly take place as soon as the public sentiment of the country will render it prudent and safe. At the present time, the hierarchy in the United States is constituted as follows:

THE PROVINCE OF BALTIMORE is composed of the following sees, embracing the cities, together with the adjacent territory, to wit:

| | | | | |
|---|---|---|---|---|
| The City of | | Baltimore, Md., | Archbishop | Francis Patrick Kenrick. |
| " | " | Charleston, S. C., | Bishop, | Ignatius Reynolds. |
| " | " | Erie, Pa., | " | Michael O'Connor. |
| " | " | Wheeling, Va., | " | Richard V. Wheelan. |
| " | " | Richmond, Va., | " | John McGill. |
| " | " | Philadelphia, Pa., | " | John N. Newmann. |
| " | " | Pittsburgh, Pa., | " | Josue M. Young. |
| " | " | Savannah, Geo., | " | Vacant. |

THE PROVINCE OF NEW ORLEANS comprises

| | | | | |
|---|---|---|---|---|
| The City of | | New Orleans, La., | Archbishop, | Anthony Blanc. |
| " | " | Mobile, La., | Bishop, | Michael Porter. |
| " | " | Galveston, Texas, | " | John M. Odin. |
| " | " | Little Rock, Ark., | " | Andrew Byrne. |
| " | " | Natchez, Miss. | " | James O. Van de Velde. |
| " | " | Natchitoches, Texas. | " | Augustus Martin. |

THE PROVINCE OF NEW YORK comprises

| | | | | |
|---|---|---|---|---|
| The City of | | NewYork, | Archbishop, | John Hughes. |
| " | " | Albany, N. Y., | Bishop, | John McCloskey. |
| " | " | Boston, Mass., | " | John Fitzpatrick. |
| " | " | Buffalo, N. Y., | " | John Timon. |
| " | " | Hartford, Conn., | " | Bernard O'Reilly. |
| " | " | Brooklyn, N. Y., | " | John Loughlin. |
| " | " | Newark, N. J., | " | James R. Bayley. |

| | | |
|---|---|---|
| The City of Burlington, N. J., | Bishop, | Louis De Gœsbriand. |
| " " Portland, Me., | " | Vacant. |

THE PROVINCE OF CINCINNATI comprises

| | | |
|---|---|---|
| The City of Cincinnati, O., | Archbishop, | John B. Purcell. |
| " " Louisville, Ky., | Bishop, | Martin J. Spalding. |
| " " Detroit, Mich., | " | Peter P. Lefevere. |
| " " Vincennes, Ind., | " | Maurice De St. Palais. |
| " " Cleveland, O., | " | Amedeus Rappe. |
| " " Covington, Ky., | " | George A. Carrell. |

THE PROVINCE OF ST. LOUIS comprises

| | | |
|---|---|---|
| The City of St. Louis, Mo., | Archbishop, | Peter Richard Kenrick. |
| " " Dubuque, Iowa, | Bishop, | Mathias Loras, |
| " " Nashville, Tenn., | " | Richard P. Miles. |
| " " Milwaukie, Wis., | " | John P. Henni. |
| District of St. Paul's, Minnesota, | " | Joseph Cretin. |
| The City of Santa Fé, N. Mex., | " | John Lamy. |
| " " Chicago, Ill., | " | Anthony O'Regan. |
| " " Quincy, Ill., | " | Vacant. |

THE PROVINCE OF OREGON CITY comprises

| | | |
|---|---|---|
| Oregon City, Oregon, | Archbishop, | Francis N. Blanchet. |
| Nesqualy, " | Bishop, | Magloire Blanchet. |
| Fort Hall and Colville, | | By the Archbishop. |

THE PROVINCE OF SAN FRANCISCO comprises

| | | |
|---|---|---|
| The City of San Francisco, Cal., | Archbishop, | Joseph H. Alemany. |
| " " Monterey, Cal., | Bishop, | Thaddeus Amat. |

THE APOSTOLIC VICARIATE of the Indian Territory is administered by John B. Miege, Bishop of *Messena*.

The Apostolic Vicariate of Upper Michigan is administered by Frederick Baraga, Bishop of *Amyzonia*.

With these statistics, gathered from the official sources, we are enabled to form a reasonable estimate of the papal population in the United States at the present time, or rather in 1854, because the statistics published in 1855 were collated during the previous year. Doubtless, many of the American people will be surprised to learn that the hierarchy of the Romish Church in the United States of *Protestant* America, is far more numerous than that of *Roman Catholic* Ireland, and nearly equal to those of Ireland, England, and Scotland, combined; yet such is the fact. In the United States there are forty bishops and archbishops.

In Ireland, there are but twenty-eight bishops and arch bishops, viz.: In the diocese of Ulster, *ten;* in Leinster, *four;* in Munster, *eight;* and in Connaught, *six*.

In England, there are thirteen bishops, including the Cardinal Wiseman, and in Scotland there are four bishops, making a total of *forty-five* in England, Ireland, and Scotland, and *forty* in the United States of America! With these statements before us, we are left to solve as we may, the following problem, namely:

If *twenty-eight* bishops are sufficient to guard the spiritual and temporal welfare of seven millions of Roman Catholics in Ireland, how many Roman Catholics should there be in the United States to require the temporal and spiritual guardianship of *forty* bishops?

How complete is this politico-religious organization in Protestant America! How pervading, how subtle, how audacious! The ramifications in our land are but the arteries and veins that receive their life's blood from the great heart at the Vatican, in Rome, and return it again to its source! It is that power which *denies the right of the people to govern*, and which claims to itself all the attributes of authority over all mankind, by *divine dispensation*. It denounces liberty of conscience as a "*a pestilential error*," and liberty of opinion as "*a pest of all others most to be dreaded in a state*." It asserts its authority to "overturn governments," to "*depose heretical rulers*," and declares its determination to "*exterminate*" all who do not subscribe to its faith. It denounces the liberty of the press, that highway of popular thought, as a license "*to be execrated and detested*." Denying to all mankind the right of opinion, conscience, speech, and research, it demands of them their substance, and taxes its people without accountability. It is the foe of all liberty,* the foe of the Protestants, the foe of our government, and yet *we sleep* while it is insidiously but rapidly fastening its deadly coils about us, and all that is dear to us! Americans! Protestants! Ye who have been cradled in the lap of freedom, shake off the slug-

* When the Congress of New Grenada, in 1851, adopted their new Constitution, which required the clergy to submit to the civil law in matters of a temporal nature, the Archbishop Mosquera, finding it impossible to coerce the government into a repeal of the act, left the country and appealed to the Pope. The appeal brought forth a bull from the Vatican against the Congress of New Grenada, in which, among other heresies committed by that body, his holiness sets forth the following:

"Nor must we pass over in silence, that, by the new Constitution of that Republic, enacted in these recent times, among other things, the *right, also, of free education* is defended, and *liberty of all kinds* is given unto all, so that each person may *even print and publish his thoughts*, and all kinds of monstrous portents of opinions; and *profess privately and publicly whatever worship he pleases*."

gish torpor of your souls, cast away the partisan traitors who would have bargained away your inheritance, look about you, read, think, hear, *believe* and *act* for yourselves! You have been too long confiding in mere seekers after office. Let, now, your own judgments and your own reason speak to you and for you. They will call to you, not as whigs, not as democrats, not as freesoilers, not as abolitionists, not as secessionists, no, not as factionists, fusionists, or sectionists of any grade, but by the sacred title of *Americans*, as *Unionists*, as *patriots*, they will call to you; and your own conscience, your own interests will respond. In your hands is the destiny of your country; you hold the charter of rational liberty, you must not, you will not, you *dare not* be false to the trust.

## CHAPTER XI.

### THE RIGHT OF SUFFRAGE.

FREEDOM of the press, and of discussion; the right of suffrage; the right of trial by jury, and the right of petition, are essential ingredients of American Republicanism. It would not be complete if either of these were withdrawn from its charter, and where they are not, there can be no popular liberty. The suffrage franchise, however, involves, measurably, all the others, because with the power to choose their lawgivers, the people hold, indirectly, the power to shape the laws themselves, and as the choice of rulers involves one of the most important and delicate duties of the citizen, so the right of suffrage is one of the most valuable and dignified of all the social privileges.

In the choice of public officers, especially those of a legis lative and judicial character, the people, for the time being, surrender their sovereignty into the hands of those whom they have chosen as their representatives, and agree to submit their public interests and individual safety to the guidance, care, and control of the chosen government. When the vote is given the sovereign power of the voter passes away, and he voluntarily becomes a temporary subject, with the full understanding that he is to remain obedient to the authority he has assisted in creating, until the return of the periodical elections, when he again assumes the sovereignty, reviews the acts of his public agents while in authority, and with his vote, censures or applauds their course.

Under a system like this there is no merit in being able to to say, "the Americans are a law-abiding people," however gratifying the fact may be, because if they elect bad men to office, and thus become afflicted with bad laws, or an unjust administration of the laws, the people have only themselves to blame. They realize a full consciousness that the result is one growing out of their own heedlessness or neglect, and while they submit to the infliction, they resolve to be more prudent in the choice of men for the future. The exercise of the franchise of the suffrage, then, involves something more than the mere mechanical act of voting. Associated with that act are the requisites of *thought, judgment, reflection ; a knowledge of men, an understanding of the effect of measures, a fixedness of principle and purpose, and a general appreciation of the effect which the vote is calculated to create.* In other words, the act of depositing a vote is an act of intelligence. It is an expression of individual opinion, and no opinion can exist without a basis of some sort in the mind of its possessor. But it is more than this. The act of voting is an act of fealty. It is the most solemn duty that the citizen is called upon to perform towards the sovereignty of the country, and it cannot be legitimately performed by one who is either prejudiced against or indifferent towards the institutions of the land. It is the act of patriotism as well as of intelligence. The man who votes with any prejudice against the institutions of the country, will vote to suppress or destroy those institutions, and he who is indifferent towards them, or he who does not realize and appreciate the purpose and effect of the vote, will be swayed to and fro by every conflicting influence that may be brought to bear upon him, and he is quite as likely to vote against his own best interests, and the best interests of the community, as he is to vote for them. Such men should never be permitted to exercise the right of suffrage. They are, at the best, but the allies of demagogues. The man who would barter or sequester his vote disfranchises himself. He is unfit for a freeman, and doubly unfit to direct the interests of freemen.

In this I take direct issue with democracy. As I understand the term, I am no democrat. If democracy implies universal suffrage, or the right of all men to take part in the control of the State, without regard to the intelligence, the morals, or the principles of the man, I am no democrat. If democracy implies freedom without restraint, license without control, or impulse without judgment, I am no democrat. As soon would I place my person and property at the mercy of an infuriated mob, and hope to save them, as place the liberties of my country in the hands of an ignorant, superstitious, and vacillating populace. How can the greatest of all sciences—the science of government—be appreciated or attained by the mind that is besotted in ignorance? How can liberal institutions be conserved without patriotism in the masses? How can the security of a people be guaranteed by the vacillating impulses of depravity? How can true and rational liberty be maintained by those who recognize it only as the outlet of their passions and desires? Men who cannot govern themselves, whether from imbecility or venality, must not essay to govern others. Men who are lax in principle, will make laws and elect lawgivers in conformity with their own notions of right and wrong; hence the utmost prudence should be observed in granting or extending the right of suffrage.

It was a custom with the democracy of Athens to ostracize, that is, to banish, for ten years, such of their citizens as, from their wealth or influence, might be deemed dangerous to the state. The act of ostracism was performed at a public assemblage of the people, who voted by writing the name of the person to be ostracized upon a shell, and delivering it to the archons, or inspectors, who counted the votes, and if six thousand or more votes appeared against an individual, he was so banished. It is related that on one occasion the people were assembled for the performance of this singular public duty. The name of Aristides, a man proverbial for the purity of his character, and surnamed "The Just," had been announced as a fitting subject for banishment. Aristides being present in the assembly, was accosted by a citizen who, being unable to write, requested him to write the name of *Aristides* upon his shell. Taking the shell in his hand, Aristides said to the man:

"Do you know Aristides?"

"No," answered the citizen.

"Why, then, do you vote to ostracize him?"

"Because I am tired with hearing him called '*The Just*,'" was the petulant answer.

Aristides immediately wrote his own name on the shell, and having returned it to the voter, passed on in silence.

If such are the results of universal suffrage, or "*pure* democracy," the system, is certainly, little calculated to promote good government.

The legitimate qualifications of a voter in the United States do not, by any means, involve the highest grade of intelligence, nor even the most perfect standard of morality. They require intelligence sufficient to form the basis of an independent opinion on the prominent measures of national policy, and the honesty and capacity of men; and they require morality sufficient to form a firm and inflexible political integrity, and an unwavering patriotism, or love of the *home* country and its institutions. These qualifications are sufficient, and there are but few Americans who have not acquired them by intuition, before they arrived at the age of manhood.

The first political idea that is presented to the mind of one reared under the influences of American Republicanism, is *equality*. Through the avenues and surroundings of republican custom, the mind of the American boy steps naturally upon the platform of equality, as soon as he is old enough to comprehend any general principles. He finds no privileged class above him to subdue and neutralize his youthful spirit—no aristocracy to overawe the innate impulses and aspirations of the free soul. He looks around, and finds himself the peer of his associates; he encounters no superior of his own age—no master except over his imperfections. His mind roams at large, and gains strength by activity; he reads, he listens to his elders, he forms opinions on topics within the scope of his mind, and fearlessly expresses them, and thus, by early habit learns to demand of others "nothing but what is right, and to submit to nothing that is wrong." It is the character of righteous independence, and thus fortified, he enters with a firm step and a reflecting mind, upon the duties of a citizen. This independence of character gives force to his principles, and vigor to his integrity. It quickens his perception, encourages a becoming self-respect, expands his understanding, and thus qualifies him early for a rational comprehension and a free exercise of the prerogatives of an intelligent and moral citizen.

These qualifications are rarely found in one trained to submission, and imbued with a sense of his own inferiority. Such a man, coming from the twilight of bondage into the broad meridian of freedom, is dazzled with the unaccustomed glory that surrounds him. His confused senses cannot endure the light. He is lost, bewildered. He can neither comprehend nor realize his new position. Accustomed to cringe in the presence of his "betters," he looks in vain for a living shrine that will accept the homage of his bended knee. By slow degrees, he at length imbibes a faint idea of the transition that he has encountered. He is told that he inhabits a land of liberty and equality. He gets a confused notion that a great change has taken place in his condition, but the nature of the change is yet unrevealed to his mental faculties. He has heard something about "liberty" before, without knowing what was meant, but the word "equality," is not found in his lexicon, and he can't make out how it is that he is "as good as other people." His mind is not a blank, it is worse than a blank. He has had engraven thereon, by the hand of a stern artist, thoughts and fancies adapted to his former state—lessons, not of rational obedience, merely, but of low, slavish, abject submission, and it is difficult to rub out the impression, and make a clean surface.

Is such a man in a condition to exercise the right of suffrage side by side with the free-born, and free-cultured intelligence? Should the vote of such a man be permitted to neutralize and render nugatory the vote of the most enlightened mind in the nation? Such is its effect. I leave common sense to answer the question.

But the man does not always remain thus? No. Let us pass to the next transition. The tablets of his mind are undergoing a further change. The attrition of surrounding elements are gradually making their mark upon them, obliterating the old impression only by new excoriations, the one commingling with the other without order, and the whole presenting an unintelligible mass of cross hatchings, etchings, lines, and interlines. The old memories are imperfectly hidden while yet the new impressions are equally indistinct. The man realizes his new position without comprehending its moral. He experiences an awkward relief from time-honored restraint. He perceives that he has a right to speak his mind, and he does so, freely; giving off, like a blurred copper-plate, the confused impressions of the matrix. He talks of *democracy* like a parrot, and seasons his essays of partisan devotion, with reminiscences of the "ould counthry," the "Faderland," or "La Belle France." St. Patrick and General

Jackson are synonymous; the "Marseillaise" mingles with the homespun air of "Yankee Doodle;" Washington and Victoria are blended in a halo around the brim of the same wine-cup, and beer-bibing infidelity pours out its boisterous libations over the quiet surface of an American, Christian Sabbath. The unshackled mind asserts its crude estimate of freedom, and degenerates into licentiousness. The flood-gates of passions and desires, long pent up, and closed by unnatural restraints, are now thrown apart, and the individual, having conceived a false estimate of liberty, rushes forth to the opposite extreme. Is this man qualified to perform *rationally* the duties of an American citizen? Is he fit to exercise that delicate and momentous trust, the power of the suffrage, and to choose men to make laws for a well-governed community? The use of the ballot presupposes illustration, a clear perception of moral right and wrong, an understanding of the governing principle of the nation in which it is employed, a stern political integrity, and, above all, an *unadulterated and inflexible* patriotism. In a political point of view, this man possesses not one of these qualifications.

We might pursue this character in illustration of the qualities of the suffrage, until we find it personifying the adage of "a beggar on horseback," or the slave with a whip in his hand—the most unscrupulous and despotic masters being those who, through the freaks of fortune, have been raised to authority from beneath the hand of oppression. But it is needless. The truth and the force of my illustration will be recognized and inwardly confessed, even by those who have most cultivated and *forced* the growth of an alien vote in the land—those who have hastened the process of naturalization, and then *dragged* their uncomprehending victims by thousands to the polls, and through their unmeaning votes made null and void the legitimate judgment of the people! The spirits who, for years past, have clustered around the council fires of "the old wigwam," can attest, if they will, the frauds committed upon our laws, and the outrages inflicted on the popular sovereignty and the popular right, by the falsehoods and perjuries practised under their sanction, upon the sacredness of the ballot-box.

Viewed in the abstract, popular suffrage is not the *peculiar* adjunct of liberty. It may be employed as the ægis of freedom, or the weapon of the despot; or it may become itself a despotism, trampling upon the rights of a minority. What despotism more positive than the ostracism of *democratic* Athens, where the unthinking and ignorant populace voted into exile their most virtuous citizens and benefactors, for no other crime than their wealth and talents? What has been done before, may be done again, wherever ignorance, jealousy, prejudice, superstition, or bigotry point the way.

Classes have ere now been arrayed against classes; the poor against the rich, the rich against the poor; the evil against the good, until the very *virtues* of men have been made a justifiable cause of popular hatred, and popular outrage upon the persons of their possessors.

The suffrage, then, is not exempt from the necessity of a careful surveillance. It will bear watching. It is the shield of liberty only where a just equilibrium exists in the popular mind; where intelligence, justice, and morality go hand in hand, and where an unequivocal patriotism pervades the masses of the people.

When Louis Kossuth was in New York, a body of malcontent foreigners, styling themselves "The Industrial Congress," determined to be in the fashion of the time, and present an address to the distinguished Hungarian. These men, who were mostly of the working class, but unable to appreciate the blessings of true and rational liberty, exhibited their love of *industry* by quitting their shops, and in an organized body discussing, for weeks together, the imperfections of the American system of government. In their address to Kossuth, they made use of the following language:

"Warm and devout, however, as our welcome is, we are pained to confess that freedom, as yet, exists *but technically* with ourselves.

"We are free, but only free *to improve* the privileges bequeathed to us by our sires, *through popular opinion and the ballot box.*"

In reply to this, Kossuth rebuked them, uttering one of the finest sentiments that ever fell from his eloquent lips.

"I believe," said he, "every nation has got all it can desire when, by the blessing of God, it has got freedom and the faculty to be master of its own fate; and if a nation has obtained this faculty to be master of its own fate, but has not the understanding, nor the will, nor the resolution to become happy, why, then, it deserves to be not happy, and it is not for a stranger to meddle in its affairs."

There is a fund of wisdom and a volume of truth in this little paragraph. This fact will be painfully manifested if the people of the United States relinquish into the hands of the stranger the freedom and the faculty which they now possess to be the masters of their fate. The suffrage is too sacred, and too delicate a faculty, to be permitted to pass from them into the hands of those who cannot appreciate genuine freedom, nor distinguish between liberty and licentiousness.

# CHAPTER XII.

## NATURALIZATION—ITS NATURE, EFFECTS, AND ABUSES.

"You may adopt a child, but he will not transmit your likeness."

The word naturalization may be appropriately called a *misnomer*, because the process of naturalization is one of the most *unnatural* of all proceedings. You may, indeed, invest an alien with the rights and privileges of a native citizen, or subject, but you cannot invest him with the *home sentiment* and feeling of the native. You cannot make him *natural* to the soil, institutions, customs, or government, or fuse into his mind the patriotic sentiment of those born on the soil, and reared under its institutions, customs, and government. Patriotism is *love of one's own country;* that is, the country of birth, and the man who could coldly renounce that natural allegiance to his home, is not the man who ought to be trusted in his professions of fealty in any other country. If he is false in his sympathies to the land that gave him birth, his professions of fealty to another land, would doubtless be prompted solely by selfish motives, and we have strong grounds to believe him unreliable in his professions to loyalty. If, on the other hand, his heart and sentiments remain true to his natural instincts, while yet he forswears those instincts, and renounces all attachment, association, or allegiance to his native land, his trustworthiness is still in doubt, because, in making the oath of allegiance, there is a mental reservation, not palpable, perhaps, at the time, even to his own perception, but liable to development through the pressure of after circumstances. You may engraft a twig of the *russet* upon the tree of the *golden pippin;* yet the twig, while it sucks subsistence from the pippin, will bear only *russets.*

You may pass a man through the formality of an oath of allegiance, and yet he may not understand a thousandth part of the stupendous purport of that oath. Ask an Irishman if he is willing to join an invading army, land on the soil of the Shamrock, shoot down his own countrymen, Catholics, Protestants, and all, burn their cabins, silence the harp, and spread desolation over the "Green Isle" of his birth, at the command of America, and he will understand you. And his reply, in ninety-nine cases out of every hundred, would be precisely what it ought to be, a loud, sonorous, indignant No! That would evince true patriotism, true love of country. Yet, when he takes the formal oath of allegiance to the United States, he promises to do all this.

The same rule applies to all men of all nations. The Englishman, proud of his national ancestry and achievements, his home customs, and even the lineal pageantry of royalty, and the grandeur of aristocracy, still loves his queen, find him where you will, and realizes nothing abroad that will compare with the productions of his own island home. Would he coolly and deliberately swear to enter the heart of that home, sword in hand, at the demand of any nation on earth? No. Yet when he places his hand upon the Holy Testaments, and the cold conventional oath of allegiance to another government trembles upon his lips, *he swears to do this thing!* Can he mean it in his heart? By no means. The oath is a mockery to the soul!

But we have something more than mere speculative and hypothetical authority for this declaration. The sentiment of real patriotism is demonstrated in a thousand forms. We see it in the brightening eye, we hear it in the joyous laugh of the emigrant, when he hears "good news" from home. The sigh of the exile is a mournful tribute to it, and the gush of honorable pride which swells in the bosom of the wanderer when he hears of some new record on the tablet of his country's glory, attests the ever living flame that is within. We behold it in that fraternal instinct which draws countrymen to countrymen as they meet, for the first time in their lives, in a strange land. It is witnessed in the gathering of new communities of one people in the land of adoption; in their reverence of early customs and habits, and especially is it presented to our notice in the organization of benevolent, political, and other societies, by persons of the same country. In the gatherings of these societies, their members enjoy an uninterrupted interchange of the *old* national sentiment. The present is forgotten in their dreams of the past; the home of their adoption is lost in the cloud of patriotic reminiscences, which cluster around the homes they have left, and too often, perhaps, the attachments thus recalled are permitted to burst forth like a smothered flame, consuming and obliterating their oath-bound fealty of adoption.

The St. George Society, an incorporation of English gentlemen, in the State of New York, have kindly placed the proof of my statement on the record. At the anniversary gathering of that association in 1852, the following occurrence took place. I repeat the account precisely as I find it reported in the New York journals of that day. After the usual dinner ceremonies of such occasions,

"The president gave the second toast, prefacing it with a few remarks. He would beg to call attention to the portrait of her gracious majesty, Queen Victoria, now ornamenting their walls. Some five or six years ago it was determined that the society should procure a portrait of her majesty, and he would inform them what was done in the matter. He then read the following communication on the subject :'

*To the Queen's most excellent Majesty.*

"May it please your Majesty :

"We, your majesty's *most dutiful and loyal subjects,* a committee duly appointed by the St. George's Society *of the State of New York,* a corporate body, formed for the relief and support of *our countrymen* who may be in distress within this State, humbly beg leave to tender to your majesty, in the name of our society, our most grateful acknowledgments for the high mark of favor which your majesty has been so graciously pleased to confer upon us, in permitting a copy of the portrait of your majesty, by Winterhalter, to be made for our society. This signal proof of the benevolent regard which your majesty has condescended to entertain for *a body of your majesty's subjects,* who, though removed from the immediate sphere of your majesty's beneficent rule, and the lustre of your majesty's bright example, *yield to none in devotion to your majesty,* and to your majesty's illustrious family, will be regarded with the sentiments which so gracious an act must call forth. In venturing, therefore, to intrude upon your majesty with this expression of their gratitude, the committee beg to assure your majesty that the members of their society, *though far from the land of their fathers and of their love, can never cease to think of it with tenderness*, and that the prayers which they offer to God from *their home in this friendly republic*, for the long continuance of your majesty's health and prosperity, *flow from hearts as loyal*, and are uttered *by lips as true*, as can be found in any part of your majesty's almost boundless dominions."

This missive of superlative loyalty to the sovereign of England, was uttered by and on behalf of men who had taken the oath of allegiance to the United States of America, and renounced all allegiance to every other prince, potentate, and government, and especially to this same sovereign and government of Great Britain! This fully sustains the hypothesis that men are not to be sworn out of their natural allegiance and affections. It evinces an irrepressible fidelity, not only to the home of childhood, but also to the government and institutions of the land of nativity. It is patriotism in all the essentials of that sentiment, and therefore beyond the reach of censure or reproach. The error by which men swear an allegiance which they cannot give, lies not in the individual, but in the system itself. That system is a moral fraud—a subterfuge by which men are inveigled through the promptings of personal interest, to compromise their noblest instincts. Could not a system be devised that would protect alike the individual interest of the alien, and the interests of the State, without demanding this unnatural sacrifice ?

Laws of naturalization must be regarded in the light of a system of contracts, by which the contracting parties agree to render an equivalent for services rendered. Upon the understood and recognized principles of international law, an alien possesses no intrinsic rights in the land where he is a resident, beyond that of protection for his person, and this accrues under the common law of humanity: and in return for this protection he is required to defend with his person, and sustain with his means, the government which gives him shelter.

The system of naturalization was created for the double purpose of affording to the alien increased privileges, and adding to the resources of the State by binding the alien more closely to its interests. Thus, its *intention* is both *politic* and *humane*. The system is calculated, under some circumstances, to give strength to the government especially in its infancy, and at the same time afford desirable facilities and a fixed protection to those who, from any cause, may have cast their lot in a land of strangers These objects would, however, be as completely secured without violence to the sentiments of the alien, and with safety to the State, by the adoption of a system of *affiliation*, instead of that which is called naturalization. A system that would identify the respectable resident immigrant with the *social family*, but not with the *political* family of the country and afford to him all the advantages of citizenship, except the right to take part in the government, would satisfy al the requirements of humanity and hospitality, and relieve the State from all the dangers of internal foreign influence.

In order to complete the contract of naturalization two pre-requisites exist, and two results are contemplated in its consummation. The first pre-requisite is, that the individual shall have left the land of his nativity, and alienated himself utterly and for ever from its government, binding himself, at the same time, politically and socially, to the country that receives him as its citizen or subject, to adopt it as his own, to obey its laws, and to defend it against all other governments, but especially against the government and country of his former fealty; and second, on these conditions the government that receives him must have made solemn promise to shelter and protect him in his person and property as one of its own, and to extend to him certain of the poli. litical privileges, and the social immunities enjoyed by its natural born citizens or subjects.

These are the pre-requisites of the condition of naturalization; the *results* contemplated are therefore—first, to strengthen and enhance the moral and physical resources of the government, and second, to improve the condition and secure the safety of the individual.

The government, then, is the first contracting party, and it remains for it to say what the terms of naturalization shall be —what amount of concession shall be made to the individual, if any, or whether it will receive him as a citizen or not, on any terms; because the government is under no moral or legal obligation so to receive him unless the interest of the country will be enhanced thereby. With the government, it is a question of mere policy, with the individual it is a matter of safety and direct personal interest.

The contract of naturalization, then, is solely of a mercenary character. It is a bargain made for value received, and it involves no more of sentiment than the purchase and sale of a house or a horse. The whole question of *humanity* and primitive right is settled in the normal relationship of *resident* and *country*, in which connection the resident demands and receives from the country protection to his person. All beyond that is purely conventional.

The government of a nation is intrinsically the trustee of its own people. It is the custodian of the public safety, the public peace, the public prosperity and honor. To watch over and guard these interests is its sole duty and responsibility, and it is bound to ward off and turn aside any and every influence that is calculated to impair them. If, therefore, it shall at any time appear that the naturalization of aliens is in whole, or measurably, detrimental to those interests, it becomes the duty of the government to alter and amend its terms of naturalization, and, if deemed necessary, to abolish them altogether.

As the government possesses the sole power of fixing the terms of naturalization, it is fair to infer that those terms will be so framed as to ensure an advantage to the state, or that the state shall not give to the alien more than an equivalent for what it is to receive from him in return. The principle is precisely the same as that where a man of business takes into his establishment a workman, who is to perform certain duties at a stipulated price, and as an employer would be accounted a bad manager who would agree to pay to the employed more than he could earn, so that government must be deemed incompetent, or unfaithful to its trust, which would grant to the alien advantages superior to those required of, or desirable from him to the state. Thus, according to circumstances, the terms of naturalization vary essentially with different governments, the government of the United States, being the only one of any importance on earth, which makes its contract entirely favorable to the subordinate party.

The privileges granted by Russia, and most of the northern European powers to their naturalized subjects, extend but little beyond those enjoyed by every foreign *resident* in the United States, viz. protection in person and property to the same extent that the person and property of their natural subjects are protected. In the Turkish empire the naturalized subject is required to renounce not only his country, but his religion—and after this, his advantages are but nominal—he has no political power or rights whatever, except so far as the civil relates to the military.

England, perhaps, comes nearest to an equitable distribution of relative advantages between the state and the naturalized subjects. She concedes to the person naturalized, all the minor immunities of her natural subjects, together with the right of suffrage based on a possession of freehold property, and the *right* to hold subordinate, or local offices, *if he can get them*—a contingency which seldom occurs. He cannot, in any case, hold a legislative office, or a seat in the privy council. Thus the state keeps within her own hands the entire duties and control of its own government; *the English governing England.*

Before the act of naturalization can be consummated under

the British law, the applicant is required to send to the home secretary a memorial, praying that a certificate of naturalization may be granted to him. This memorial must set forth the name, age, and profession of the applicant, whether he is married, or single, if he has any children, or not, of what friendly state he is a native, and if he intends to continue and reside in the United Kingdom. This memorial must then be substantiated by an affidavit of the petitioner, and the declaration of *four householders* of good repute, affirming his repectability and loyalty. The cost to the applicant is about thirty dollars of our currency.

The United States, in the early history of their government and nationality, adopted a more liberal policy, a policy corresponding with the necessities of an infant nation. The territory of the new government was vast and fertile, and its population comparatively trifling, and utterly inadequate to the natural resources of its domain, and the requirements of a young, but vigorous independency. Under such circumstances, it was a wise stroke of policy to encourage a healthy immigration, and the most liberal inducements were offered. The naturalization law first adopted by the American Congress in 1790 required only *two years' residence* in the United States in order to qualify an alien to take the oath of allegiance, and by taking that oath he became at once invested with all the prerogatives, social and political, of a natural born citizen, with the single exception, that he was not made eligible to the office of President, or Vice President of the Republic. The primary effect of this law was rapid immigration from the most valuable classes of Europeans; men, who brought with them respectability, intellect, industry, and capital, and whose presence was an immediate and valuable acquisition to the *morale* and the *materiel* of the country.

But this result was succeeded by an inordinate ambition on the part of the newly-created citizens, to reach the honors and emoluments of public office, and to take a leading part in conducting the public policy of the country. Such a disposition, on the part of the adopted citizens, although not anticipated by the framers of the law, was, nevertheless, predicated upon a distinct right; a right guaranteed by the contract of naturalization, and as it soon became evident that under the law as it then stood, Europeans were converted into active and influential American politicians, before they could possibly become Americanized or perform the functions of citizens understandingly, the act was so far altered in 1795 as to fix the term of probationary residence at *five* years instead of two. The privileges of the naturalized citizen remained, however, the same.

But even this term of probation, taken in connection with the vast political influence bestowed on foreigners by the act of naturalization, was at the time regarded by many statesmen as being too short to qualify the alien for a safe exercise of the delicate responsibility of the suffrage, and a participation in the affairs of a government, the very antipodes of all their pre-established ideas of state policy. Thomas Jefferson entertained a peculiar distrust in the system. He noticed the avidity with which the adopted citizens seized on the political privileges accorded to them under it, and apprehensive of disastrous results, which, to his far-seeing mind, appeared to hover over a policy so unusual, he did not hesitate to express his fears, and urge a still further amendment to the law of naturalization. He perceived an anti-republican sentiment, and an anti-American influence gradually but steadily, though to the common mind imperceptibly, fusing themselves into the new system, and even at that early day he seemed to entertain a prophetic dread that his country was nursing in its own bosom a dangerous and insidious viper. "I hope," said Jefferson, "we may find some means in the future, of shielding ourselves from foreign influence, political, commercial, or in whatever form attempted. I can scarcely withhold myself from joining in the wish of Silas Dean, 'that there were an ocean of fire between this and the Old World.'"

An expression like this exhibits the intensity of his dread for the results of a system of naturalization so liberal to the alien as the one then in force; and in 1798, while president of the senate, he succeeded in obtaining the passage of a further amendment, changing the probationary term to *fourteen years* instead of *five*. This act contained, also, other restrictions intended to guard against fraudulent evasions of its provisions; but in 1802 the whole act was repealed, and a new act, restoring the *five years'* probation, was enacted in its stead. Two years after, viz. in 1804, this last act was in turn repealed, but was re-enacted in 1816, and continued in force until 1828, when, in order to facilitate the election of a partisan candidate for the presidency, the law was modified by repealing the clauses which required the alien to obtain certificates of registration, and the declaration of intention.

Thus, our laws of naturalization, which should have been

made more stringent as the necessity for immigration diminished, have, on the contrary, been relaxed, and the inducements to immigration increased. Citizenship in the United States, has by this process been rendered so facile and cheap, that political parties have been able to enter largely and safely into the business of speculating in voters. They persuade men by thousands to become naturalized, who are themselves unconscious of any such right, or of the use to be made of it. They pay the paltry expense of the process for men who have no money of their own, and especially none to expend in what appears to them an unmeaning ceremony; and when they are found to hesitate about accepting citizenship even on these terms, the persevering demagogues urge, coax, and even coerce them, and lead them listlessly before the proper authorities (and sometimes *improper* authorities, as, for example, the "Naturalization Committee," at Tammany Hall, or the Broadway House) and there the poor wondering aliens take an unmeaning oath of allegiance to the United States! Even the judges of some of our courts have not hesitated to lend their offices to this system of arrant knavery, and to attend, either in person or by their clerks, the sessions of these vile committees.* The process of

* On this subject, Judge Dean of the Supreme Court of the State of New York, says:

"There are, probably, no laws of a public character so imperfectly understood and *so badly administered* as those for the naturalization of foreigners."

* * * * * * * * *

"It was never intended by those who enacted the act for the naturalization of aliens, that persons who had been transported for crime—that those who came over here merely because Europe was too full for them—but who retained their naturalization (!) over, the ignorant victims are led directly to the ballot-box, the "right ticket" is placed in their hands, and under a careful and oft-repeated injunction, "not to allow any person to take their ticket from them, or to exchange it for another," they are pushed forward like automatons, and made TO VOTE!

This mode of procedure is now common under the present naturalization laws of the United States, and its demoralizing and denationalizing effects are palpable to every mind that is not utterly blinded by the selfish instincts of the demagogue. The spirit of patriotism shudders as it contemplates this prostitution of the sacred attributes of freedom and intelligence.

However well the liberal policy of our naturalization laws may have been adapted to the necessities of the republic in its infancy, it is apparent that that policy is little less than suicidal in the present attitude and condition of the United

loyalty of feeling for the monarchies they had left, should, because they remained here for the period of five years, be entitled to admission to citizenship. The intention was to permit those who came here from abroad, seeking a permanent home, who, by five years of continuous residence, manifested that intention,—and by good behavior during all that time, and an attachment to republican principles, which could be proved to the satisfaction of a court, had shown themselves worthy recipients of the benefits to be derived from citizenship, and safe depositories of the powers it confers, to be admitted to these rights and the exercise of these powers, by an order entered in open court, after an examination into the facts of each case, and a judical decision upon the application—an examination which should be conducted with the same care, and a decision which should be made with the same deliberation and solemnity as that which should accompany every other judicial act. Those courts which, instead of administering this law, have, by their negligence and inattention, practically repealed it, *admitting thousands to the rights of citizenship who want all the requisites to entitle them to such admission*, have been guilty of a gross violation of duty, and have made the law itself odious in the public estimation."

States. And as it is the first duty of government to adapt its public policy to its own interests, it is plain that those laws should be modified as occasion suggests, to the exigency of the time. This would be the true policy of the nation. The individual policy of the partisan or the demagogue may be the reverse, because the "loaves and fishes" depend for the time being, not upon the ultimate fate of the country, but upon the number of votes that a particular party or faction may be able to cast at an election.

There exist many visible and incontrovertible reasons why the system of naturalization requires essential modifications at the present time. They are as follows:

1. The necessity for a rapid increase of population has passed away. The nation is in perfect vigor, both moral and physical. It has reached an altitude of power which requires no adventitious aid.

2. The intellectual character of the great mass of immigrants who have, for several years past, come to the United States from foreign lands, is not adapted to the political duties of the citizen, and is liable, if vested with full political rights, to subvert rather than strengthen our institutions of civil and religious liberty.

3. The number of this class of immigrants amounts (directly and indirectly) to the enormous sum of half a million, annually, or nearly so. The immigration of a single year being sufficient to exert a perceptible influence on our public policy through the ballot-box.

4. This aggregate of the European elements in our midst, has already become so great as to demand for itself peculiar

political privileges, and arrogantly to assume rights and powers subversive of the interests of the natural-born citizens of the country, and dangerous to the national identity, both as it regards our civil and our religious institutions.

5. It is already asserted by foreign residents that the country is homogeneous—that it has no distinct identity of population, character or interest, and hence, that the rights of aliens are equal to those of the natural-born citizens.

6th and last; whatever the natural or acquired rights of foreigners in the United States may be, they are certainly unqualified to govern the American people, and generally incapable of understanding the principles upon which the American Republic is constructed.

## CHAPTER XIII.

ALIEN SUFFRAGES—VATTEL ON THE RIGHTS AND DUTIES OF ALIENS—RESERVED POWERS OF THE STATES.

As some of the new States of our Union have construed the reserved power by which the several States are permitted to establish the terms on which its citizens may exercise the right of suffrage, in a liberal sense, and under that construction have conferred the right of suffrage upon persons who are not citizens, it is well worth our while to analyze the subject, and learn how far such a construction will bear the constitutional test, and what may be its ultimate effect upon the States in which it is practised, or upon the institutions and policy of the United States.

The Constitution of the United States is silent on the abstract question of suffrage; hence to the States is reserved the power to regulate the terms on which its citizens may exercise the right of suffrage, and the manner in which it may be enjoyed. But although the Constitution is silent on this subject, it is not silent on the subject of *naturalization*, which involves the entire political rights of residents who are citizens or subjects of a foreign power. By the Constitution the sole power to establish a uniform rule of naturalization is vested in the Congress of the United States; and by the present rule adopted by that body, no alien can become a citizen by naturalization until he has resided at least five years within the United states, or their territories; nor until five years after he shall have made a declaration under oath, of his "*bona-fide* intention to become a citizen of the United States, and to renounce for ever all allegiance and fidelity to any foreign prince, potentate, state, or sovereignty whatever." The first question presented in that examination, is therefore this, namely:

Does a subordinate State, in granting the right of suffrage to the citizens or subjects of a foreign power, resident within the State, exercise only a reserved right, or does she assume a power delegated to the nation of which she is but a component State or integral member?

*M. Vattel*, in his elaborate work on international law, says:

"It belongs to the nation and its rulers, to fulfill the duties of *humanity* towards strangers *in everything that no longer depends on the liberty of individuals.*"

He also says:

"It exclusively belongs to each nation to form her own judgment—of what her conscience prescribes to her—of what she can or cannot do—of what it is proper or improper for her to do; and of course it rests solely with her to examine and determine, whether she can perform any office for any other nation, without neglecting the duty which she owes to herself."

The same rule applies to her intercourse with individuals, as well as with nations. Hence, while it belongs to the nation to fulfill the duties of humanity to strangers, the nation is also to be the sole judge of what she can do for others, without neglecting the duty which she owes to herself.

In the United States of America, the national power, or the national weakness, lies solely in the popular suffrage. Upon that suffrage depend alike the policy, the probity, and perhaps the very perpetuity of the nation itself in its primitive form and character. The first duty, therefore, that the nation owes to itself, is to watch over and control the popular suffrage, because, if that is neglected, the nation may be destroyed. This, as I understand it, is a fixed principle of international law, and it seems to have been so recognized when the several States relinquished into the hands of the national government the sole power to establish a uniform rule of naturalization. We are now led naturally to inquire, What are the rights and duties of aliens, as established by the law of nations?

On this subject *Vattel* says:

"The inhabitants, as distinguished from citizens, are *foreigners*, who are *permitted* to settle and stay in the country. Bound to the society by their residence, they are subject to the laws of the State while they reside in it; and they are obliged to defend it, because it *grants* them protection, *though they do not participate in all the rights of citizens.*"

Now, the most important right of the citizen of the United States is the right of suffrage—the right to take part in its government and policy—the right to choose its rulers, make its laws, and direct its destiny. It can never for a moment be supposed, then, that, by any law regulating the intercourse of nations, so important a right can be claimed by the citizens or subjects of a foreign nation, who, according to Vattel, are only *permitted* to reside in the United States; much less can this nation grant to them so delicate and important a privilege, without neglecting the most solemn duty which it owes to itself; and if the nation cannot grant that privilege, by what rule may it be granted by a subordinate State? "Foreigners," says Vattel, "do not participate in *all* the rights of citizens." This implies clearly that they *do* participate in some of the rights of citizens, but not in others. Where, then, is the discrimination? What are and what are not their *rights?* The first quotation, which I have made from the highest authority on this subject, is plain, and to the point; the nation is bound to the stranger in all the duties of *humanity;* it is compelled to protect him in his social character and necessities; to afford him the opportunities of commerce with its own citizens; to protect him in his person, his property, and in his lawful endeavors to acquire property; to watch over his life, his liberty, and his pursuit of happiness, and he has a *right* to demand such protection. Here ends the duty of the nation, and the right of the alien. The rights of the citizen, which, according to Vattel, are not enjoyed by the foreigner, are those which pertain to the conduct and safety of the State, or, in other words, they are *political rights*, and as the right of suffrage is the highest political franchise known to our citizens, that right especially does not belong to the alien. But, says Vattel,

"A nation, or sovereign who represents it, may *grant* to a

foreigner *the quality of a citizen*, by admitting him into the POLITICAL SOCIETY. This is called *naturalization*."

This principle sustains my last position, because it declares that until the foreigner is naturalized, he is not a member of the *political society* of the nation, and, consequently, is incapable of exercising any political function whatever. He is subject to its laws, and obliged to defend it, because it grants him protection, but he does not participate in the political rights of the citizen, until he has been admitted into the political family, by *the process of naturalization.*

The conclusion, therefore, is, that the unnaturalized subject, or citizen of a foreign power, has no innate *right* to claim the privilege of voting, and that no separate or individual State has the legal right or power to confer that privilege upon him. The nation, in its intrinsic power, may, it is true, concede that privilege, provided it can be done compatibly "with the duty which she owes to herself," but a State is not the nation, and possesses no such power; she cannot admit the alien into the "political society," having relinquished that power to the nation; hence, the nation alone can determine what citizen or subject of a foreign power may be admitted to the privilege of the suffrage within her States and territories. The United States never having granted that franchise to those who are aliens, it follows that every vote given by an alien is in direct violation of the spirit and the letter of the national Constitution and laws, and therefore *void ;* because,

1. By the recognized principles of international law, an alien possesses no political rights in the country where he resides,

2. The general government, or nation, may alone confer political rights upon the alien by the formula of naturalization.

3. Any subordinate State which confers the privilege of political suffrage on an alien usurps a prerogative which is vested solely in the nation, and

4. The exercise of a political privilege by an alien, without having been naturalized, is an illegal act.

Yet this delicate privilege has been, and is, so conferred upon aliens in some of the Western States. By the Constitution of Illinois, for example, all white male *inhabitants* above the age of twenty-one years, having resided in the State *six months* next preceding an election, have the privilege of electors, and are allowed to vote for all public officers, *even to members of Congress and electors for President of the United States.* There is no reservation whatever. Under that Constitution, the immigrant subject of Austria, Russia, the Roman Pontiff, or any other despotism of Europe, possesses and exercises, within *seven months* from the day that he first sets his foot on American soil, either at New York or New Orleans, as potent a voice in the choice of national representatives, and in directing the policy of the American government, as the most intelligent citizen, who was born and has been reared under our own institutions! A result certainly never contemplated, either by the framers of the Constitution of the United States, or by the original States, when they relinquished to the general government the sole power of naturalization, or by the Congress of the country, when it declared that an alien must reside *five years* in the United States before he could be eligible to become a citizen.

The only ostensible, and doubtless, real motive for this singular construction of the Constitution as applicable to the reserved rights of the several States, is, that it offers inducements to immigrants to settle in, and populate, the tenantless lands of the great interior; a motive not only plausible, but intrinsically meritorious, because, if the United States are to become the receptacle of the laboring masses of Europe, certainly their labor could not be better employed, either as relates to their own interest, or the interests of the country, than in cultivating and developing the agricultural resources of the wide, uncultivated West. But whatever merit this view of the subject may, at first sight, present, it is entirely absorbed in the vast and momentous results to be apprehended in the exercise of political power by a class of residents, who, from the very nature of the case, must be incapable of appreciating the trust, or of wielding it for the good of the State.

The subject is not merely a local one, nor one in which the States of the West are alone concerned. The influence exercised by the unappreciating alien voters of Illinois, Ohio, or any other State, is felt in every State of the Union, and imparts a color to the very policy, even, of the national government; nay, it is very plain to perceive that it may actually determine that policy through a preponderating influence or balance of power in the national councils; and thus we may have forced upon the country, through the votes of foreign subjects, the European intervention policy of a Kossuth, the red republican and infidel policy of French and German theorists, or the more subtle, and no less dangerous policy of the

Romish despotism. Those States, therefore, which retain this irrational construction of what pertains to the reserved rights of the States, may perceive that others than themselves have an interest in the subject, as broad and as abiding as their own, and that with this interest they are vested, also, with the right to defend it.

When the Constitution of the United States declared that "the powers not delegated to the United States by the Constitution, nor prohibited by it to the States, are reserved to the States respectively, or to the people," it was certainly intended that this provision, so eminently due to the sovereignty of the States, should apply only to the internal affairs of individual States; that, while acknowledging the sovereignty of the Constitution in all matters of national or general import, a local domestic independence should still be maintained and reserved to the States as separate and free commonwealths. Thus far, these reserved rights are sacred and irrefragable, but when an individual State, in the exercise of what it deems its reserved rights, shall perform any act detrimental to, or in any way affecting the public policy and interests of other States, or of the United States, it transcends its privilege, and violates the sovereignty of others. And this I hold to be the precise attitude of those States who permit the subjects or citizens of foreign princes, potentates, or states, to exercise the privilege of the suffrage within their borders.

But, apart from this view of the subject, I think it will not be difficult to show that the act of granting the suffrage franchise to aliens, so far from being an act of wisdom, and a source of benefit to the States which grant it, is, in fact, the worst measure of policy that could be adopted by them. In the first place, I do not hesitate to say that *it fails in its ostensible object.* It does not, in any perceptible degree, increase either the population, the wealth, or the resources of any State that has adopted it. The class of European emigrants, from which the new States seek to derive a rapid population, give no thought to the political institutions of the State in which they determine to settle. Their choice of location is governed by its physical adaptation to their wants. They know no difference, they seek no difference, between the *political institutions* of the several States, and naturally give the preference to those localities which afford the most ready employment. They regard *America* as a unit, and, politically, they know no difference between the State of Missouri and the State of Illinois. They seek, as I said before, those localities which afford the best facilities, and the best return for labor. In proof of this, let us make a comparison: Missouri *does not* give the privilege of the suffrage to aliens; Illinois *does* give the privilege. Both are Western States, lying side by side, but with the inducements to immigration greatly on the side of Illinois.

| | |
|---|---|
| In 1840, the population of Missouri was - - - - | 383,702 |
| In 1850, the population of that State had increased to - | 682,044 |
| Showing an increase in ten years of | 298,342 |
| In 1840, the population of Illinois was - - - - | 476,183 |
| In 1850, the population of that State had increased to - | 851,470 |
| Showing an increase in ten years of | 375,287 |

The greatest *natural* increase of population by birth has

been estimated at five per cent., or equivalent to a double in twenty years. At this rate, the natural increase of population in the State of Missouri, during the years mentioned, would have been 191,851, which, taken from the aggregate increase of 298,342, leaves, as the result of immigration, an increase of 106,491.

At the same rate, the natural increase of population in the State of Illinois would have been 238,091, which, taken from the aggregate increase of 375,287, leaves, as the result of immigration, an increase of 137,196, being only 40,705 more than that of the State of Missouri, in ten years.

When we take into consideration the vast inducements offered to immigrant laborers by Illinois over Missouri, my declaration, that the gratuity of the suffrage to aliens does not, in any perceptible degree, increase the population of the State, is sustained. These inducements are found in the following facts:

1. Missouri, being a slave State, does not so much require the labor of the white immigrant in tilling her soil. Illinois, being a free State, the immigrant laborer does not find in her borders that source of unequal competition.

2. Missouri has had in progress no great public works to demand laborers from abroad. Illinois, on the other hand, has constructed her immense canal, and built over two thousand miles of railroads.

Here are good and sufficient causes to account for all the additional increase of population which Illinois has exhibited over Missouri, leaving nothing as the result of her liberal construction of the principle of State sovereignty. They prove, conclusively, that the immigrant will seek those localities which afford the readiest means of subsistence, without regard to any political advantages that may be offered. Those States, therefore, who seek to increase their population by vesting aliens with extraordinary political privileges, utterly fail in their object.

The next, and most important view of this extraordinary construction of the principle of State sovereignty, is its probable effects upon the ultimate prosperity and character of the States who entertain it, and upon the rights and happiness of their citizens. The first duty of government, after the security of the people, is self-preservation, because even a bad government is better than none at all; but most especially is this the duty of a government so happily constituted as ours, which derives all its just powers from the consent of the governed. Our government and institutions are peculiar to themselves; there are none other like them on the face of the globe; hence, to understand and appreciate them, it is necessary to be educated *to* them; and, without an understanding of their construction, it is impossible to take part intelligently in their management. This axiom is so well admitted that our own countrymen, however intelligent they may be, are not permitted to exercise any political power whatever until they have lived twenty-one years under the workings of our system. My next proposition is, that the sole conservative principle of the nation is in the people, or those who, by their votes, form the government out of their own opinions.

The American people, those born and reared on American soil, have but one opinion as to the general principles which embody our institutions, or, in other words, our system of government. They differ only in measures of immediate or local policy. Out of that difference, political parties arise, and at our elections we determine, by the expressed wish of a majority of the people, what measure, or what course of local policy shall be adopted; but whatever it is, it is sure to be in conformity with the general principles of our government. The intelligence, the fidelity, the *home sentiment* of our countrymen are a sufficient guarantee of such a result. But what guarantee have we, where the votes of those bred under our institutions are overborne or neutralized by the votes of those who regard our system as not sufficiently democratic; or those who deem it too puritanical in its respect for the Sabbath; or those who declare that no government can be perfect unless it is subordinate to "the Church?" What guarantee have our sister States of the West, within whose fruitful borders the tide of European emigration is pouring like a living flood; what guarantee have they that their too liberal constitutions and laws will not melt like wax,. before the consuming heat of imported opinions, and through the manipulation of foreign voters, be remodelled and made to assume new aspects, repulsive to rational liberty, subversive of religion, and hostile to the true interests of the State? None whatever. The chances are in favor of some such result, or at least, that the American residents of those States will be made to endure severe mortification growing out of this cause. They will find that they have encouraged a clannish sentiment among their foreign population, directly hostile to those of American birth and sentiment, and political demagogues are not wanting who will seize upon this very hostility and employ it to the detriment of the best interests of the State.

The mere process of naturalization, recognized and legalized as it is by civilized nations, is a precautionary measure, and presupposes the existence of *a necessity* in one of two forms, perhaps in both; namely, first, in the incapacity of the alien to take part understandingly in affairs of the State, and secondly, in the importance of guarding the State against the introduction of foreign and antagonistic influences. By granting the franchise of the suffrage to aliens, this principle is ignored, and the State is made to assume the attitude of a suitor. The very sovereignty of which she is so tenacious is absorbed in humiliating overtures. Instead of making her own laws, and dictating the conduct of the stranger who settles within her borders, she meekly resigns her most dignified prerogative, and solicits where she ought to command.

# CHAPTER XIV.

## IMMIGRATION—ITS CHARACTER, EXTENT, AND RESULTS.

"Behold, therefore, I will bring strangers upon thee, the terrible of the nations; and they shall draw their swords against the beauty of thy wisdom, and they shall defile thy brightness."

EZEKIEL, *chap.* xxviii., *v.* 7.

So far as the vital interests of the United States are concerned, there is, perhaps, no feature of political economy more deserving the careful consideration of the statesman than that of immigration. The distinguishing features of our form of government, as adapted to the happiness and prosperity of its individual citizens—the diversity of climate and the physical resources of the United States, have conspired to pour upon our shores a vast and still increasing tide of people, fleeing from the oppressions, restraints, and the burdens of life, engendered in the overgrown communities of the Old World. The loftiest intelligence and the meanest intellect—the man of wealth, and the starving millions—the statesman, the philosopher, the idiot, the criminal, and the insane, have been alike attracted from the scenes of their nativities, and, in one common flood, have cast their destinies and their opinions, their worth and their mendicity, their morals and their vices, their superstitions, their traditions, and their prejudices, upon the social bosom of America.

To believe that a mass so crude and incongruous, so remote from the spirit, the ideas, and the customs of America, can be made to harmonize readily with the new element into which it is cast, is, to say the least, *unnatural*. It is a belief at war with reason and common experience. As well might we hope to harmonize the tribes of the forest with the tribes of the commercial mart—the savage of Minnesota with the money-changer of Wall street. Man is the creature of habit and custom, wherever, and under whatever auspices his lot is cast. Opinions, morals, usages, are all the fruits of training and education, and all these, by training and education, become, not *impressions* merely, but absolute *convictions*, or what is sometimes termed the *second nature*. To root out these convictions, to annul this second nature, to *unlearn* the mind of what has been learned through years of precept, example, and discipline, is not the work of a day or of a few years. Where the new element, thus thrown into a community, is trivial and unimportant, and the surroundings of old habits and customs are few, the mind of the possessor is more easily reached and moulded to the new associations. A single savage may be readily civilized; a whole tribe never. So it is with the immigrant. A few individuals, scattered here and there throughout a whole people of opposite notions and customs, will yield, in the absence of pervading reminiscences of their past habits, readily and easily to the notions and customs which surround them. But if, on the contrary, those individuals are thrown together, where the opportunities of an interchange of old thoughts, old memories, and old associations are uninterrupted, the *home* sentiment will wrestle with the new influence; a clannish spirit will grow up among them, and the recollections of the past will cluster tenaciously, and almost holily, about their hearts.

This is the condition of the immigrants from Europe, residing, and still pouring into the United States, and so palpable and pervading has the foreign element become, that its deleterious effects upon our welfare, as a nation, is no longer a problem. European immigration is unquestionably the "Grecian horse" of the American Republic.

The opinion of the father of our country on this subject is worthy of being read and re-read. His patriotic and prophetic mind, ever jealous of foreign influence, could not remain silent on a subject of such magnitude, and as early as the year 1794, he expressed his views upon it in the following letter, addressed to the elder Adams. The letter is dated

"PHILADELPHIA, *Nov.* 17, 1794.

"*To John Adams, Vice-President of the United States.*

"DEAR SIR:

"My opinion with respect to immigration is, that, except of useful mechanics, and some particular descriptions of men and professions, there is no need of encouragement.

"I am, &c.,

"GEORGE WASHINGTON."

Washington saw that the social advantages to be derived by the foreigner who should make this country his home, would prove a sufficient inducement to immigration, without the addition of those extraordinary *political* inducements, which have, from time to time, been offered by Congress, and through which alone immigration is rendered dangerous to our institutions.

The total number of passengers arriving in the United States, *on shipboard*, during the last eleven years and one quarter, viz. from September 30, 1843, to December 31, 1854, as I find by the record in the office of the Secretary of State, was, 3,174,395
Of these, there were citizens of the United States, about, 226,742

Total number of aliens, 2,947,653

*Three millions within a fraction!*

During the first of these eleven years, viz. from September 30, 1843, to September 30, 1844, the number of passengers was but 84,764; and during the last, viz. from December 31, 1853, to December 31, 1854, the number of passengers amounted to the enormous sum of 460,474! of whom only 32,641 were citizens of the United States. This vast immigration does not include the thousands who silently enter upon our territory by crossing the northern frontier from the Canadas. Those, if it were possible to enumerate them, would doubtless swell the aggregate to nearly or quite HALF A MILLION!

The immigrant aliens thus cast promiscuously upon our soil, may be divided into four distinct classes, thus:

1st. MEN OF BUSINESS, CAPITAL, AND RESPECTABILITY, who take little or no interest in politics.

2d. RED REPUBLICANS, AGRARIANS, AND INFIDELS, a

restive, radical, discontented people, at war with all government.

3d. PAPISTS; men who will obey their priests *first*, and the law of the land *afterward.*

4th. PAUPERS;* men, women, and children, who are sent to us by the municipalities of Europe, to be supported at our expense. The great proportion of this class may be included, also, in class No. 3.

The first of these classes is comparatively far from numerous. They come to America to make fortunes, with the intention, generally, of returning and enjoying their wealth at home. They care little who governs, so long as trade is good, and profits large, and if they go through the formula of naturalization at all, it is solely for the purpose of facilitating their means of becoming rich. Citizenship affords them an opportunity to purchase, hold, and convey real estate, and that is all they gain or care for by the operation. Caring little for the country or its institutions, and less for its politicians, they very seldom avail themselves of the political rights of the citizen. They are to be found punctually at their counting-rooms, warehouses, and on Change, but seldom at the polls. This class of immigrants is always desirable. It adds to the mercantile wealth and character of the country; it gives an impetus to commerce and finance, and without tampering with the public policy of the nation, enhances its power, and contributes to its general prosperity.

* The census of 1850 shows that pauperism in the United States is in the proportion of one American to ten foreigners. Of the native-born population, only *one* in every 317 is a pauper; whereas, of the foreign-born population, *one* in every 32 is a pauper.

It is a circumstance worthy of note, that this class of immigrants, the most qualified to perform, in a rational manner, the duties of citizens, and the most interested in our public policy, is the last to avail itself of the prerogatives of the citizen. The United States can well afford to spare the occasional fortunes borne back to Europe by these visitors, as a *quid pro quo* for the practical services which they render while on our soil.

The second class differs from the first in many important essentials. They are generally working-men and tradesmen, respectable in their sphere, and possessing the physical elements of usefulness. So far, they are, to a limited extent, desirable residents. In qualifying this desideratum, I mean to be understood that it is possible to overstock the country with that class of operatives. It is possible to increase the competition in mechanical labor to an unnatural extent, and thereby destroy the healthy equilibrium that should exist between that class of labor and the capital of the country. The result of such excess is to reduce the wages of the mechanic to a standard below its relative value, and drive the native artisan out of employ. It must be apparent that, when imported industry produces that effect, it becomes injurious to the country at large, and oppressive to one of the most useful and important classes of our own countrymen. The offset of cheap wares, which this competition produces, can bear no comparison with the injury inflicted upon the vital interests of the American mechanic.

The home-born and home-educated mechanics and tradesmen of the United States constitute, not only the numerical, but also the *moral* power of the country, and when you strike a blow at their interests, you lacerate the interests of the country itself. Political demagogues are accustomed to characterize these classes of citizens as the "bone and sinew" of the nation; they are more; they are the muscle and blood, with no small share of the brain. They are generally intelligent, and always law-abiding and industrious. They are patriotic, brave, and generous, not mercenary. Proud, too, as every American freeman ought to be; proud of their country, their liberties, their independence, their national history, and their own manliness, and may God forbid that this pride should ever be humbled! It is the moral bulwark that stands between the nation and its foes, and, as such, demands the most earnest solicitude of the government. As an ingredient of its public policy, it is of vital moment that the producing interests of the country should be both encouraged and protected on its own ground, against an undue competition created by immigration.

The theory that capital and labor will naturally establish their own equilibrium, holds good where natural causes only are brought to bear; but the excess of the producing element caused by immigration, is unnatural and extraneous, and the theory ceases to apply; more especially where, as in this case, the element of immigrant labor exceeds the element of immigrant capital, in a ratio at least fifty to one. A discrepancy so wide is well calculated to create an aristocracy of wealth, fatal to the moral and social interests of the producing classes, and liable to lead to the wildest schemes of retaliation towards a government, or a system that fosters and encourages it.

But it is the immediate *political* and moral aspects of this class of immigrants to which I purpose mainly, now to call the reader's attention. They are mostly from France and the German principalities, to which we may add a few from Italy, and a very few of the most illiterate from England; and although embodying distinct theories, they are found sufficiently in harmony in their general political ideas to warrant their classification as a unit. They are the malcontents of the Old World, who hate monarchy, not because it is monarchy, but because it is restraint. They are such men as stood by the side of Robespierre, and aided him in pouring out the best, as well as some of the worst blood of France; men, who established a horrible republic upon the corpses of their own countrymen, and who advanced through carnage, only to retreat again from their own encrimsoned handiwork, and, with white hearts and red hands, seek, under a restored monarchy, that safety which they could not find in the licentious and ungodly fabric of terrors which their own brutal passions had erected. These are your red republicans! red with the blood of the innocent! Men who would gladly abolish both law and Gospel at a single swoop! Such men clamor for "universal suffrage," "free farms," and "intervention in European affairs." They demand the abolition of all laws regulating the Sabbath" they forget their oath of allegiance to the United States, and call themselves "*European democrats.*" Here is one of their cards, published in the New York papers during the Kossuth *mania.* I republish it, as showing the drift of the political thought of this class of *adopted* citizens.

"UNITED COMMITTEE OF THE EUROPEAN DEMOCRACY. The members of the French, German, Italian, Hungarian, Polish, and Czecho Sclavish committee, invite the democrats of all the nations of Europe, to meet on Wednesday, the 10th of December, at 9 o'clock, A. M. in the Shakespeare Hotel, corner of Duane and William streets, for participating at the great manifestation for delivering to the citizen, KOSSUTH, *the flag of the European democracy.*

"GENERAL Z. AVEZZANA,
"President of the United Committees.
"W. RAVENEAU, Secretary."

Some of these men are naturalized citizens, probably some are not; but it is known that General Z. Avezzana, who signs the above card, as president of the "United Committees of the European democracy," *is a naturalized citizen of the United States*, and that he held a commission as captain of a military company, composed of "European democrats," in the State of New York, under the broad seal of the State, long before Louis Kossuth was heard of in America. His title of "General" is derived, doubtless, from his association with this Red Republican organization, and will probably take effect when the people of Europe fight the great battle of democracy on European soil. The last that I knew of General Avezzana, he was a quiet and respectable segar-dealer, in Broadway, in the city of New York, an occupation far more rational than that of organizing seditious or revolutionary parties in the home of his adoption, against the sovereignties of the Old World. His association with these revolutionists proves, however, that he has not become *Americanized*, notwithstanding his formal naturalization, and it also leaves the inference that he does not intend to become Americanized. He, doubtless, stands ready, with his associates, to spring into the vortex of European revolution whenever a favorable opportunity is presented; not in the character of an American citizen, but as *an Italian.*

This exhibits the true *sentiments* of these men in regard to their home attachments. They are patriotic, perhaps overzealous, and founded on unreal notions of what constitutes rational liberty; but springing from the pure fountains of Nature. It presents them in their true light as *Europeans*, not as Americans.

But it is, after all, perhaps, more important that we should know their sentiments in regard to their *adopted* country, than what they intend to do on the other side of the Atlantic, because that is what most interests our immediate welfare. This ranting about European revolution is of little importance to the American people, so long as the ranters deport themselves as law-abiding citizens, loyal to the Constitution of the country, and attached to those institutions, of which that Constitution is the basis. It is when they attempt to engraft their crude, radical notions upon our system, and to subvert that beautiful fabric of government which alone can ensure to us the blessings of civil and religious liberty—it is then that we are called upon to meet them with the sturdiest weapons that patriotism can devise, and beat down their seditious and treasonable aims. In order that the reader may understand how far this class of adopted citizens appreciate the glorious boon of liberty which we present to them, let us quote from one of their manifestoes, published in the city of Richmond, Virginia, in the year 1851. It was issued by the German branch of this "European democracy," and is entitled the "PLATFORM OF THE SOCIAL DEMOCRATIC SOCIETY OF WORKINGMEN."

From this "platform" I make the following quotation. After an appropriate preamble, in which they declare that the American people "have proven their incapacity to develop and build up the true democratic principles of the Constitution" of their own country, these men say: "The Workingmen's Society, in Richmond, has therefore resolved to publish the following fundamental principles of reform :"

"A. *Reform in the Laws of the General Government, as well as in those of the States.*"

"WE DEMAND, 1. Universal suffrage. 2. The election of all officers by the people. 3. The abolition of the presidency. 4. The abolition of senates, so that the legislature shall consist of only one branch. 5. The right of the people to recall their representatives at their pleasure. 6. The right of the people to change their constitution when they like. 7. All lawsuits to be conducted without expense. 8. A department of the government to be set up for the purpose of protecting immigration. 9. A reduced term for acquiring citizenship."

These are the alterations they would make in the *internal* government of the country. I do not republish them with a view of controverting their theories—they are too ridiculous for anything like serious argument, and too insolent for any other notice than that of contempt. The object is to give the platform as much publicity as possible, in order that the American people may see what kind of citizens we manufacture out of these red republican, agrarian infidels, by the process of naturalization. But I pass now to the second plank in their platform. It is marked and entitled as follows:

"B. *Reform in the* FOREIGN *Relations of the Government.*"

"1. Abolition of all neutrality. 2. Intervention in favor of every people struggling for liberty."

It is not assuming too much to suppose, that, with the guardianship of the whole world upon his shoulders, as this idea suggests, Uncle Sam would have his hands full, and plenty of exercise. The idea is certainly a brilliant one! But in the next plank we are to have:

"C. *Reform in what relates to Religion.*"

"1. A more perfect development of the principle of personal freedom and liberty of conscience. *Abolition of laws for the observance of the Sabbath. Abolition of prayers in Congress—abolition of oath upon the Bible.*"

What a blessed *reform* this would be in religious matters! I do not think the American people are prepared to follow out the suggestion, yet this is what these adopted citizens want, and they do not hesitate to say so. The next feature of this interesting platform relates to:

"D. *Reform in the* SOCIAL *Conditions.*"

1. Abolition of landed monopoly. [This means simply that those men who, by their industry and talent, have acquired a large estate, shall be compelled to divide it with those who have neither the

industry nor the talent to acquire for themselves.] 2. Advalorem taxation of property. 3. Amelioration of the working classes—by lessening the time of work to eight hours for grown persons, and five hours for children. By incorporation of mechanics' associations and protective societies. By granting a preference to mechanics before all other creditors. By establishing an asylum for superannuated mechanics without means, at the public expense."

Our American mechanics are willing to work ten, twelve, and sometimes, voluntarily, *sixteen* hours a day, and, consequently, they are not likely to become "superannuated without means." It is a capital idea, though, of these "social democrats," that the State shall first pass laws to encourage and sustain them in their laziness, and then build comfortable asylums, in which they may enjoy their *otium cum dignitate*, drink lager-bier and puff the meerschaum without money and without price. What an admirable incentive to industry such a system would afford

"4. Education of poor children by the State. 5. Taking possession of the railroads by the State. 6. Promotion of education. By the introduction of free schools, with the power of forcing the parents to send their children to school, and prohibition of all clerical influence. *By instruction in the German language. By establishing a German University.*"

The last two *demands* illustrate, in a striking manner, the extent of *national*ization, which they have undergone by the process of *natural*ization.

"7. The supporting of the slave emancipation exertions of Cassius M. Clay by congressional laws. 8. Abolition of the Christian system of punishment, and introduction of the human amelioration system. 9. Abolition of capital punishment."

This platform was signed:

"*For the name of the Social Democratic Society,*

"DR. C. HEINMETZ, President.

"J. BIESER, Secretary.*

DATED, "RICHMOND, VA., *Oct.*, 1851."

Here our fellow-countrymen may see at a glance the moral, social, and political predilections and aspirations of this class of immigrants. We receive them with the arms of hos-

* On the basis of this platform, an association of foreign radicals was formed in the city of Philadelphia, entitled "THE AMERICAN REVOLUTIONARY LEAGUE FOR EUROPE." The plan was arranged on a grand scale, and provided for the organization of subordinate leagues and *military corps* in every city and county in the United States, with a congress of delegates for the general government and direction of their seditious plan. At a meeting of the congress, held in Philadelphia, on the 29th day of January, 1852, a constitution was adopted, giving a full account of the plan, and the manner of carrying it out. That constitution will be found at length in the Appendix of this volume.

Prior to the arrival of Kossuth in America, Dr. Kinkle, the celebrated German socialist professor, had done much towards forwarding these seditious movements, aimed alike at our system of neutrality and our form of government. In the accomplishment of their ends, those radicals did not hesitate to seize upon every subject which had taken hold of the popular mind, and in their efforts to raise the proposed revolutionary fund, they took sides with the abolitionists, as indicated in the 7th subdivision of their article on "Reform in the Social Condition," hoping to gain their sympathies, and glean, at the same time, a few pence from the free colored men in the United States. Thus we have the resolutions passed at a meeting of the German Political Club, of Cleveland, Ohio, in the following words:

"*Whereas*, The colored people, in their meeting, held on the 17th inst., have expressed their sympathy with the German Nation by a resolution to actually aid the German National Loan, the German Political Club resolves:

"1st. To express its hearty thanks, and avails itself of this opportunity to declare the conviction that *the German people, as soon as they shall have obtained the Democratic Republic in the coming struggle, use all means which are adapted to abolish Slavery*, an institution which is so wholly repugnant to the principles of true Democracy.

"2d. That this resolution shall be published in all the newspapers of this city."

pitality and sympathy wide open—we embrace them; we feed and clothe them; we protect them from the despotisms that would pursue and destroy them, we give them liberty, social and religious; we make them our peers, our equals; we marry them to our children; we say to them, partake with us of the bounty which, under the Divine blessing, and through our gracious institutions of freedom, have been bestowed upon us—and they repay us with ingratitude, and, under the very license that we give to them, they coolly, ignorantly, and deliberately set to work in pulling down the humane fabric which generously protects them. They would destroy the very system which has afforded them a refuge, when they had no other refuge on earth, and, in that destruction, they would involve themselves and their benefactors in one stupendous ruin.

A few words on this subject, from one who never erred in his judgment, nor swerved in his patriotism, may be appropriately quoted in this place. In the farewell address of Washington, we find the following passage:

> "Citizens, by birth or choice, of a common country, *that country has a right to concentrate your affections.* The name of AMERICAN, which belongs to you in your national capacity, must always exalt the just pride of patriotism more than any appellation derived from local discriminations. With *slight shades of difference*, you have the same religion, manners, habits, and political principles. You have, in a common cause, fought and triumphed together; the independence and liberty you possess are the work of joint counsels and joint efforts, of common dangers, sufferings, and successes."

That country has been far from successful in its right "to

concentrate the affections" of the citizens by choice; and, at the present day, how bold and distinct have become "the shades and difference in the religion, manners, habits, and political principles," which, in the days of Washington, were so "slight!"

Viewing this subject philosophically or practically, we find that these men realize in the country of their refuge more liberty than they are capable of "enjoying and employing rationally." Bred to a hatred of their own home-government, they have acquired an almost instinctive hostility to all government. Taught by sad experience to regard the rulers of their native land as tyrants, they do not realize the possibility of a government of equal and liberal laws. Never having seen liberty, they know not what it is, and with the first taste of its sweets, all restraints, civil and religious, become alike irksome to them. They soon begin to regard all laws as oppressive, whether they emanate from the edict of a despot, or the openly-declared will of a free people. Thus, having nothing to lose, and, as they think, everything to gain, by agitation, they thirst eternally for change, fondly believing that the time is at hand when they can ride indolently into power or wealth, by the effect of the suffrage, or mount to them on the blood-red waves of Revolution!

I pass now to the third class of emigrants, viz. "Papists—men who will obey their priests *first*, and the laws of the country afterwards." I refer to this subject again, only in its connection with immigration. The *morale* of the papal influence in the United States has been as fully discussed, in preceding chapters, as the limits of the present work will permit; and it remains only to state in this place, that it is to immigration that the United States are indebted for the introduction of this element into the public policy of the nation.

To the fourth class of immigrants, viz. "Paupers," we may appropriately add Felons, because it is proven to a demonstration that both paupers and felons have been systematically sent from European governments and municipalities to the United States, in order to rid themselves of the support of the one and the villainies of the other. Within a short period, several nests of convicted felons have been actually intercepted on their way into the port of New York. Among them, I will mention the case of the British vessel, the *Crocodile*, which, in August, 1854, arrived from Bermuda, having on board *seven convicts*, who had been released from sentence, on condition that they would "emigrate" to the United States. Also, the British ship *Falcon*, which arrived soon after the *Crocodile*, having on board *ten more convicts*, released on the same conditions. Another batch of *ten convicts*, from Belgium, was detected and arrested on entering the same port, during the winter of 1854 and '55, and lodged in prison; but, while the mayor of the city was engaged in obtaining the proofs of their infamous characters, they were taken from prison, on writs of *habeas corpus*, and discharged summarily by his honor Judge Roosevelt.

These cases are cited merely to prove that this infamous system is carried on under the name and prestige of "immigration," and thus our hospitality is abused, and the moral atmosphere of society contaminated. The extent to which this species of imposture has been carried on is beyond the reach of estimate. Probably the most accurate data on which an opinion can be based is the enormous disproportion of European criminals in the United States, as compared with those of American birth; a majority of all the capital crimes, the felonies, larcenies, and misdemeanors being committed by foreigners, whereas the foreign population of the country is only about *one-seventh* of the whole.

"In December, 1853, I visited the city prison, for the purpose of examining the record of capital offences, and I found that within the eleven months past there have been fully committed for trial, on the charge of murder, twenty-three persons.

"Of these only eight were Americans, including two blacks.

"There were committed for the crime of manslaughter, six persons, only one of whom was an American.

"On a charge of assault with intent to kill, there were committed thirty-five persons. Of these only eight were Americans, including five blacks.

"On a charge of arson, there were committed four persons, all of whom were foreigners.

Here we find *sixty-nine* commitments of persons charged with the most heinous crimes known to our laws, and of the whole number so charged there are only TEN white Americans (five of whom are of foreign parentage) and *seven* American negroes, the remaining *fifty-two* being all immigrants from foreign countries!

What an appalling picture of imported crime does this present!

And, in continuation of the subject, we may add the following:

"At the October term of the Court of Oyer and Terminer, in New York, in 1851, Judge Edmonds, in passing sentence on certain murderers, used the following expressive language:

"'Eight persons have been arraigned at this term for murder. Five of you have been convicted, and upon three of you the last punishment known to our law is denounced. All of you owe your crimes to your indulgence in the ruinous habit of intoxication. All of you are foreigners, who have sought our soil that you might enjoy the benefit of our free institutions, and, in return for the protection which our laws so freely offer to you, violate them without scruple, and apparently without remorse, even unto the shedding of blood. The preservation of peace and good order among us, and the security of human life, admonish us, in a peculiar manner, under such circumstances, to enforce the law upon you.'"

If we look at the catalogue of minor offences we behold the same glaring disproportion. By the return of the Warden of the New York city prison, for the year 1850, I find the total number of commitments made during the year as 21,299, of whom 5,777 were natives, and 15,522 foreigners. Nearly three foreigners to one American are thus placed on the record of crime.

It is needless to enter upon further details in proof of the magnitude of this class of immigration; the records of our courts; the prisons of the several States; nay, even the gallows itself, stand forth, a grim, but incontestible witness of the fact, that to immigration alone we are indebted for the vast excess of crime which so often startles the moral sense of our communities, and casts a stain upon our national reputation.* And yet, through our liberal system of naturalization, these same criminals, if they can manage to avoid conviction of crime long enough, become citizens and *voters* in five years after their arrival on our soil!

The magnitude of pauper immigration is readily measured at the overflowing eleemosynary institutions of the country, and especially those established for their especial benefit. The Reports of the Commissioners of Emigration of New York, for the years 1852, 1853, and 1854, exhibit the following facts. The Commissioners of Emigration are a body organized by the laws of the State to look after the interests of immigrants, and provide for those that are needy; and it is only from their annual reports that a correct statistical view of this interesting subject can be obtained by the public. Their report for the year 1852 exhibits the fact that, during that year, no less than 300,992 aliens arrived in the port of New York alone, and passed under their supervision; and, during that year, no less than 141,992 were either supported entirely or pecuniarily assisted by the commission! Thus, there were received into their institutions, totally destitute, the following:

| | |
|---|---|
| In the Marine Hospital, destitute and diseased, | 8,887 |
| " Refuge and Hospital on Ward's Island, | 15,182 |
| " Lunatic Asylum, | 355 |
| Total in the Institution, | 24,424 |
| Besides these, there were boarded and lodged, temporarily, in the city, | 117,568 |
| Total number cared for, | 141,992 |

* See the Appendix to this volume.

In 1853, the number of alien passengers was 284,945.. There were supported—

| | |
|---|---|
| In the Marine Hospital, | 4,796 |
| " Refuge and Hospital on Ward's Island, | 14,365 |
| " Lunatic Asylum, | 362 |
| Total in the Institution, | 19,523 |
| Boarded and lodged, temporarily, in the city, | 44,514 |
| Total number cared for, | 64,037 |

In 1854, the number of alien passengers was 319,223. There were supported—

| | |
|---|---|
| In the Marine Hospital, | 4,762 |
| " Refuge and Hospital on Ward's Island, | 15,950 |
| " Lunatic Asylum, | 260 |
| Total in the Institution, | 20,972 |
| Boarded and lodged, temporarily, in the city, | 44,514 |
| Total number cared for, | 65,486 |

By this, it will be seen that the authorities of New York support and provide annually for a population of diseased and destitute aliens, the very refuse of Europe, to an extent equal to the entire population of any one county in the State, excepting the four or five largest counties, and far greater than that of many of the most thriving counties! In fact, there were, at the Census of 1850, ten counties in the State of New York whose entire population, severally, was less than the number of foreign paupers entirely and permanently supported *in the hospitals and asylums* of the Commissioners of Emigration, during the year 1852! With these facts before us, I feel justified in classifying "paupers" as one of the great subdivisions of immigration at the present day. They are fairly entitled to that dignity; and it should be a question—a prominent question—with the American people, whether this class of immigrants ought to be encouraged or tolerated. They are not merely useless, they are worse than useless—they are a moral sore on the body politic—a disease, both moral and physical—a leprosy—a contamination; and the American authorities and people are made to be their servants, their physicians, their nurses, their hewers of wood and drawers of water!

The plea, that the commutation tax paid by immigration supports this aggregation of moral filth in our community, is paltry, if not meanly mercenary. It is as much as to say, "If Europe is willing to pay us for doing her dirty work, we are willing to do it for her;" and for the sake of a few officials, who grow fat and lusty by their speculations on this capital of infamy, the people consent to suffer it. It is a system of low, miserable fawning to the political influence of the foreign element in our midst, and it needs reforming at the hands of an honest but confiding community.

European immigration to the United States will be found, on a clear and impartial view, to have been attended with its advantages and its disadvantages—the latter greatly preponderating. It has afforded us limited advantages in commerce—it has supplied us with servants and laborers, and it has added to the numerical power of the nation. But it has also brought upon us a train of evils not easily eradicated.

Immigration has given us too many servants. It has left too little for American boys and American girls to do. It has deprived them of those opportunities for practical study in the duties of ife which are absolutely essential for their welfare as men and women. Our boys are gentlemen, and our girls are ladies, at ten years of age; and the consequence is, that, at twenty-one, they are too often neither the one nor the other. Dennis and Bridget have usurped the place of our own children, our apprentices, and our clerks, at the house, while Patrick takes down the shutters, sweeps the floor and arranges the goods at the store.

The light labors of the house, the workshop, and the store, are essential to a proper discipline of the young mind of both sexes; and the performance of them is the prerogative of the rising republican generations. Excessive immigration, by cheapening servile labor, deprives them of this prerogative; and, as a consequence, our youth very often become precocious aristocrats at sixteen years of age

Immigration has produced a discord of moral and political sentiment in the land. It has engendered a clannish spirit uncongenial with the national feeling; it has inculcated theories at variance with the principles of American republicanism—it has brought infidelity, and a disregard for those habits of religion and morality which were inculcated by our forefathers—it has implanted the papal influence, that poisonous foe of civil and religious liberty—it has invaded the time-honored customs of our ancestors: customs closely associating the social, moral, and political duties of the citizen with a firm and implicit reliance on the providences of God; it has inflicted an unequal competition on the industry of the people, and brought about a dangerous and temporising disposition among those on whom the people rely for the safe and judicious management of their public affairs.

These are facts, and, with such facts before us, the duties of the American statesman, in his dealing with immigration, are no longer problematical. They are manifest. If he cannot check the moral evils resulting therefrom, he can at least stay the current of national emasculation, and throw a safeguard around the altar of American liberty.

## CHAPTER XV.

### INTERVENTION—THE PLANS OF LOUIS KOSSUTH—HENRY CLAY.

"Who would be free, themselves must strike the blow."

THE influence of American example has been developed in a diversity of forms, but in none, perhaps, more forcibly than in the eagerness of monarchical subjects to throw off the senseless incumbrance of "legitimacy," and assert the broad principle of popular sovereignty. The ruling powers of Europe have naturally and invariably united in support of the system of legitimacy and aristocracy. To have done otherwise would have been to falsify their own theories of government, and to jeopardize their own schemes of personal aggrandizement. The word "legitimacy," in this sense, implies simply a political right by primogeniture; a right to govern, acknowledged by the mere circumstance of birth. By this system, all the attributes of sovereignty are claimed and held by the rule of simple descent, from father to son.

The success of the principle of popular sovereignty, as developed in the expanded power and influence of the United States, has inspired the "legitimately" governed peoples of Europe with new ideas and new impulses. They desire to imitate our example, and with that desire arises, almost instinctively, a call to us for aid. They ask us to make war upon their tyrants, and free them from the yoke of subjection. This is not unnatural; but it is unreasonable. To yield to their several demands would be a dangerous departure from the precepts of that great "first law of nature," self-preservation, and a direct infraction of the long-settled policy of the Republic—the policy of non-intervention in the political affairs of other nations. This policy of our government is coeval with the government itself. It was urged and sustained by the founders of the nation, and especially enjoined upon the people by WASHINGTON himself. Nothing can be more unequivocal on the subject than the following extract from a letter, written by WASHINGTON, to the Earl of Buchan:

"PHILAD., *April* 22, 1793.

"MY LORD:

The favorable wishes which your lordship has expressed for the prosperity of this young and rising country cannot but be gratefully received by all citizens, and every lover of it; one means to the contribution of which and its happiness, is very judiciously portrayed in the following words of your letter, '*to be little heard of in the great world of politics.*' These words, I can assure your lordship, are expressive of my sentiments on this head, and I believe it is the sincere wish of United America to HAVE NOTHING TO DO WITH THE POLITICAL INTRIGUES OR THE SQUABBLES OF EUROPEAN NATIONS, but, on the contrary, to exchange commodities, and live in peace and amity, with all the inhabitants of the earth; and this, I am persuaded, they will do, if rightfully it can be done. To administer justice to, and receive it from every Power they are connected with, will, I hope, be always found the most prominent feature in the administration of this country; and I flatter myself that nothing short of imperious necessity can occasion a breach with any of them. Under such a system, if we are allowed to pursue it, the agriculture and mechanical arts, the wealth and population of these States, will increase with that degree of rapidity as to baffle all calculation, and must surpass any idea your lordship can hitherto have entertained on the occasion."

From this policy our government has never departed, and under it the magnificent prophecy of Washington has been fulfilled. "The agriculture and mechanical arts, the wealth and population of these States," have increased "with that degree of rapidity as to baffle all calculation."

In adopting and sustaining this system, the United States has stood alone among nations; yet it has been admitted by eminent statesmen, in England, to be an important element in the most perfect system of neutrality in existence. But, with all its admirable qualities, we can scarcely hope to find the doctrine of non-intervention in practice in Europe, so long as "legitimacy" continues to be the ruling theory of governments. Intervention is essential to the maintenance of that theory, as well as to the preservation of dynasties. It was this element which brought together the several sovereignties of Europe against Republican France, and led to the brilliant achievements of Napoleon Bonaparte.

In that protracted contest, however, the efforts of intervention were not directed solely against Republicanism. This is shown in the fact that the most decided energies of the combined Powers were put forth after the Republic had been merged in the empire, and while Napoleon, who was not of "blood royal," bore the sceptre of France. It was an intervention on behalf of "legitimacy;" and its immediate purpose was the restoration of the Bourbon dynasty. It was successful—Napoleon, deserted by his own countrymen, and basely betrayed by England, became a prisoner for life, and the Bourbon resumed the throne. Every event of that tremendous contest bears witness of the fickleness of France, and the last of all stands forth in bold relief, a monument of her ingratitude.

Intervention in the affairs of other nations is an element in the policy of monarchical governments. With them it involves the principle of self-preservation. With Republican America the opposite is the case. Our policy is as extreme as our institutions, from everything which characterizes the monarchy; and, although our sympathies must, and will, ever be with those who struggle against oppression, it is neither our policy nor our duty to involve ourselves in their affairs, to jeopardize our peace, or embroil our nation.

The eminent Hungarian, Louis Kossuth, was the first and only man who could, even momentarily, shake the sentiment of the American people on this question. His struggles (ostensibly for freedom), his sacrifices, his misfortunes, his imprisonment in Turkey, and his out-spoken appeals, touched the American heart, and it vibrated under his hand like a sweet-toned instrument at the touch of a master. But his real character and his real purpose were misunderstood, until, standing upon our own soil, and speaking from his own lips, Kossuth made himself known to the people of the United States. The transition of public sentiment which followed, was almost unpardonable. To him it was terrible. He came among us alike misunderstanding and misunderstood. The generosity of our government in rescuing him, and offering him a place of safe exile, was misconstrued; and, instead of evincing that gratitude which seemed due to an act so august, he had no sooner set foot upon our land than he assumed the authoritative bearing of a monarch, and unhesitatingly demanded a renunciation of our national policy, and the violation of a sacred neutrality. It is almost painful to revert to the contrasted events of his arrival upon, and his departure from, our shores. He came the honored guest of the popular heart. He was received with a succession of triumphs, unparalleled, perhaps, in the annals of our country. He departed in obscurity, and, to his own discredit, *under an assumed name.* His approach was glorious, his sojourn seditious, his departure disgraceful.

His appeal to the Germans in this country, urging them to quit their allegiance, and cast their suffrages on behalf of the European revolutionists, was an act of sedition the most gross and ungrateful.* His attempted perversion of the language and precepts of Washington, was an insult to the intelligence of the nation; and his demeanor, while amongst us, marked as it was, from first to last, with an air of egotistical *nonchalance*, was that of a master, rather than a guest.

It is not surprising, therefore, that the flood of generous sympathy, which welcomed the persecuted exile, should have been withdrawn from the unscrupulous agitator. Yet, Kossuth was not alone to blame in this matter. He had, with unequivocal frankness, declared his views on the course

* See the Appendix to this volume.

which he believed the United States ought to pursue towards the revolutionists of Europe, long before his eyes were greeted with the cheering view of our republican hill—long before he had set foot upon the deck of an American vessel, or taken shelter under the ægis of our national flag. While yet a prisoner on parole in the dominions of the Sultan, he addressed a letter to Mr. Marsh, our representative at Constantinople, foreshadowing all his subsequent proceedings. In that letter, he did not hesitate to define a new line of policy for the United States, and to announce his conviction that it was *the duty* of our government and our people to cast away that system of neutrality, which had been so fruitful of peace and prosperity, and make war upon the governments of Europe on behalf of the struggling peoples.

This letter, which was at the time published throughout the United States, should have opened the eyes of the people to a correct view of his intentions. But it did not have that effect; and his whole career, while with us, was but a reiteration of the theory therein expressed. He came to the United States with no false pretensions. In his first speech—his reply to the Mayor of New York, at Castle Garden, Kossuth unequivocally declared that he should ask of the people of the United States, not their sympathies alone, but "material aid," for the independence of Hungary. Could he have been at that moment undeceived; could he have been assured that the United States would not abandon their system of neutrality, the whole aspect of his mission would have been changed. But, misled by hollow-hearted demagogues, who expected, in the exhibition of a feigned sympathy, to secure to themselves and their parties the united support of the Red Republicans, he was permitted to remain a victim to this error until, after a long series of ovations, he stood in the death-chamber of "the sage of Ashland." There he encountered the withered frame but the undaunted spirit of the American patriot. In that presence, the stern Hungarian quailed before the invincible truth. Standing upon the threshold of eternity—spared, as it seemed, a few brief days of mortal life for this emergency of his country, HENRY CLAY revealed to the perception of the misguided exile the fixed and irrevocable policy of the United States—*non-intervention.*

"No greater calamity," said Mr. Clay, "could befall this government than the doctrines of intervention proposed by M. Kossuth." He, therefore, earnestly deprecated any such policy. The vital principle of this country, he said, rested upon its republican character, as seen in the capacity of the people for self-government, and in its practice of confining its action to its own duties. Our example is one of Christian progress, and the United States, as the only living Republic, and example of man's capability for self-government, was bound to encourage progress and prosperity on this continent. All this would be endangered and destroyed by foreign wars, and with them all hopes of free institutions. The reply of Mr. Clay to Kossuth will be found at length in the Appendix to this volume.

But Kossuth was the victim of yet another error, equally incompatible with that degree of intelligence and political sagacity which had been accorded to him. He *individual-*

*ized* the American people and the American government as distinct powers, possessing distinct and separate interests. An idea so absurd was inexcusable in one claiming to be so well versed in the economy of nations ; yet, unwilling to give up his hope of American intervention, he did not cease to entertain the idea that, by arousing the sympathies of the people, and enlisting them to his views, he could *command* the favorable action of the government. His appeals to the Germans, both in public and by a secret circular,* urging them, by the power of their suffrages, to *compel* the government of the United States to adopt his policy of intervention, was one of the fruits of that idea. This may have been the result of his disappointments; and that, failing to enlist the coöperation of the government to his plans, he adopted the European method, and appealed to the popular heart. His manifesto to the Germans was certainly in contradiction of his previously-expressed views, because, while in New York, on one of those festal occasions at which he was the honored, *only* guest, Kossuth, as usual, addressed the assembly. When he had concluded his address, an Irishman arose and expressed his surprise, that the Magyar had not alluded to *his* countrymen, "notwithstanding there were of them, 7,500,000 in the United States." To this Kossuth replied, in these words:

"GENTLEMEN:

"I beg leave to tender my thanks for the sentiments and feelings of sympathy which the gentleman has expressed ; but he was pleased to remark that, in my humble speech, I did not say a

* This circular will be found at length in the Appendix.

word about Irishmen. I feel it my duty to explain why I did not. On the first step which it was my good fortune to put on the glorious shores of the United States, I declared that, claiming for my own country the sovereign right of every nation of the world, to dispose of its own domestic concerns, I, during my stay here in the United States, would feel it my duty to respect the same principle; consequently, not to address myself to whatever single distinction of birth —to whatever single party—but to address the united people of the United States; and I was and am convinced, that when I addressed the people of the United States, I addressed every man who, proud of his own freedom, feels a sympathy for the principle of freedom in those who are oppressed. I believe that there is the world in the United States, which embraces every man who has the high honor and immense benefit to be a citizen of the United States; and that the world is the people of the United States. *I know no Irishman --I know no Anglo-Saxon—I know no Germans, here,* but I know the people of the United States, and, with these words, address them, and ask for their general support."

Nothing could be more chaste and appropriate than this brief reply, yet he did afterwards depart from the purpose therein expressed, and, most offensively, appeal to the distinctive German character and predilections.

Kossuth was also inconsistent in his professions. The world knew him at first, only, as a leader in the Hungarian revolution against the authority of the House of Hapsburgh. The ostensible purpose of that revolution was the restoration of Hungarian independence; but, to this day, it does not clearly appear whether, in case of success, it was the intention of Kossuth to restore the "Iron Crown" of his father-land, or give to his people the advantages of a popular government. In America he spoke as a republican; but in England he spoke as a monarchist.

The history of this man is that of one who is ambitious, but erratic; of one whose mind is capable of projecting great deeds, but too unbalanced to accomplish them; of one who would be great and virtuous, if greatness would follow the virtuous intent; yet who would be great even at the sacrifice of virtue, if virtue fail to accomplish his desires. He would prefer to be called great and good; but to be great was his ambition. His misfortunes and his eloquence gave him his immense popularity out of his own land; a popularity which, if it had been husbanded with wisdom and deliberation, might have carried him well forward in the accomplishment of his design; but, like a wayward child, spoiled with over-kindness, he cast the golden opportunity away.

# CHAPTER XVI.

## STATE RIGHTS—SLAVERY.

"In contemplating the causes which may disturb our Union, it occurs as a matter of serious concern, that any ground should have been furnished for characterizing parties by geographical discriminations."

GEO. WASHINGTON.

WHEN American Republicanism was in its chrysalis, or transition state, and while its destiny was suspended between the extremes of monarchy and popular sovereignty, one of the first important elements of interest was that of social independence among the several colonies and commonwealths. Emerging at the close of the Revolution from a condition rather of servitude to, than dependency upon, the British Crown; and with a distinct remembrance of the imperative inflictions of the parent government, whose authority they had just cast aside, the people were naturally jealous of any positive centralization of power in the reorganization of their system of public policy. With this feeling prevalent, the construction of a constitution became the theme of universal anxiety, and a work of critical responsibility. But, in addition to this, there was yet another obstacle in the way of establishing a comprehensive and harmonious constitution, growing out of a diversity of geographical interests. The commercial necessities of extreme localities were found to be as remote as the localities themselves; and through the arbitrary demands of climate, the social habits and customs, and the economy of labor, were entirely and irretrievably dissimilar. Thus, a people thoroughly united in political sentiment and political interest, were as utterly divided in their local and social necessities.

Under these circumstances, it is plain that a constitution which should be found to invade the local necessities of any portion of the embryo nation, would fail to receive the concurrence of the people, and result in animosities prejudicial, and, perhaps, fatal to the harmony of the Confederation. It became apparent that the Constitution must be framed, not only in a conciliatory spirit of compromise, but on a basis of the utmost liberality toward the domestic interests of the several States. The great conflicting geographical interests were, therefore, called upon to surrender a portion of their favorite notions of policy for the general good, and the several States, while they surrendered to the General Government the power of controlling the foreign and domestic policy of the nation—to regulate its commerce, coin money, establish post-offices and post-roads, to declare war, to support an army and a navy, to regulate the distribution of the public lands, to establish an uniform rule of naturalization, and, in fine, to exercise all the functions of a free and distinct nationality—yet retained within themselves certain sovereign and inalienable rights, which were deemed to be essential to their several domestic necessities, and not incompatible with the duties and the sovereignty of the nation, or the rights of individual States.

On this basis the Constitution of the United States was framed, and American Republicanism stood forth the paragon of social governments. Like Minerva, as she sprung from the brain of Jupiter, the Republic emerged in an instant, as it were, invincible and mature.

The rights reserved to the States by the compromises of the Constitution were of a domestic or local character solely. The several States took upon themselves the condition of separate and distinct families, each family constituting an absolute component of a complete society, governed by general laws, the family retaining within itself the management of its own household, in matters purely local. All subjects relating to the General Government were surrendered into the hands of the General Government; each State possessing a voice in the management of the public policy of the nation only through the system of representation. Each State also conceded to the neighboring States the common right to an uninterrupted and peaceable management of their own affairs, the enjoyment of their own opinions and customs, and the enactment and execution of their own laws, *provided* that those laws should be made consistent with the Constitution of the Confederacy, and in unison with the rights and prerogatives of the individual States and their citizens.

This was the first great compromise ever entered upon by the people of the United States—a compromise remarkable alike for the fraternal spirit in which it was accomplished and the unprecedented glory of its results. It enunciated an untried and perfect principle in the science of social government; it signed and sealed the charter of civil and religious liberty, and it reared an example of popular sovereignty, worthy of the emulation of all mankind.

It is a noteworthy circumstance that the men who, at the present day, denounce the violation of the Missouri Compromise of 1820, are themselves striving to violate this great compromise, which, in 1789, confirmed the Union of these States, and pronounced them one nation, one government, one people.

Among the rights thus reserved, and one in which every State participated to some degree, at the period of the Revolution, was the right to retain the institution of African slavery, although Congress was empowered to prohibit the importation of slaves after the year 1808. The institution had been fastened upon the soil of the colonies by the parent government, and the slaves held by individuals under British laws, before the Revolution, were confirmed as the property of those individuals, under the Constitution and laws of the United States, after the Revolution. This proprietary right was re-affirmed by the local laws of the States severally, and, with the right of possession, was involved the further right to sell or purchase.

The right to entertain the institution of slavery was a *reserved*, not a mere *permissive* right. The States entertaining the institution held, within themselves, severally, the sovereign power to abolish it at their pleasure, within their own jurisdiction, and at their pleasure to restore it. The institution is, therefore one of a local or domestic character, beyond the reach or control of the General Government, except so far as relates to the *conceded* authority to suppress the importation of slaves after a stated period, and to compel the restoration of fugitives from one State to another. It is also equally beyond the control of any other State than the one in which it exists by the local laws, and any interference with the institution where it so exists, by another State, or by the people of another State, must be in direct violation of that neutrality of interest so solemnly guaranteed by the great national compromise.

The States of the northern portion of the Union, finding the institution unprofitable, very naturally adopted the suggestion of a wise policy, and abolished it from their soil as speedily as the interests of individual owners would permit; and, in order to hasten the event, large numbers of slaves were sold by their owners, at the North, to those who had more profitable employments for them, at the South—thus perpetuating the bondage of the slave, while in the act of abolishing the institution of slavery. The *morale* of the procedure seems to have been one of dollars and cents, rather than a question of right and wrong. It would be well if the political humanitarians (?) of the North would remember this circumstance while clamoring for the abolition of slavery at the South. Free territory, so called, is free territory only so long as the people who inhabit it elect that it shall be so, and whenever the people of the State of New York, or Massachusetts, or Connecticut shall elect to restore the institution of slavery within their borders, they will insist upon their reserved right to do so, and justly too, as tenaciously as South Carolina or Georgia now insist on their right to the uninterrupted enjoyment of their election.

In a political view, the question of slavery is not an open question. We may vote it from our own State borders, but we cannot vote it from the territory of a sister State, without perpetrating a broad and distinct violation of the principle of State sovereignty, and subjecting ourselves to the endurance of retaliatory inflictions whenever a majority of the States may see fit to impose them upon us. As well may the States of the South enforce the institution of slavery upon the States of the North, through a preponderating majority in Congress, as that the North should enforce the South to abandon it; the principle is the same, the right to do so is equal, and the process of accomplishment must be through the same channel. But neither of these results can be attained without ignoring the just compromises of the Union, and removing the foundation-stones of the Republic. It would lead to an interminable warfare of local interests and local prejudices. Let the barrier of State sovereignty be once broken down, and causes of contention would be multiplied an hundred fold. The conflicts of individual States, like those of the South American confederacies would be unceasing, and in the vortex of anarchy thus set in motion, the arm of the General Government would fall powerless. A total, and open dissolution of that Union, distinctly avowed, and embodying the free States on the one hand, and the slave States on the other, with all its repulsive and disloyal features, would be a condition far preferable to that national chaos which would be the certain fruit of a violation of the great principle of

State sovereignty. The political abolitionist, who seeks upon free soil, to disturb the domestic institutions of other States, is no less than a political incendiary! He would apply the blazing torch to the great temple of civil and religious liberty, and like Nero, rejoice over the conflagration!

But all this is apart from the abstract subject of slavery. Our national policy does not permit us to deal particularly with the question of right and wrong on the subject, except within our respective State sovereignties. In those States where slavery does not exist, we may treat the subject in its moral aspect only, but in that aspect we may discuss it fully, freely, and unreservedly. If it is an institution repulsive to our conscience we may so declare it, and, by every element of moral and religious suasion, persuade those who entertain it to abandon it. But the people of the free States have no political responsibility resting upon them in the matter, nor do they possess any coercive power over it. Whether they are under a *moral* responsibility or not, is entirely a matter of conscience with each individual. So far as their political power extends they have cleared their skirts by abolishing it from their borders and each man is left to himself to determine whether or not it is his moral or religious duty to go further and persuade his fellow citizens of other States to do as he has done at home.

I do not hesitate to affirm that slavery is the result of natural laws. But the laws of nature do not always accord with what our moral and religious conscience declares to be right. The act of adultery, for example, and the act of theft, are the results of natural laws, instincts, or necessities, yet the moral and religious sentiments revolt against them. The laws of Christianity, civilization, and common decency are opposed in this to the laws of nature. The child born out of wedlock is, in law, denominated *a natural child*, or a child born under the natural law; yet the poor unoffending offspring of nature is branded with disgrace and the mark of infamy is set upon him, by the laws of moral and religious conscience. Thus it is with slavery, in the view of those who deprecate it, and like all other themes in ethical science, the more remote we are from it, and the less we are accustomed to it, the more repulsive it appears to us. In matters of this nature it is not "distance" that "lends enchantment to the view."

Slavery is the offspring of that principle in nature which gives supremacy to mind over matter—and to the superior over the inferior. It may be an act of ferocious cruelty, in our view, for the wolf to gorge himself upon the palpitating flesh of the dying lamb, or for the vulture to feed upon the dove. If so, it is no less a cruelty in man, when he revels upon similar *viands;* still he does not hesitate to draw the keen carver through the juicy sirloin, or to garnish his table with the canvas-back duck, the woodcock, and the barn-yard chanticleer. Even so it may be an act of cruelty and injustice in a race of superior intelligence to enslave, and command for its own purposes, the labor of a race of inferior intelligence; yet it is the result of natural laws. If it be a wrong, however, it is a wrong without limit, because an actual wrong is not susceptible of compromise—it is a wrong based upon some fixed principle—not to be measured by the degree of intelligence in the slave, but by his innate or natural right to be free. It is not the black skin, the ungainly form, nor the obtuse intellect that shall either justify his bondage or plead for his emancipation—he must claim the latter by the law of personal *right.* If it be, as the abolitionists avow, upon this principle alone that we find a wrong in slavery, the same principle must be universal and eternal, and it will apply with equal force to the ox and the horse as to the man, because the law of nature is the same in either case. It is simply urging one principle against another, the principle of natural *right* against the principle of natural *might*, a rule not generally observed by mankind either by races, communities, or as individuals, when their several interests are at stake. The highest law usually recognized is the law of power, whenever that law can be enforced with safety to its possessor. It is therefore, folly to attempt a combat with the institution of slavery, as it now exists, on the abstract question of *natural* right. The owner of slave property possesses a *legal* right, and that, for his purpose, is worth at least twenty of the other. But there is a nearer and a more practical way to relieve our consciences and eventually remove the institution from the soil of our country.

The wrong of slavery which comes nearest to the heart of the freeman, both South and North, is a *social* wrong. It grates harshly upon the best sympathies of humanity and casts a blight on the progressive genius of the age. If the abolitionist is honest he will confine himself to this view, and make his appeals to the sympathies, or if you please, the interests of the slave-owner, rather than to the politician and the demagogue. Threats, imprecations, and foul epithets, avail nothing so long as the slave-owner has the bulwark of the Constitution, the laws of his own State, and the ultimate fiat of the supreme court as his ægis. Every political assault upon his proprietary character is purely Quixotic; it is a battle with a windmill; it can make no other impression than that of confirming him in his legal right, and drawing more closely the fetters of the slave. Convince his moral sympathies and his interests that slavery is every way wrong, that it is a curse alike to the bondman and his possessor—make him believe, as you do, that it is a burden to the community in which it exists; that its influence is enervating to society; that wherever it goes it carries with it the corrosion of inactivity, and that it sows the seeds of imbecility in the moral atmosphere that surrounds it—show him that it paralyzes the energies of the people, disturbs the equilibrium of society, and that it sweeps away that healthy distinction between labor and capital which is essential to the development of great enterprises—let him once realize that it is opposed to the spirit of progress, that it is neither inventive nor suggestive, but that it is, on the contrary, morally and physically an element of social emasculation. Accomplish this, and the barriers that have so long stood, with the solidity of adamant, between you and emancipation, will crumble at your touch, and fade away like the mists of the morning.

Armed with such a spirit the abolitionist may travel on foot from Virginia to Texas, and carry his arguments with him, not only in safety, but with the certainty of a hospitable reception. Heretofore, instead of appealing, the abolitionist has *demanded* when he had no power to enforce—instead of convincing he has *exasperated*, and, as a natural consequence, instead of advancing in his purpose, he has been driven back; slavery has steadily increased while he has been fighting a shadow. His ground has been untenable, unnatural—he has been trying for twenty years to catch flies with vinegar, instead of using molasses, wondering all the time, in the simplicity of his heart, why it is that the game eludes him. The solution is plain. He has used the wrong kind of bait.

I mean to apply this charitable train of remarks to the *honest* people of the North, who, through motives of a pure philanthropy, *really* desire to witness the abolition of slavery. But these are not the men who promote a political agitation on the subject; these constitute *the many*, the agitators are the few. Their consciences and their dreams would never have been disturbed by the spirit of slavery, had not the apparition been conjured up by men of sinister motives. The question of slavery has ever afforded a theme for the demagogue when all other themes have been exhausted. They who make a trade of politics, and who thirst eternally for place, power, and emolument, *must* have a stimulating theme to sway the popular mind, and when the great political questions and measures of *party* are settled, or grown stale and insipid, their ingenuity is taxed to find new themes for excitement, new aliment for the popular stomach. Subjects which appeal to the sympathies and the moral sentiments of man are avoided by statesmen of honor and talent, because of their inflammable nature. It is only the man of small mind, of limited intellect, the political pettifogger, who resorts to them. Your statesmen of real talent are never long at a loss for *legitimate* work on which to employ the popular mind. From the suggestive fountains of their own genius they draw topics of public interest and public necessity, real or imaginary, but never, no, never will the patriotic statesman suggest themes of national discord for popular discussion.

Our ADAMS, the champion of the right of petition—our WEBSTER, the giant expounder and defender of the Constitution—our CLAY, the stern and unwavering advocate of American protection and internal improvement—our JACKSON, the Ajax of the national honor, who, in tones of thunder, vowed "the Union *must and shall* be preserved!" these, and many more whose names glorify the tablets of our country's history, these never stooped so low, never prostituted their talents so far, never compromised their own patriotism, or their country's peace to such a degree. But they have passed away, the conservative power of their great minds is withdrawn, and a race of demagogues, emulating only their renown, *sans* principle, *sans* talent, *sans* patriotism, *sans* everything but ambition, are struggling to seize upon the helm of the nation! These men, incapable of conceiving or executing a noble enterprise—and unable to rally their parties through the ordinary channels, stoop from their high calling, and the commanding altitude of the statesman, and with whining, canting, hypocritical appeals to the moral sentiments of the people, kindle the scathing fires of fanatical rancor and plunge the nation into a war of ethics. Brother is arrayed against brother, father against son, State against State, the

North against the South, not upon questions of great public policy, involving the general good, but upon a mere abstract idea, involving the question as to whether the institution of slavery is right or wrong in the sight of God!

This is a theme for the pulpit and the consistory—a labor of the churchman and the philanthropist, not for the hustings or the politician. Divest the subject of the borrowed political trappings which now hang about it, and try it by the test of conscience and religion. Take it away from your Sewards, your Weeds and your Greeleys, and leave it to the eloquent artillery of your Chapins, your Beechers, and your Coxes. If the right or wrong of slavery could be discussed in this wise, upon its own ground, with argument instead of vituperation, aiming at conviction rather than coercion, its opponents would find strong allies in the very vortex, the hot bed of the institution itself.

Philanthropy has nothing to gain, but our country has everything to lose in a crusade against State sovereignty and individual rights and possessions. There is no theme upon which human nature is more tenacious. Men and States will fight upon these issues, even against principle. It becomes with them a point of honor to resist the aggression, and their argument is this, *We will settle the questions of sovereignty and possession first, and the principle afterwards.*

In the present agitation of the subject of slavery as a political question, by people at the North, the entire people of the South are placed on the defensive, upon the broad basis of State sovereignty, and the legal rights of individuals; and thousands who might deprecate slavery in its moral aspect, will unite with others in resisting the attack upon their local integrity, and their social rights and customs. And they will resist it to the last—till every spark of national sentiment is absorbed in sectional animosity, till the name of "country" becomes a by-word, and that great and sublime fabric of patriotism, the UNITED STATES OF AMERICA, which no despotism could awe, and no combination of despotisms subdue, torn piecemeal by internal discord, has fallen, the victim of fraternal hatred, and been destroyed under the fratricidal hands of its own children. Such is its *ultimate* tendency, but apart from this, there are *intermediate* results of grievous magnitude and importance.

It alienates the national sentiments of the people, and destroys that harmony of intercourse essential to the general prosperity and social happiness of our citizens.

It encourages fanaticism and bigotry, and affords an unfailing source of inflammatory material for the demagogue, both at the North and the South.

It perverts the purposes of legislation from measures of State policy to measures of conscience and ethics—combining the elements of religion with politics.

It draws millions of money from the pockets of the people to pay for the useless and protracted debates on the subject in Congress—and the printing of speeches which are never read.

It has already divided the Baptist Church and the Methodist Episcopal Church in the United States into two parts—a Northern Church and a Southern Church—a forcible illustration of the deep-seated hostility already engendered between the two sections of our country—the men of the North refusing to worship at the same altar with the men of the South

It affords a theme for hostile discussion and bitter sentiment among people who should be more amicably and more profitably employed.

These are among the immediate results of a discussion which evolves everything of evil, and nothing of good—it is alike unprofitable and dangerous. Set on foot by men of humane motive, it has been seized upon by political tricksters, and fomented by European influences, in the earnest hope that through internal agitation they may subvert what they cannot otherwise overcome; viz. our powerful and happy union of States, and our system of popular government. No crisis has ever fallen upon our country which more especially demanded the exercise of a stern and inflexible patriotism among the people.

I shall introduce into this chapter a brief extract from the opinion of Washington on this very subject. I do so with every reliance on his wisdom and patriotism, yet with a certain sense of diffidence, because I remember that when the Hungarian, Kossuth, while in this country, controverted some of the opinions of Washington, and even went so far as to give novel interpretations to them, assuring the American people that they had misunderstood the language of their own great statesman, he was not only listened to with profound deference, but actually cheered by men of every rank. The opinions of Washington were, at that time, secondary to the opinions of Louis Kossuth. It may be that at this day his opinions are secondary, in the estimation of some, to those of George Thompson,* Wendell Phillips, William Lloyd Garrison, and the like, but I venture to give them notwithstanding. Applicable to this theme, and coming from a fountain, the purity of which no man has dared to question, they may touch a dormant chord in the bosom of some reader, and awaken notes and emotions of patriotism, which have been bound in silence and sleep by influences inharmonious but more immediate.

"The *unity* of government, which constitutes you one people, is also now dear to you. It is justly so, for it is *the main pillar* in the edifice of your real independence—the support of your tranquillity at home, your peace abroad; of your safety, of your prosperity, *of that very liberty which you so highly prize.* But, as it is easy to foresee that, from different causes and from different quarters, much pains will be taken, many artifices employed, to weaken in your minds the conviction of this truth; as this is the point in your political fortress against which the batteries of *internal* and external enemies will be most *constantly* and actively (though often covertly and insidiously) directed, it is of infinite moment that you should properly estimate the immense value of your national Union to your collective and individual happiness; that you should cherish a cordial, habitual, and immovable attachment to it; accustoming yourself to think and speak of it as of the palladium of your safety and prosperity; watching for its preservation with jealous anxiety; discountenancing whatever may suggest *even a suspicion* that it can, in any event, be abandoned; and indignantly frowning upon the

* George Thompson, *a member of the British Parliament*, has been one of the most violent abolitionists in the United States. While actually a member of Parliament he has visited this country to deliver abolition addresses and excite sectional discord between the North and the South.

first dawning of every attempt to alienate any portion of our country from the rest, or to enfeeble the sacred ties which now link together its various parts."

"In contemplating the causes which may disturb our Union, it occurs as a matter of serious concern, that any ground should have been furnished for characterizing parties by geographical discriminations—Northern and Southern—Atlantic and Western; whence *designing men* may endeavor to excite a belief that there is a real difference of local interests and views. One of the expedients of party to acquire influence within particular districts, is to misrepresent the opinions and aims of other districts. You cannot shield yourself too much against the jealousies and heart burnings which spring from these misrepresentations; they tend to render alien to each other those who ought to be bound together by fraternal affection."

There are men now in the land who do not hesitate to denounce that Union which Washington characterizes as "*the main pillar* of our independence, our tranquillity, our peace, our safety, our prosperity, nay *even of that very liberty which we so highly prize*," as "an atrocious bargain" and "an infamous compact!"

As I have given the opinion of Washington on the value of the Union, it is but fair that I should give the opinion of a person of much influence at the present day, on the same subject. I quote, therefore, from a speech delivered by William Lloyd Garrison, at a meeting held at Jamaica, Long Island, in the month of August, 1855. Mr. Garrison, in the course of his speech, said:

"There is no Union, therefore, I say down with it. Union is equality; there is no equality, therefore there is no Union. First I want the liberty of the slave; *let everything else go by the board.* I do not address myself to the slave-holders. I do not talk to them, they are incapable of an argument; they do not understand argument; they are insane men. We shall have *a northern republic of our own.* Oh! for the jubilee to come. Then we shall be a free people, and have the blessing of Almighty God showered upon our heads."

Now this Mr. Garrison is either sincere or insincere. He professes to be the champion of emancipation; he professes to labor for the liberation of the slave, and in the same speech he went so far as to say: "The slaves of our country must and shall be free; this is a certain thing." If he is sincere in this profession, it would not be impertinent to inquire how he intends to free the slave by dissolving the Union and establishing a "northern republic?" By such a procedure not a slave would be liberated, and he knows it; but, on the contrary, the bonds of the slave would be more closely drawn. A slave-holding *nation*, a nation recognizing the institution in its organic law would be established, side by side with *his* "northern republic," and all the moral influences which may be now employed in favor of emancipation would be shut out for ever. Taking Mr. Garrison's own words, he stands self-convicted, *a disunionist* and not an abolitionist! And yet there are men and women who will be led away by such frothy and treasonable declamation!

Now if the institution of slavery is, as I have shown, panoplied in a vested right, and solemnly guaranteed to the several *States*, or such of them as may choose to entertain it, and if, in consequence of this right, every attempt on the part of the "free States" to abolish it from other States has proven futile, any similar attempt to prevent its introduction upon the free soil of any of the territories of the United States must prove, indirectly, equally abortive; because, although Congress possesses the power to refuse the admission of any such territory into the sisterhood of States, with a constitution that recognizes slavery as one of its domestic institutions, it cannot prevent any State adopting such a constitution after it has been admitted into the confederacy. Thus, if any Territory applies for admission as a slave State, and is refused on that account, she has only to return, remodel her constitution, omitting the slavery clause, apply again, and be admitted. This accomplished, she may assert her sovereign right as a free and irresponsible State, re-enact her original constitution, and in spite of Congress and all other powers, save her own sovereign will, she may take her place as a slave-holding State in the confederacy of the Union.

The people of the United States have been more than once brought to the painful conviction that even the compromises of the Constitution are insufficient, on this subject, to give peace and harmony to the country. As the Northern States, one by one, cast away the institution of slavery from their borders, and as the States of the South, without exception, retained it, it became at length a marked, distinguishing feature between the local, domestic policies of the two extremes of the Union. Thus circumstanced, it afforded a pretext for geographical discriminations, and a basis for sectional animosities, out of which political aspirants might hope to obtain an advantage. In order to encourage, and mark more distinctly an imaginary diversity of interests in the two sections, and to familiarize the popular mind with the idea of a sectional individuality, North and South, every means within the scope of the imagination have been, and are still, employed. The distinguishing epithets, "Free States," as applied to one section, and "Slave States," as applied to the other, were not the least effectual in promoting this sense of individuality in the minds of the people.

Upon this pretext the struggle for sectional power and aggrandizement commenced. And so evenly were the parties in the contest balanced—so deep-seated the jealousy—so violent the raging conflict of local sentiment—the one party contending furiously against any further acquisition to the political power of the South, by the admission of new States into the Union *with* slavery, and the other as strenuously maintaining the principle of local sovereignty, and the right of admission, irrespective of that feature of domestic policy —that all nationality of sentiment or feeling has at times been absorbed, and a dissolution of the Union has seemed inevitable.

It was at a crisis like this that the famous act known as the MISSOURI COMPROMISE was conceived and enacted. The people of that territory having applied for admission into the brotherhood of States, presenting a constitution recognizing the institution of slavery, was, after a long and embittered struggle, admitted into the Union, with the *proviso* that no more slave States should be thereafter admitted north of the line 36° 30′. This compromise stilled for a time the sectional storm, and gave a temporary peace to the country.

But the fate of the Missouri Compromise exhibits the instability of all such measures as are left to the vicissitudes of sentiment, the venality of political parties, or the corrupt purposes, even of the government itself. It proves that upon the compromises of the Constitution alone, rests the sovereign rights of the people. The Missouri Compromise, the creature of one Congress, is made the foot-ball of a succeeding Congress, and the executive arm of the nation is lent, and made an instrument, in consummating the violation of the national faith. The act known as the Missouri Compromise, passed by Congress in 1820, was repealed by Congress in 1854, and the act repealing it, known as "the Kansas and Nebraska Act," bears the signature of Franklin Pierce, President of the United States!

This act it is not difficult to characterize as a gross and wanton violation of the national integrity; because, although the compromise existed only by the frail tenure of a congressional act, and, like any other act, was liable to repeal whenever necessity, or the caprice of the government should demand it, yet it was, from its very surroundings, and the circumstances under which it was created, of a nature more sacred than any ordinary act of legislation. It partook, so to speak, of the character of a treaty. It was a pledge—a promise—a solemn guarantee made by the government to the people, and as such it was invested with peculiar force and dignity.

It is not surprising, then, that the unceremonious rupture of such a pledge should have aroused the indignation of a deceived and betrayed people. It is not surprising that an outraged public sentiment should have spoken loudly and forcibly in denunciation of so foul a wrong, or that the men who participated in the act should have been branded as the foes of the public peace, and the national honor. Such *was* the effect in the States of the North, though, strange to say, the act repealing the Missouri Compromise was originated by Northern men, and consummated by the aid of Northern men.*

But the most deplorable effect of this act has been the renewal of that sectional discord to which we have before alluded. It re-opened the casket of evils under which the Union had once been placed in jeopardy, and sent abroad again the self-same spirit of geographical hatred. As a natural result, the first impulse of public sentiment at the North, demanded a restoration of that line of compromise which had so summarily been torn from the statutes of the country,—and that demand is still urged by many, through the strongest convictions of right and justice. Such a course would seem, at the first glance, to be the true one. But when we reflect upon the mutability of those public pledges which rest solely upon the sandy foundation of congressional enactments, and which are liable at any moment to be broken, and torn into shreds at the dictation of partisan demagogues, the utter uselessness of the procedure becomes apparent. It is plain that the sectional discord that would be engendered in the progress of that measure of restoration, would more than counterbalance any benefit to be derived from its accomplishment.

* *Sixteen* Senators from Free States, and *forty-four* Representatives from Free States, voted for the repeal of the Missouri Compromise. The act was introduced by a Senator from a Free State, and Franklin Pierce, President of the United States, a citizen of a Free State, signed the act, and confirmed it as the law of the land.

Again, the act of repeal cannot, with truth, be characterized as peculiarly that of the Southern section of the Union, because, as has been already shown, it was sustained by one half of the senators, and by about one third of the Representatives from the Free States, receiving at last, the sanction of a President from the Free States. The act was one of a *partisan*, rather than a sectional character. This fact also contributes to the difficulty and the inutility of a restoration, because, having employed it as a measure of partisan policy, they who so employed it will be compelled, from motives of consistency alone, if from no other, to stand by and maintain it. The restoration of the Missouri Compromise, therefore, would exist only to be again repealed, whenever the party opposed to it may reach the power to accomplish that repeal. Heart-burning agitation and a continuous war of opinions between the North and the South would, it is evident, result from such a course. Every public measure would hinge on that one idea. The popular mind would be diverted from matters of national import into the channels of a sectional feud. The elections of the whole country would be determined on that basis, and not a constable would be chosen, nor a street scavenger appointed, unless it should be known that he was "sound" on the *Compromise question.*

Besides, it is a question of serious doubt, whether an act like that establishing the Missouri Compromise line can constitutionally exist. Or, if it can so exist as applicable to the *Territories*, its powers must certainly cease the moment those Territories are elevated to the position and dignity of free and sovereign *States.* Its effect, therefore, can be but temporary, or continue during the territorial existence. To deny this, we must advance two new and startling propositions, either one of which, if established, would be sufficient to hurl the Union into fragments. The first of these propositions, would be to the effect that the reserved rights of the States, as guaranteed by the Constitution, do not apply to States subsequently admitted into the Union; and the second would be to the effect that Congress has power to regulate the domestic concerns of all the States.

Such would be the effect of an attempt to enforce the terms of the Missouri Compromise upon any new State formed from a Territory over which those terms had been recognized during the territorial existence, or from any other Territory. It would be to assert that Congress possesses certain powers over the sovereignty of new States which it cannot exercise over the original States of the confederacy; or, maintaining the principle of equality among the States, it would lead to the conclusion that Congress possesses the power to direct the domestic concerns of any and every State in the Union. This, no man is willing to admit, and hence the utter fallacy of attempting to legislate slavery out of the new States against the will of the citizens of those States.

# CHAPTER XVII.

## POLITICAL PARTIES.

" Here runs the mountainous and craggy ridge,
That tempts Ambition. On the summit see
The seals of office glitter in his eyes;
He climbs, he pants, he grasps them! At his heels,
Close at his heels, a demagogue ascends,
And, with a dext'rous jerk, soon twists him down,
And wins them—but to lose them in his tnrn."

COWPER.

POLITICAL parties are intrinsically the legitimate offspring of opinion. They exist as a necessity, and when founded upon sound principle, they are valuable as eliciting the popular ideas on important public measures, and also as a healthy balance of power between the public interest and the seductive tendencies of office—the one party operating as a check upon the other. The legitimate, adhesive property of parties is a public necessity and the measures applicable to that necessity; hence, when the necessity is past, and those measures have been either adopted or abandoned, the adhesive property ceases to exist, and the public mind is restored to its natural, social equilibrium.

But in the managment of a political party there are always a few men who have at stake deep personal interests. During the contest of principle, these men have occupied honorable and lucrative positions in the public service. They have been presidents, governors of States, senators, members of Congress, legislators, mayors of cities, aldermen and judges—or they may have occupied subordinate positions in office, wherein the emolument surpasses the honor—or they may have been only seeking after these several stations of profit and honor without obtaining them.

With all these the dissolution of a party is fatal. Having long "fed at the public crib," or set their hearts on the attainment of support from that source, it is difficult for them to let go their possessions or their anticipations. The destruction of their party is the destruction of their hopes, and it is only in conformity with the natural law of self-preservation that they struggle to hold the *material* of their party together for future triumphs. Finding it impossible to do this on the old issues, they resort to new ones which they designate *party measures.* If they are shrewd and able, they will adapt these measures to some feature of public necessity in the nation, and make them consistent with their former doctrines. By so doing they may for a time keep up their organizations and rally their partisans under the old banner, and still divide the chances of success with their opponents. This has been done from the establishment of our government to the present time.

The parties originally formed in the United States were the result of a diversity of opinion as to the plan upon which the new government should be formed and administered. Sifting out the chaff, this was the basis of that hostility of sentiment which characterize the parties of our young Republic. The adoption of the Federal Constitution was practically a settlement of that question, but it remained unsettled in theory, and parties were rallied upon the original issue long after popular sentiment had settled down into a satisfied conviction, in the enjoyments which the constitution afforded. The "Democrats" on the one hand, and the "Federalists" on the other, kept up their hue and cry, although neither Democracy nor Federalism existed, or were likely to exist in the country.

Even to the present day, the so-called "*Democratic party* struggles to rally its partisan host under a variety of extraneous issues, but with nothing in fact to hold it together beyond the antiquity of its empty title. In this matter it has been more successful than its rival. The Federalist leaders have, with their party, undergone numerous mutations both in their professions and their cognomen. They have been best known of late years as "National Republicans," and still later as "Whigs," but whatever they may have lost of their original identity they have gained in the practical utility and patriotic character of their measures, having always advocated the protection of American industry and American genius, against European competition or what is called "Free-trade;" and also the development of the internal resources of the country by a system of public improvements at the expense of the general government. Both of these measures of national policy have been opposed by the "Democrats," with all the virulence of partisan rancor, and these issues, together with the question of finance, involving the existence of an United States Bank, have been the themes by which the two "old parties" have wheedled the people during the last quarter of a century.

But these issues at length grew stale. The question of finance was settled by the establishment of the sub-treasury, and it was apparent from the first, to every statesman of talent, that the *extreme* of protection and the *extreme* of free trade, would neither of them be of practical utility to the country. The people at length caught this idea, and, as a natural consequence, the difficulty of holding parties together was greatly enhanced, because, say what we may about party ties, the popular mind of the United States acts, as a general rule, upon *conviction*, and upon conviction only. Conscientious in their attachment to the measures of party, they cling tenaciously to those measures until their object is accomplished or by common consent abandoned, and when either of these results have been consummated, it requires more than the prestige of a mere name to bind them to their party affiliations. Veneration for old attachments, and the social influences which grow up among men long associated either in public or private duties, go far to fasten the bond of unity and hold the friable components of a party together, yet it is more difficult for men of honest motive to act against their solemn convictions of right and wrong.

For many years past the political organizations of our country have been held together only by the "cohesive attraction of public plunder," and the measures set forth to the public as party measures have been but the subterfuges of ambitious men. And as by degrees the chains of partisan attachment became gradually looser, and the difficulty of binding free men in "the traces" without the existence of any apparent public necessity, increased, the stratagems of the designing became less scrupulous and more varied. Driven to the extreme of desperation, they have stooped to the lowest acts of demagoguery, and pandered to the deepest vices and the most dangerous influences. Their contests have been like the contests of the freebooter, a war for the spoils.

When political parties arrive at this crisis they part with their legitimate character, and become incumbrances on the body politic; mere festering excrescences on the science of government. As their contests are but forays upon the public treasury, each party recognizes the right of the other to enjoy the spoils after gaining a victory, and thus the conservative and purifying balance of power is lost and the public moneys squandered. An economical administration is a thing to be talked about but not seen; the interests of society are forgotten, public offices are multiplied, and salaries are increased to feed the greedy demands of clamorous partisans; peculations on the treasury are winked at, and in order to supply these extraordinary demands the taxes must be increased. The people groan under the burden, yet cling to their parties, because each promises "reform," until at last corruption is made manifest and the game can be played no longer. Men discover that they have been held by artificial ties to parties professing great though effete principles, merely as a cloak to public robbery and individual aggrandizement, and they can be rallied under the old banners no longer.

The old parties in the United States have been long

approaching this crisis in their history, and they have at length reached it. The climax is attained, and their followers have turned their backs upon them. Utterly disgusted with the venality of public men, the honest sentiment of the people rises in the majesty of moral supremacy, and rebukes those who have betrayed it. The old parties have been broken, scattered and ground to powder by the overwhelming force of public sentiment, yet never despairing, never at a loss for *some* expedient, good or evil, on which to hang their hopes of future successes, and continued plunder, they have renewed their machinations in new directions. Men who are politicians by birth, education, and instinct, have been suddenly converted into *humanitarians!* Those whose sympathies have hitherto been expended only on defeated partisans, have been softened to a charitable consideration of *the negro;* statesmen who have never been suspected of entertaining an excess of the Christian virtues, have become solemnly convinced of the unchristian character of that "peculiar institution" of the Southern States.—Those, too, who have been the sternest advocates of "State rights" have evinced a most earnest desire to superintend the affairs of the people of Louisiana and Kansas—in a word, the desperate political leaders have as a last resort, become abolitionists and free-soilers.

And they have given an importance to this heart-burning topic, which its originators could never have accomplished. They have applied the Herculean shoulder to the car of abolition and disunion, which had long been fast in the mire of public prejudice, and sent it forward on its mission of civil discord. They have given vitality, vigor, activity to a limping demon, and they must live or die in the breath of his nostrils. The ancients possessed a belief that certain evil spirits were easily raised, but that the sorcerer who conjured them from the realms of darkness possessed no power to send them home again, and was consequently forced to keep them employed, because, although they would obey his commands, yet, if he failed to keep their devilish propensities occupied, they would turn upon him and destroy him. The political sorcerers of our country have raised such a devil in the spirit of abolition, and they have not the power to lay it if they would. If it fails of employment, they fall. Their political existence is identified with it, and dependent upon its activity, and however the country may be distracted, and the Union shaken by its ravages, they will continue to ply it with evil works. This spirit can be laid only by the united energies and patriotism of the American people. Like no other devil, it professes good works; but like all other devils, it accomplishes nothing but evil. It is a hypocrite, a fiction, a spirit without a soul. Skulking like a dastard under the cloak of humanity, it hurls its insidious shafts at the heart of the nation, and exults at every groan of its victim.

When we see statesmen who have occupied many of the most responsible positions, following in the wake of Wendell Phillips, Fred Douglass, and William Lloyd Garrison, we are forced to confess that nothing but the sternest convictions and the most sincere repentance could have produced a moral wonder of such magnitude. The partisan leaders of the Southern States are not behindhand in expedients; and taking their cue from the elastic consciences of the North, they adapt their note to the local interests of *their* section, and sing the song of slavery or disunion, and thus, under the guidance of decaying partisans, the North of our country is arrayed against the South of our country, and we are rapidly becoming two distinct peoples! This deplorable result grows out of the simple fact, that the ancient parties of the country having outlived the purposes of their existence, now send up only the effluvia of decaying mortality. The beautiful symmetry of their construction is seen no more. The watchful eye which flashed in glances of terror upon the foes of the land, is sodden and spiritless. The heart which once beat only for the glory of the nation and the happiness of the people, is still, pulseless, and cold; and the once noble, but now inanimate forms, festering in their cerements, lie repulsive at the door of the sepulchre, and send forth only the exhalations of decay. Let the dead carcases, with all their pestilent fragments, be entombed, that the nostrils of the people may be no more offended, and the equilibrium and peace of the nation be restored.

## CHAPTER XVIII.

### THE NATIVE AMERICANS—THE PARTY OF 1834.

"Breathes there a man with soul so dead
Who never to himself hath said,
This is my own, my native land."
SCOTT.

Among the most patriotic men of the United States, from the time of Washington, Silas Dean, and Thomas Jefferson, down to the present day, there has existed a deep solicitude, amounting at times to an actual jealousy, on the subject of European interference in American affairs, and the deleterious effects of imported influences upon our national characteristics and peculiar institutions. The political facilities afforded to foreigners by our liberal system of naturalization and suffrage, coupled with an unprecedented immigration, have been well calculated to increase rather than diminish this anxiety, and efforts have from time to time been made to check the seeming inroads upon our prosperity and safety, growing out of these causes. But every attempt thus made has been met with the most determined hostility by the old partisan leaders, and however warmly the popular pulse has beaten towards the new movement, the character, objects and *morale* of the effort have been so misrepresented and vilified as to have effectually withdrawn from it every prestige of success, and after a brief struggle it has been for the time abandoned.

The avowed motives of those efforts have been, first: an amendment of the laws of naturalization in such manner as to extend the probationary residence of aliens to twenty-one years as the first qualification of citizenship; and, second: an abridgment of the rapidly-increasing political influence of the Papal power in the United States. As I have, in previous chapters of this work, exhibited, at some length, the evidences of a necessity for the adoption of these salutary measures as proposed by the so-called "Native American Party," it is needless to recapitulate them in this place. Neither one nor the other of the objects above mentioned were in themselves hostile to the interests of either the adopted citizens or the resident aliens already in the country, because in no respect were their rights invaded, or their prospective privileges abridged by them, and the men who urged those measures of policy upon the attention of the country were as much entitled to the sympathy and coöperation of those classes, as to the sympathy and coöperation of the native-born citizens.

The interests involved in the adoption of the American policy were universal, because the interests of the foreign resident and the native citizen in the destiny of the country are identical. If the American people, by maintaining their institutions of civil and religious liberty in their perfection, perpetuate the sources of their own happiness and prosperity, and enable themselves to transmit the same elements of enjoyment to their children, the adopted citizen shares equally with them in the result. If, on the other hand, the social, religious, and political privileges of the American people are to be by any means swept away, mutilated, or abridged, the adopted citizens must share with them in the common calamity.

Thus it may be seen that when the foreign residents of the United States, whether naturalized or otherwise, oppose the measures of the American party, they do no less than oppose the best interests of themselves and their posterity. They have, by the mere act of immigration, acquired rights under our Constitution which cannot be taken from them. The moment they set their feet upon our soil they acquired the right to become citizens by naturalization, and in the act of naturalization they are invested with all the prerogatives of the native citizen, with the single exception that they cannot be allowed to administer the government of the country. These rights, acquired under a solemn compact, are sacred to them and their posterity so long as the Republic, with its American republican institutions, is permitted to occupy a place on the scroll of nations. The Constitution of our country is as much the charter of their liberty as of our own, and if that charter is ever violated, the outrage will be as fatal to the interests of the adopted as of the native citizen.

Some of the foreign population, as I have shown, have already expressed their determination to take that most perfect instrument into their own hands, and remodel it according to their agrarian and atheistical notions, but this only shows that we have already too many politicians of that stamp in the country, and proves the necessity of adopting the conservative American policy.

But it has ever been the study of the political American gamblers, to misrepresent the motives of their own countrymen in this simple and conservative matter. For many years past, the wire-pullers of each of the organized parties, both Whigs and Democrats, have encouraged foreigners to acquire and exercise their political privileges, with a view of securing the combined foreign vote for their several parties; and in order to accomplish this, they have committed themselves and their governments, both State and national, to the immediate interests and ambition of foreigners, by pledges and promises of appointments to public offices, and even the passage of laws adapted to their peculiar wants and fancies. The foreigners had become so numerous, and the Roman Catholics were found to be so clannish, that to secure their coöperation at an election, was deemed equivalent to success, so well equalized were the forces of the contending parties. It is not surprising, therefore, that when partisans grew unscrupulous, there should exist between them a spirit of rivalry in fishing for this foreign influence; or that each party should struggle, by excessive concessions and liberal promises, to secure so valuable an ally.

The advent of a party, hostile alike to the corrupt practices of the home demagogue and to the concentration of a powerful foreign element in the political arena, was naturally the cause of intense commotion among the spoilsmen, and the party itself was regarded by them as a common enemy. They laid aside, to a great extent, their immediate feuds, and together, like good friends, set to work belaboring the intruder. Their first step was to poison the minds of the whole foreign population against the American policy, and to accomplish this, they have made it to appear, that *the purpose of the American party*, or the "Natives," as they scurrilously denominated them, *was to take from the foreigner his acquired rights*, both social and political. They went even so far as to establish, with some of the ignorant adopted citizens, a credence in their declaration, that if the "Natives" were successful, they would either send the foreigners all back to Europe, or else "hang them up like strings of onions." They denounced the new party as a horde of "selfish, persecuting bigots;" as "narrow-minded fanatics;" as "a party with one idea," &c., &c., not forgetting to interlard their abuse of their own countrymen with copious adulations of foreigners. In fact, their pretended solicitude for those classes was redoubled, and their praises, promises, and pledges were lavished upon them to such a degree that the very aliens, at length becoming impressed with an unwonted opinion of their own talent, interest, and importance, united in the crusade, and cried, "Down with the d——d Natives," as lustily as any. They also began to dictate terms to their patrons, and to demand the fulfillment of promises. The political sorcerers discovered that they had raised one of those imperturbable spirits which I have before alluded to. This was especially the case with the Roman Catholics. The hierarchy was first persuasive, then pressing, next clamorous, and finally, imperative.

It was a bitter pill to the austere American demagogues, thus to listen to dictation from those whom they regarded and used only as instruments for their own advancement, but they were forced to swallow it. They had gone too far to recede—the raised devil could not be laid—it must be pacified, and in order to appease it the constitution of the State of New York was amended in such a way as to render a foreign bishop eligible to the executive chair of the State! the Holy Bible, which had been the guide of our forefathers, was cast out of the public schools;—Roman Catholic teachers were appointed over Protestant scholars, and the school-moneys contributed by Protestants were given to the education of Papists in their own anti-republican seminaries.*

As the oppressive burden of a large foreign population was very naturally first developed to an offensive degree in the larger cities of the sea-board, in consequence of the greater numbers there congregated, so the first organized movements to counteract their influence took place in those cities. In New York, Boston, Philadelphia, New Orleans and other cities, their effect upon the social and political interests of the people became intolerable. The mechanic was crowded from his workshop by the cheap

* All these features still exist in the State of New York as monuments of the perfidy of her rulers. The Romish schools, which draw upon the school-fund, are cloaked under the title and semblance of "Orphan Asylums." The character of the instruction afforded, and the bigotry which prevails in these "Asylums" may be gathered from the following. In the year 1852, the Pope issued a mandate on the subject of education, the purport of which is found briefly condensed in the *Freeman's Journal*, which says:

"The Pope, to whose voice pastors and people alike *are bound to listen*, has called on all bishops to see to it, that Catholic youth are educated in schools *where all, and in all things are Catholic;* that is in schools under Catholic teachers of approved faith and morals, where the instruction given in secular science shall be in conformity with, and accompanied by the religious teaching *of the church*, and where, during the years of their study, *they shall not be exposed to the company of children who are heretics or infidels.*"

labor of European competitors, and many a family that had lived comfortably on the proceeds of the honest industry of the husband and father, was driven to actual want, and often forced to seek subsistence in other cities. Taxation was swelled in furnishing a support to the thousands of indigent and diseased paupers, who were conveyed from the wharf on which they landed direct to the alms-house, or the refuge assigned to them by the authorities. The streets were overrun with imported mendicants, and the dwellings of the citizens were invaded by them from morning till evening. Crime of every degree was increased five-fold, and the prisons were peopled with exotic felons. The spirit of drunkenness lurked in low haunts and fetid groggeries, or reeled obscenely through the public thoroughfares; and the loose brawl and the midnight scream usurped the places of order, decency, and sobriety. These were the *social* aspects of an overgrown foreign populace.

But the *political* aspect was no less repulsive and oppressive. *I write only what I have witnessed.* I have seen bands of foreign bullies, regularly organized, and *under the direction of an Irish alderman,* placed at the polls, with a supply of bludgeons close at hand, for the purpose of preventing Amecans from approaching the polls to exercise their birthright of the suffrage. I have seen that, when Americans attempted to enforce their right to enter the place of voting, these foreign bullies have, by the word of command, seized their bludgeons and beat down grey-haired Americans like dogs in the highway! I have seen foreigners, the most illiterate, and bloated with dissipation, placed in the responsible office of inspectors at elections, and made the judges of the political rights of men who claimed their three score years and ten of residence on their native American soil; and I have seen the suffrage right of these old citizens *challenged* by the ignorant and besotted refuse of European municipalities. have seen the most talented of my countrymen made to give way, and stand aside to make room for the ambitious desires of foreign aspirants to public office; and I have seen both the enactment and the execution of laws perverted from justice and the public necessities, to feed the clamorous demand of imported prejudices. In the city of Philadelphia Americans have been shot down in cold blood by *foreigners in ambush*, while holding a peaceable public meeting on their own soil, in one of the public places of the city. These men had dared to avow themselves AMERICANS, and in favor of an American policy, and they paid for their independent assertion of an inborn right, with the price of their blood! Yes, in the year 1844, Americans were deliberately *murdered* by foreign Roman Catholics in the public streets of Philadelphia, *for opinion's sake!* and the proud flag of America was at the same time torn contemptuously into fragments and trampled to the earth by the ignorant and superstitious minions of Rome! Ten years later, viz., in the fall of 1854, at one of the polling-places in Williamsburgh, N. Y., Americans were not permitted to approach the ballot-box unless they were known to be of the party favorable to the Irish, and, in attempting to do so, one of our countrymen was brutally murdered with bludgeons, and several others horribly beaten and mangled, by the overwhelming throngs of

*Irishmen!* Again, during an election held at Louisville, Ky., in the summer of 1855, Americans were shot down by foreigners, who, sheltering themselves in their houses, deliberately, and without provocation, levelled their deadly weapons at men who were peacably passing along the streets, and murdered them merely *because they were Americans!*

It was from elements and influences like these that the Native American Party has, of late years, started into existence, in the great cities, only to be beaten back by the combined efforts of native demagogues and imported brutality. Yet it is a circumstance worthy of note that, in all these efforts, the intelligent foreign residents and adopted citizens; those who read for themselves and thus obtain a correct view of facts, have been, almost without exception, the advocates of the American policy. But they comprise *the few*, and moreover, they are not the kind of stuff from which our party leaders have been accustomed to manufacture voters for a political emergency.

Now if the circumstances to which I have briefly referred, are any indication of what Americans and Protestants are to expect under foreign and papal rule, then certainly the law of self-preservation, the first law implanted by the Almighty in every human breast, if no other, will justify us in the sight of the world, if we erect between ourselves and these modern Goths and Vandals, the loftiest barriers of political restraint.

The Native Americans have never yet assailed the foreigner or the Romanist because of either his birth or his religion. It is only against their moral and political idiosyncrasies, hostile to our social and political interests, that the voice of remonstrance has been raised, and if ever a war of classes or of religion occurs on American soil, it will be the fruit only of their clannish hostility, intolerance, and brutality. With a law-abiding and a forbearing spirit, the American people have endured much, too much, at the hands of imported bigotry and superciliousness, and it is not in the nature of events that this state of things can endure much longer.

The foreigners and the Roman Catholics are the masters of their own destiny in the United States. They *may*, perhaps, *become* the masters of *our* destiny; but if so, the precursors of such an event will be appalling—and the result fatal to human liberty. The latter event we must not anticipate; it is too terrible for contemplation! but of the former we may reason together. I say these classes are the masters of their own destiny, because that destiny depends on their deportment. If they will be not only *with* us but *of* us; if, when they swear to be Americans, they will realize the *spirit* of political baptism and prove themselves converted to our political faith, our institutions, and strive to assimilate with our habits, customs, and language; if they will abide by and respect our laws, and use without abusing the privileges and freedom which our institutions afford to them; if they will be content to enjoy religious liberty, and hold their church aloof from the State; in a word, if they will become truly Americanized, and deport themselves as good citizens, their destiny will be peaceful, happy, and glorious. But if, on the contrary, they cling to former attachments; if they take an unmeaning oath, swearing one thing, and regarding another;

if they study to preserve their foreign peculiarities, habits, customs, and language; if they assail our Constitution and our laws, and make war against our institutions; if they drag their religion into the political arena, and declare their determination to make their church the ruling power of the nation; if they attempt to coerce and rule over the people who have given them an asylum from the despotic oppressions and starvation of their own native lands: if this is to be their deportment, their destiny is already written, for, assuredly, the Genius of America will not strive always with words of *persuasion* against them. There is a point beyond which patience ceases to be a virtue, and the dictates of that law which teaches us that "Charity should begin at home," the law of self-respect and self-preservation, must be enforced; the American people may be constrained to adopt such measures of policy as will for ever put these assumptions at rest, and change materially the social and political aspect of the foreigner and the papist in the United States. Their fate, I repeat, is in their own hands: if they are wise they will mould it to happy results.

At various periods of our national history distinct signs of apprehension, in regard to the subversive influence of foreigners acting on a political equality with the native citizens, have been manifested, but no attenpt to organize a distinct party, devoted to the American policy, occurred until the year 1834. This took place in the city of New York, and was ushered upon the public attention by a temperate address, in which was recounted the rapidly-increasing dangers of foreign and papal influences upon our republican institutions, and setting forth the necessity of radical amendments to our system of naturalization as a shield against their encroachments. To the citizens of New York the address made especial appeals, exhibiting the increased burden of taxation imposed upon them for the support of the European poor who made that city their refuge, and exposing the ambitious arrogance of foreigners in their efforts to control the municipal affairs of the city.

This address had the effect to arouse a strong popular sentiment in favor of the new party, and in a short time an organization was so far effected as to warrant the nomination of a distinct American ticket for the local offices. Professor SAMUEL F. B. MORSE, whose genius has added a brilliant and imperishable ray to the halo of American glory, and whose writings have stamped him with the mark of a sterling and pure-minded patriot, was chosen as the American candidate for the office of Mayor of New York, and at the election which immediately followed *nine thousand* citizens responded with their votes, in favor of the American party and its principles. This vote, although not sufficient to elect the American candidates, was enough to throw consternation into the camp of the old parties. Besides, the movement of the New Yorkers was quickly followed in various other cities in different parts of the Union, and for a short time there existed the most marked indications of popular sympathy and encouragement.

This result was unexpected by the old political leaders, and forthwith their batteries were directed through the port-holes of a thousand partisan presses, in every portion of the land, against the new organization. The most effective implements of party discipline were immediately brought into requisition; those of their camp followers who had ventured to speak approvingly of the American party were denounced and vilified, and those who had sustained it by their votes were formally excommunicated, branded with a *pseudo* infamy, and declared to be among the proscribed for ever.

The artillery of parties, powerful, thoroughly organized in every portion of the country, with an army of presses, and a phalanx of prejudices, proved too much for the little band of Spartan-spirited patriots, whose only weapon was a good cause and a virtuous purpose, and, after a struggle of two or three years, the first American party was overwhelmed, and utterly obliterated.

But although the organization was abandoned, the broad principle which it had enunciated was immutable. The ingredients of that party were scattered, but with them were scattered the seeds of a future harvest of opinion, that should, at some future day, bring forth fruit of its kind from every pore in the soil of American Nationality.

"Truth crushed to earth will rise again,
The eternal years of God are hers,
But error wounded writhes in pain,
And dies amid her worshippers."

The array of facts brought to light, during this brief effort, and the logical deductions drawn from them, went forth, and when the storm came on they nestled silently in a quiet recess of the *American mind*, and there, stript of all extraneous vesture, and away from all counter-influences and prejudices, they underwent the test and scrutiny of calm reflection.

# CHAPTER XIX.

## THE AMERICAN REPUBLICAN PARTY OF 1844—ITS RISE AND FALL.

——— "When the Deity conversed with men
He was himself a Patriot!—to the earth,—
To all mankind a Savior was he sent;
And, all he loved with a Redeemer's love;
Yet still, his *warmest* love, his *tenderest* care,
His life, his heart, his blessings and his mournings,
His smiles, his tears, he gave to thee, Jerusalem,
To thee, *his country*."

Z. Wolfe.

In consequence of the annihilation of the American Party, the demagogues grew bolder, and the foreigners and papists more audacious and presuming. A very few years sufficed to develop this fact. Before the year 1840 had passed away, the footprints of Romanism were distinctly visible on the political field of the country. This was especially the case in the Empire State, where William H. Seward occupied the executive chair. At the commencement of that year, under the instigation of his "friend,"* Bishop John Hughes, the Romish prelate of New York, Mr. Seward put forth that re-

* In a letter to a gentleman in New York, dated November 15, 1840, Mr. Seward says: "Bishop Hughes is my friend, I honor, respect, and *confide* in him." This is at least an inferential justification of my statement that it was at the instigation confidential friend Bishop Hughes, that he made the recommendation.

markable recommendation to the Legislature, which I have before noticed in this work. In 1841 the plot thickened,—Mr. Seward reiterated his formerly-expressed sentiments in favor of the Romish and foreign aggression upon our educational system; and the year 1842 witnessed the consummation of his recommendations. Romanism took possession, to a considerable extent, of the public schools of the State, and the Bible, which had been implanted in those schools at the foundation of the system, and used as a reading-book for religious and moral, but not *sectarian*, instruction, *was banished* from them. It was plain to every eye and every mind that this infamous outrage was the result of *a deliberate bargain between the authorities of the State and the Church of Rome*, and it is not remarkable that thereby the fires of popular indignation should have been kindled.

And those fires *were* kindled. On every hand the voice of public condemnation was heard; the quiescent spirit of Americanism was re-awakened, and the party was reorganized in the City of New York under the title of "AMERICAN REPUBLICANS."

This party proceeded forthwith in the organization of ward committees or associations, in each of the several wards of the city, and the creation of a general committee, to be composed of delegates chosen in the several wards. They also prepared and published a "Declaration" of their general principles, which were the same as those of the party as it existed in 1834. The "declaration of principles," or, in modern *parlance*, the "platform," issued at that time, and which I republish at length, while eminently conservative and patriotic, will be found to contain none of those features of "bigotry" and "proscription" attributed to it by the enemies of the party. That platform was framed in the following words:—

DECLARATION OF PRINCIPLES OF THE AMERICAN REPUBLICAN PARTY.

*Whereas*, in the course pursued by the leaders of the political parties of the day, we discover *an utter recklessness and disregard of the good government and well-being of society, a contempt for moral honesty*, and the true and proper administration of the laws to restrain vice and its demoralizing effects upon the thoughts and actions of the people, all of which is plainly manifested by the appointment to offices of honor and trust, of *men of immoral character, and individuals who are ignorant of the laws and institutions of our country;* therefore, we, citizens of the United States, have concluded to associate ourselves together, and be known and designated as the American Republican Party of the City and County of New York, for the purpose of endeavoring, as far as in us lies, and with our best abilities, to correct the evils herein complained of, and by the virtues of the men of '76, and the memory of a "Washington," a "Franklin," and a "Jefferson," the defender, the counsellor, and the apostle of our liberties, we pledge ourselves to each other, to use our best exertions to bring about a reformation at the ballot-boxes, and that we will not aid or assist in any way or manner, directly or indirectly, in electing any man to office, be his party predilections what they may, either of honor, trust, or emolument, from the lowest to the highest, *who has not at all times shown a proper respect for the decencies of society and an honest and virtuous regard for the laws and the due administration of justice ;* our inquiries shall be, "Is he capable? Is he honest?" Also, is he an American-born citizen?

*Resolved*, That as American citizens, having at heart the purity, permanency, and honor of our institutions—jealous of our rights and liberties, and fearful of the evils of foreign influence, *which have already exhibited themselves*, we will not recognize nor support, for any office of honor, trust, or emolument, for General, State, or Municipal Government, any person or persons who are directly or indirectly subjected to or influenced by, the laws or powers, temporal or spiritual, of any foreign prince, power, or potentate.

*Resolved*, That we highly appreciate that protection and freedom in "life, liberty, and property," guaranteed to the people of our glorious republic, by that best of instruments that the mind of man ever conceived, the sacred Constitution of our country; so also do we view with abhorrence all attacks upon, or abridgment of, our free and unbiased expression of opinion in regard to the conduct of each and all of our public officers, whom we, the people, have elevated to honor, by conferring upon them offices within our gift, without fearing that they will make use of the powers temporarily conferred upon them for party or selfish purposes.

*Resolved*, That, as a party, we will not appoint to any office within our power, any person who is not American by birth, born within the jurisdiction of the United States.

We hold and maintain that the present Naturalization Laws are unequal and unjust, and we will, therefore, use all honorable means in order to effect such alteration in said laws as shall require of all foreigners, *who shall arrive in our country after such alteration shall have been made*, to remain at least twenty-one years within the jurisdiction of the United States, before they shall be endowed with the birthright of Native Americans, the elective franchise. Also, the passage of a law by Congress, prohibiting, under heavy and severe penalties, the importation of foreign paupers or convicts to any port or place in the United States.

We declare, also, that *it is not our intention or desire to have enacted any retro-active laws by which to abridge the vested rights of any*—but we do hold and will sacredly maintain the full intention of the Constitution of these United States *alike unto all, without partiality*. We are in favor of the constituted authorities enacting such laws as shall give the privilege to persons of foreign birth, after they shall have *declared their intention of becoming citizens of these United States*, in conformity with the laws regulating the same, *of holding and conveying real and personal property, and the enjoyment of the protection and privileges of all our laws and institutions, except that of holding office and the elective franchise.*

Our country, right or wrong; but still, our country, is our motto; principles, not men, our creed; our birthright is our object; and perseverance, until we obtain it, is our determination. In opposing the elevation of foreigners to office, and in seeking a change in the naturalization laws—as well as in advocating our native inherent rights, we are only reverting back to the elementary principles of our national Constitution, supported by the views and declarations of the immortal Washington, and Jefferson, the clear-headed statesmen; *we are not actuated by feelings of hostility towards adopted citizens. What we contend for is all* PROSPECTIVE. We disclaim the intention of opposing respectable and industrious foreigners immigrating to this country. But we do object to and shall use all lawful means to exclude from our country the idle, the vicious, and the unprincipled of every clime, that the morals of our citizens be not injured by their example, or our property taxed for their support.

We have, therefore, adopted this Declaration of Principles and Constitution for the purpose of more effectually carrying into operation our principles, and of preventing an increase of foreign influence, and of maintaining inviolate our Political Rights—our Civil and Religious Liberties.

In the spring of 1843 this party took the field with a full municipal ticket, and polled a vote which exhibited a large change of popular sentiment in favor of the American policy. Though not yet sufficient for success—encouraged rather than disheartened by the result, the party continued to perfect and strengthen its organization, and the patriotic example was again followed by the people of Boston, Philadelphia, St. Louis,

New Orleans, and other cities. In 1844 each of the cities above-named elected, in whole or in part, an American Republican Municipal Government.

The great point of interest in the contest of 1844, between the old party leaders and the American Republicans, was the city of New York. This was partly owing to the fact that the movement originated in that city, but mainly because of the vast foreign population residing within its limits. It was expected that the entire foreign vote would be cast in opposition to the new organization, but to the surprise and confusion of its enemies, the entire body of Protestant Europeans endorsed the principles avowed in the American creed, and voted for the candidates who favored those principles. The party, in selecting its candidates, had been governed by the Jeffersonian test. They chose men for their honesty and business capacity, rather than for their experience in the corrupting vortex of politics—men eminent rather for integrity and respectability of character, than for their skill as political managers. James Harper, Esq., the leading partner in the extensive publishing house of Harper & Brothers, a gentleman highly-conspicuous for his business talent and moral worth, was chosen as their candidate for the office of Mayor, and the same policy was observed in the choice of candidates for members of the Common Council, and heads of the public departments of the city. Mr. Harper was elected Mayor of New York by a very large majority, as were also a majority of the members of the two boards of the Common Council. The American Republican party was triumphant.

During this canvass, the same bitterness of spirit and vindictiveness were exhibited by the partisan presses and leaders, as on the former occasion. No arguments were employed to controvert the doctrines of the American Republicans, but one continuous torrent of epithets and ridicule was poured out upon them and their advocates, until the very name "American" had become a scurrilous jest. In fact, their doctrines were incontrovertible; the propriety of their policy was apparent to all, though not admitted by all, and the hostility arrayed against them was but the effect of a desperate struggle on the part of men eager to retain the grasp of power.

In Philadelphia the canvass, although marked by no distinguishing features on the part of the parties legitimately engaged in it, was nevertheless made memorable on account of the course pursued by the Roman Catholics, and the fatal result of their interference. This class of our "adopted citizens," residing in that city, not satisfied with the privilege of meeting Americans on their own ground, with their own peaceful weapon, the ballot, determined to take Time by the forelock, and break up their organization. They argued very rationally, that, *if they could but silence the American orators, and prevent public assemblages of the American people*, there would be little difficulty in destroying their party, and without sufficiently weighing the conditions on which they relied for success, they determined to adopt that plan of operations. They accordingly gave notice that no American meetings would be permitted in certain specified districts, and this notice was accompanied with threats of bloody vengeance on any who should have the temerity to violate its provisions.

The district of Kensington, in which a meeting of American Republicans had been called by public notice, was especially designated in this threat. But the meeting took place precisely as it had been advertised, at 4 o'clock on the afternoon of May 6th, 1844, and the threat was consummated. From the windows of houses, from loop-holes, and alleys in the vicinity, a murderous fire of musketry was poured into the assembly with terrible effect. George Shiffler, a young man who held the national flag on the orator's platform, was shot through the heart, and died almost instantly, and eleven others were dangerously wounded.* Thus was the constitutional right of the American people peaceably to assemble, and the sacred right of free speech, invaded by a brutal horde of Irish Romanists; thus were the lips of a free-born American sealed in eternal silence by a Papal bullet! Why do we pore over the pages of history and recapitulate the horrors of the eve of St. Bartholomew, when proofs like this, of Papal barbarity and bigotry, are breeding, ghastly and fresh, on our own soil?

As a matter of course the result produced by this bloody assault was exactly the reverse of what its perpetrators had intended. They expected to intimidate the American orators, and thus stifle their influence in the community. It is needless to say that great excitement prevailed, or that this tangible evidence of the truthfulness of the American Republican doctrines was not lost upon the community. American meetings, the most enthusiastic and numerous, were held in every quarter of the city, and to add to the excitement, a rumor was circu-

* At a meeting held on the following day the murderous assault was renewed, at which *eight Americans were killed*, and about forty wounded. See Appendix.

lated stating that arms and ammunition were concealed in the Roman Catholic Church in Queen Street. A committee was appointed to search the building, and, under the direction and authority of the sheriff of the county, the committee proceeded in the performance of their duty. The rumor was found to be true, as will be seen from the following extract from their report, under date of July 11th:—

"The first door we opened revealed to us two able-bodied Irishmen, with fixed bayonets and loaded muskets. These men were disarmed, and on opening the door at which they stood sentry, we saw twenty-seven muskets stacked along the room. Placing out of our own number a guard over these men and muskets, we proceeded on our search; and in our way found eight other men armed as above. Arriving in the room in which the religious services were held, one of the Committee brought the priest in front of the altar, and thus addressed him: "I ask you, upon your sacred word as a man and a Christian, have you any more men here? Have you any more arms? Have you any ammunition?" To each of these questions he answered positively—no. Finding nothing new in our progress, we again proceeded to the room or vestibule from which we first started. In this room were several closets, and some of them were in a case or counter which stood along the wall. We asked the priest to open it. He said it contained nothing but a few lemons and articles for making something to drink. We asked him to open it, when we discovered a keg of powder, some percussion caps, and buck shot; and on account of this quibbling of the priest, we were anxious to open a closet which was under the stairs, leading from the vestibule to the room behind the altar. The priest here said that the closet contained private property belonging to his brother, W. H. Dunn, and some few small articles belonging to himself, and objected to open it, stating that the key of that place had never been in the hands of any other person but himself and brother. No denial would be listened to, and accordingly the closet was opened ; in it was found seven single, and two double barrel guns, and several pistols ; and several hundred cartridges, some of which had eight, ten, or more slugs, and buck shot in them, and upon examination of some of the fowling pieces, they had seven, eight, and even nine finger loads in them.

"*Adopted in Committee, July* 11*th*, 1844.

"John W. Smith, Wright Ardis,

And sixteen others, having headed this committee by request of the Sheriff, I subscribe to the foregoing report.

"N. M'KINLEY, Alderman."

Thus the American party of 1844, like that of 1776, was baptized in blood, and from that day to the present the organization has never been abandoned in the city of Philadelphia.

Up to this time the American Republican movement had been but local in its operations. The organizations by which it was conducted had been confined to the municipal interests of the cities in which they originated, and but little effort had yet been made towards perfecting a national organization. It is apparent, however, that a party professing principles so closely identified with the most vital political interests of the entire people, could not long confine its energies to matters merely of municipal importance. Measures were accordingly taken for a concentration of action, and the formation of a national party, and a convention was called, to consist of delegates from the several States, and to be holden in the City of Philadelphia, on the fourth day of July, 1845.

In conformity with this call the convention assembled at Philadelphia on the Anniversary of our National Independence. Nearly three hundred delegates were present. General HENRY A. S. DEARBORNE of Mass. was chosen President. At this convention a more comprehensive "Declaration of Principles," but embracing as its general features the doctrines set forth by the party in New York, was adopted, and the title of the organization was changed from "American Republican" to that of NATIVE AMERICAN, and it was thereafter known as the *Native American Party.*

As a national party the founders of this organization soon found themselves confronted by new, and in some respects unforeseen obstacle. They had expected and were prepared to encounter the continued hostility of the leaders of the whig and the democratic parties with their Roman allies, but they had not fully anticipated, nor were they prepared for a certain luke-warmth which manifested itself among the people of the rural districts of the country, towards the new party. The influences complained of had not yet been brought home to them; they had not personally witnessed their effects, and it was impossible for them to realize the magnitude of the dangers so newly presented for their contemplation. The whig party, also, now set forth a fresh ground of hostility, charging the Native Americans with having caused the defeat of HENRY CLAY, who had been the whig candidate for the Presidency in the fall of 1844. They directly accused the Native Americans with a breach of faith in this matter, asserting that the whigs had supported the Native American municipal candidates, in the expectation that they in return would support the whig candidate for the Presidency.

This charge, it is now perhaps needless to say, was nothing more than a perfidious device of the enemy. In the primitive organizations of the American Party, and at the time of the presidential election in 1844, they made no pretensions to a national organization, and although they elected several members of Congress, took no part in the presidential contest. The individual members were left to vote on that question according to their own judgment and predilections. Whatever the whig party may have "expected," therefore, from the Native Americans, there certainly could have been no understanding between them on the subject.

But apart from any understanding between the parties, Mr. Clay did himself, at the suggestion of his own party friends, agree to attach to the whig banner a large share of the Native American creed, and the groundwork of that plan, after having been submitted to Mr. Clay, was published as an editorial article in the New York *Courier and Enquirer*, a short time prior to the election. That article was widely read, but the circumstance that Mr. Clay had given it his approval was carefully concealed from the public. This was the result of a timid policy. The immediate friends of that great and pure statesman were afraid to declare openly the sentiments of their candidate in favor of the American doctrines lest they should be deserted by their foreign allies. They were mistaken. The foreigners who sustained the whig party were mostly Protestants—for with all his subserviency to the Romish power, Mr. Seward never secured the vote of that class to his party—and, had the friends of Mr. Clay pursued a more frank course of policy on this subject—had that gentlemen's views been publicly made known and generally understood, the entire American vote would have been cast for him, and without doubt he would have been elected President of the United States. As the great champion of an American protective policy, Mr. Clay's known views were in a great measure congenial with the sentiments of the new party, and as a consequence many of the democratic members of that party, who would have otherwise supported his opponent, gave a ready and cordial support to him.

But this did not shield their party from the outpourings of that bitterness of disappointment which followed the defeat of Mr. Clay. The hostility of the whigs was redoubled, and in the spring of 1845, by a partial fusion with the democrats, they succeeded in New York in defeating the American nominees. This defeat, although regarded at the time as but temporary in its effects, was fatal to the American cause.

When the party was at the zenith of its success, many of the prominent actors in the old parties had become suddenly and surprisingly converted to the new faith, and with loud and earnest professions of attachment labored among the most zealous in the American ranks. In many instances they "out-heroded Herod" in their denunciations of foreigners and Romanists, and often in their speeches presented as the views of the party, the most ultra theories, and the most inflammatory and denunciatory sentiments. Orators and controversialists of this stamp did more to fasten upon the Native Americans the current charges of "bigotry" and "proscription," than anything that could be found in their platform, or their public addresses. Whether this was a part of the motive of these men, or not, is of course unknown, but certainly they were the first to advise a dissolution of the party, and the first to to leave it on the appearance of adverse circumstances.

The effort to enlist the sympathies of the people of the rural districts having failed, the national organization was virtually abandoned, although a certain committee was appointed, with power to call a national convention for the nomination of candidates for President and Vice President in 1848, if deemed advisable. That convention was called, more, however, with a view to another interchange of opinions, then with any intention of an immediate renewal of the organization. The convention made no nomination, but having corresponded with General Taylor, and found his views to coincide with the general features of the American Policy, they, in advance of any other party publicly *recommended him as a suitable candidate for the Presidency.* The local organizations, "growing small by degrees, and beautifully less," continued their efforts, until 1847, when, with the exception of that in the city of Philadelphia, they were all finally abandoned. The American Party was a second time in its slumber.

# CHAPTER XX.

THE ORDER OF UNITED AMERICANS—ITS ORIGIN—ITS PRINCIPLES AND OBJECTS—ITS FORM OF GOVERNMENT.

"When the skin of the Lion proves too short, we must eke it out with the Fox's tail."

RICHELIEU.

I AM now about to write of an institution which has already exerted a silent yet important influence in the political history of the United States. How far it is destined to exert its conservative power in the future, depends perhaps more upon the wisdom and the purity of its counsels than the assaults of its foes—because it is now so firmly fortified in public esteem, so consecutive, systematic, and effective, in its organization, and so numerous in its membership, that it is enabled to look with complacency and indifference upon every attempt to defeat or retard its patriotic purposes. The objects of this order have been political and social; it has studiously remained aloof from every partisan affiliation, and while sustaining entirely the doctrines and objects of the American Republicans, it has levelled its shafts as freely at the American demagogue. Its political character may be read in a single sentence of its platform, thus:—

"Our political action will be adapted to the exigency of the crisis which may arise; but our polar star shall ever be the salvation of our country and its institutions."

From this we are to infer, that, from whatever source or by whatever means that exigency may occur, whether instigated by internal or external foes, whether of a nature social, religious, or political, whether sooner or later, in peace or in war, in civil discord or domestic quiet, if that exigency shall directly or indirectly place in jeopardy our country or its institutions, it is the purpose of this society to meet it with a resolute and patriotic hostility. A purpose so noble, seconded, as it has thus far been, by an unobtrusive, orderly, and law-abiding deportment on the part of its membership, could not fail to secure the public confidence and respect.

The organization of this order took place on the 21st of December, 1844, in the city of New York. At that time several gentlemen, entertaining a solemn conviction of the dangers which overhang our institutions, from the nefarious designs of Jesuitism, from the rapidly-increasing influences exerted upon them from abroad, and from the ignorant masses of Europeans who were permitted to share in the elective franchise, as also from the glaring habits of corruption to which our politicians had descended; having witnessed also the futility of previous attempts to awaken the popular mind to a true sense of those evils, or to overcome the united and secret combination of organized demagogues by means of an open party, and anticipating that a like result would follow the effort then being made—resolved to adopt some plan by which those deleterious influences might be met on their own terms, and with their own weapons. The most potent weapon employed by the unscrupulous politicians, as well as by the natural foes of American Republicanism—the followers of Loyola—was the *secrecy* with which their machinations were planned and carried out, and it was determined that the same weapon (secrecy) should be employed to check their operations, and thwart their designs.

It was observable, also, that the political education of the young men of the country was confided entirely to the partisan schools, and very few graduated and stood forth upon the platform of manhood with any ideas of political duty beyond the mere essentials of a democratic or a whig success. They understood very distinctly, because they were so trained to believe, that to the party into whose lap they had chanced to fall when they emerged from boyhood, the whole country, if not the whole world, was indebted for every vestige of liberty remaining, and for all that might be garnered up for future use—hence, when their party was triumphant, they were given to understand that "the country was safe," and they could return to their workshops and counters, and continue their avocations with the most perfect assurance that there would be no more danger until the next election. In their estimation the highest qualification of a politician was to be found in his tact for getting the "right" votes into the ballot-box, and keeping out the "wrong" ones, and the most accomplished statesman was he who could make his measures tell best for "the party." The idea of legislating for the people was not *obsolete* with them, because they had never entertained it—it had not been among the rudiments of their education; it was a thing Utopian—heard of but unknown. Thus the *spirituel* of our political element was rapidly degenerating into a mere factional system, while the pernicious ingredients of radicalism, superstition, and ignorance, were held aloof as make-weights to be thrown into either scale which would afford the largest remuneration.

A system that would afford a school of patriotism to the young, purify the *morale* of the political atmosphere, and by awakening a *home pride*, a spirit of American nationality among the people, neutralize and stifle those imported theories which were being rapidly engrafted upon our time-honored republican customs and sentiments, was a something desirable, at least, if not imperatively necessary as a measure of self-protection. The formation of a politico-benevolent institution, beyond the reach of the corrupting influences of partisan demagogues, was therefore determined upon. An institution which, as one of its features, should receive into its membership young men who were soon to enter upon the discharge of their political duties, and thus, by bringing them into a social contact with men of maturer years and experience, afford to them opportunities for a more rational and patriotic political instruction than could be obtained under the corrupting influences of mere partisans and factionists—an institution that should be strictly national in its character, and entirely American in its policy and its membership; one that would, in its political character and action, eschew all partisan attachments and prejudices, moving unitedly in whatever direction the ultimate good of the country should demand, whether in the choice of men, or the adoption of measures—

an institution that would encourage study, oratory, and research, and impart information to the young by addresses and discussions in political science, and general history, and especially on topics relating to American history, and thus by intuition bring about a more conservative, healthy, and patriotic train of political thought in the great American mind.

Such was the general outline of a plan for the formation of a society for the purposes which I have already stated. As an additional bond of unity, a beneficiary feature, something of the nature of Odd Fellowship, was added to the plan, and upon this basis the Order of United Americans was ushered into existence.

The first meeting of this Order took place on the evening of the 21st of December, 1844, at the private residence of one of its members, in Forsyth street, in the city of New York. At that meeting there were present the following persons: viz.:—Simeon Baldwin, James Harper, Thomas R. Whitney, George P. Parker, William Atkinson, Charles A. Whitney, R. C. Root, T. B. Miner, Geo. W. Parsons, Danl. Talmage, G. E. Belcher, L. D. Burling, and E. D. Root.

These gentlemen at that time comprised the entire membership of an association which in less than eight years numbered its tens of thousands of members, distributed over the various States of the Union, and which has been as remarkable for the wholesome influence which it has exerted over the political sentiments of the country, as for its fidelity to its original purpose.

At the meeting above-mentioned, the general plan and purposes of the association were discussed, and a brief constitution for its primitive government was unanimously adopted—together with the following "Preamble" or code of principles:

PREAMBLE.

During the last few years, events of a most alarming nature have transpired, which threaten to annihilate those glorious institutions bequeathed to us by our patriot sires.

The precepts and warning legacy of our immortal WASHINGTON, to "beware of foreign influence," seem, in a fearful measure, to have fallen upon ears deaf to the cause of freedom, save that radical freedom which admits of no restraint, and acknowledges no law, except that which to-day may be enacted and to-morrow annulled, at the caprice of base demagogues, to serve some unhallowed party purpose.

With sorrow we have seen many of our countrymen unite with citizens of foreign birth, in enacting laws, and supporting principles that must inevitably end in the subversion of our liberties, unless we rally, in the majesty of our strength, now, while we have the power, and for ever stay the further progress of dangerous innovations upon our established laws.

The most alarming of these exactions is the exclusion of the Bible from our public schools. If the word of God, the *Magna Charta* of all civil and Religious Liberty, be banished from our public schools, we may look forward with certainty to the day when the blighting wand of moral darkness will usurp the seat of enlightened rectitude, and when our dearest rights will be wrested from us by ambitious rulers, who, fearing not God nor regarding man, will weave around us the galling chains of despotism, and for ever banish from our now happy shores the name of freedom, and its attributes.

Believing that the present crisis in our political condition calls loudly for the most effective coöperation of all who sincerely desire the perpetuity of our institutions, an ORDER has been organized for the purpose of more effectually securing our country from the dan gers of foreign influence, by a concert of action and singleness of purpose, that we may look for in vain through the ordinary channels of society. Coupled with this laudable endeavor to secure to posterity the civil and religious rights that we enjoy, is the ennobling and virtuous duty of aiding our fellow men in distress; that when laid upon a bed of sickness, the friendly aid of this Order may be manifested in providing for our necessities. In the silent watches of the night a friend will ever be ready to administer to our wants, and if death lays his cold hand upon us, we shall depart in the assurance that our widowed consorts will be the recipients of the imperishable friendship of the fraternity, and if need be, that pecuniary assistance which will soften the asperity of their desolate condition. The paternal guardianship of this Order will ever bring our fatherless children within their watchful care, and especially will the orphan be protected from the snares of a cold and heartless world, and placed in the path that leads to honor and usefulness here, and to a blessed rest hereafter.

In our efforts to release our country from the thraldom of foreign domination which now, or shall hereafter exist, we will act as with the heart and impulse of *one man*, and truly and faithfully conform to the will of a majority of our Order.

Our political action will be adapted to the exigency of the crisis that may arise; but our polar star shall ever be the salvation of our country and its institutions.

As the perpetuity of our civil and religious liberties is the great object, to secure which we unite our strength, we will assail no man for his religious opinions.

With these remarks upon our object and position, we submit our constitution to the examination of our countrymen, cordially inviting them to come forward and unite with us in securing our free institutions to ourselves and to our posterity.

This preamble, together with the constitution, was forthwith published to the world, and immediately thereafter a ritual for the private government, and instruction of its members, was prepared and adopted. As an evidence of the liberality of spirit towards foreigners in which the organization was conceived, I venture to quote a passage from the instruction given to their members on their admission to the order, in the following words:

"At the same time, we extend the right hand of fellowship to those who seek our shores, and with sincerity cherish their new home and its institutions."

The publication of the constitution with its preamble produced no little sensation on the public mind—and while their provisions were received with cordial approbation by the conservative and truly patriotic, they were met at the same time with the sternest denunciations of the partisan leaders and presses. The Order was characterized as an "infamous cabal," an "infernal Native American machine," a "Jacobin Club," &c. One of the New York papers did not hesitate to pronounce it an organization more vile than that of the Jesuits. To all these assaults the Order listened in silence, and "went on its way rejoicing." ALPHA CHAPTER, the first organized under the constitution, increased so rapidly in numbers, that early in the following spring it was deemed advisable to divide the membership, which was accordingly done, and by this division, WASHINGTON CHAPTER, No. 2, was created, and its organization took place on the 31st of March, 1845. On the first day of April, 1845, the first hall, used especially for the meetings of the order, was dedicated. The membership of Alpha Chapter had, during the winter, secured the lease of a suitable hall, and fitted it up in a most elegant manner, the walls and ceiling being embellished with elaborate and appropriate designs in fresco. On the occasion of the dedication the hall was open to the public, and the beautiful Temple of Patriotism, brilliantly lighted and decorated, was thronged with an assemblage of ladies and gentlemen who had been invited to witness the ceremony. The Hon. Wm. W. Campbell, a member of the Chapter, delivered an appropriate address, after which a Poem, written for the occasion, was delivered by one of the members—both of which were afterwards published in pamphlet form by the Chapter, and circulated gratuitously. WARREN CHAPTER, No 3, was instituted in Brooklyn, N. Y., on the 26th of April in the same year; MANHATTAN, No. 4, on the 9th of May, in the city of New York, and JEFFERSON, No. 5, was instituted August 13th, at Harlaem. Thus, notwithstanding the hostility of timorous politicians, five chapters of the order were instituted within eight months after the preliminary meeting of its founders.

The government of the order was made by the constitution legislative, administrative, and judicial, and the whole system is strictly American Republican, every officer and every representative being elective. The order is divided into three distinct grades or departments, viz.:

1st. The "Arch Chancery," or National legislative head, consisting of delegates, or representatives, called "Arch Chancellors," three from each State chancery.

2d. The "Chanceries," or legislative head in each several State, consisting of representatives called "Chancellors," three from each Chapter in the State.

3d. The "Chapters," or local organizations, comprising the membership of the order.

The Chapters are organized without any limit as to locality or number; for example, any number of Chapters may be formed in a single town or ward, that can be supported in such town or ward; besides, the members are not required to reside in the particular town, ward, county, or state, in which the chapter to which they may belong is situated. The presiding officer of the CHAPTER is denominated the "Sachem;" his term of office is six months. The presiding officer of the State CHANCERY is entitled the "Grand Sachem;" he is also the administrative officer of the State. His term of office is one year. The presiding officer of the ARCH CHANCERY, or National head, is the "Arch Grand Sachem;" he is also the chief administrative officer of the whole order. His term of office is one year.

The judicial power is at present vested by grades in these three bodies; the minor offences among the membership being tried by the Chapters, their verdict being subject to an appeal to the Grand Sachem, and his decision again subject to the revision of the Chancery (as a court for the correction of errors, only), otherwise, the decision of the Grand Sachem is final. Matters of litigation between Chanceries are adjusted on appeal to the Arch Grand Sachem, as are also differences between the Chanceries and their Chapters, his decisions being subject to revision in matters of law, by a permanent "JUDICIAL BOARD," chosen from the body of the Arch Chancery. The several State Chanceries have in contemplation the establishment of Judicial Boards, similar to that of Arch Chancery, with a view to separate as far as possible the judicial from the legislative departments. This feature is the only important one wanting to render the government of this powerful society as complete in its general features, as that of the national government itself.

## CHAPTER XXI.

### THE ORDER OF UNITED AMERICANS—ITS PROGRESS, INFLUENCE, AND CONDITION.

"It is time that we were a little more Americanized."
ANDREW JACKSON.

ALTHOUGH the Order of United Americans came into existence at a moment when the American party was in the ascendant in several of the principal cities of the Union, the anticipation of its founders, that that party would, like its predecessor, be submerged by the waves of political corruption which threatened it on every side, was soon realized. As stated in the last chapter, the American party was overwhelmed in 1845, and almost entirely extinct in 1847.

When the last struggles of that patriotic effort were over, and no more traces of its existence were visible on the surface of the political waters, "Nativeism" was supposed to have received its final death-blow. Then it was that the very name "American" became a term of reproach, and the offscourings of European fens rose up in the high places among the people with sneers and scoffs, deriding, and denouncing the native sons of the soil, the descendants of the sires who fought the seven years' war against the fathers of these very men, and established a nation, free and independent! A refuge for these miserable revilers! Then it was that *American* demagogues, and their prostituted retainers, listened to and applauded the detractors of their own countrymen, and seconded their sneers with boisterous mirth and acclamation! To have favored the policy of the American party was to be despised and insulted—to declare one's self an American in principle was to be shunned in public, and hated in private. In the family, in the church, in the public mart, and the private circles, in the court of justice, at the festival or the funeral, in business or at leisure, day or night, sleeping or waking, the "Native American" was avoided as one accursed! And wherefore? Because he had dared to avow and uphold the broad principle that "AMERICANS *ought to* GOVERN AMERICA."

But while these persecutions were heaped as burning coals upon the heads of all who would not openly kneel before the partisan altar, and *repent* of their *patriotic indiscretion*, all who would not join in the cry of condemnation against their fellow-countrymen *and themselves*; although that spirit of resistance to foreign influence, which had, for a brief season, prevailed, seemed to have been exorcised for ever; and on the *surface* of the political ocean no ripple appeared to indicate its continued existence, there was, gliding beneath the dark waters of corruption, a small, yet swift and steady under-current, which, though feeble as an embryo, was destined to sway in the future as a torrent. Silently, deeply, beyond the heedless gaze of the self-confident partisan, and the more wary wiles of the scheming Jesuit, the Order of United Americans moved onward, gathering strength as it progressed, and like a subterranean streamlet, gradually undermining the foundations of corrupt political structures, or, like a quicksand, absorbing the ground-plans for papal encroachment. Its watchword was passed from city to city, from State to State, and its influence, like the wind, felt, though still unseen, accumulated at every step. A few bold spirits, too independent to fear, and too firm to quail before the threats of their opponents, invincible in their panoply of honesty, at length came forth, the champions and exponents of the principles of the Order. Public meetings were held, and addresses delivered, under the auspices of the association; in the cities, in the villages, in the hamlets of the country, sometimes under the dome of the sacred edifice, sometimes in the public hall, sometimes in the village school-room, or under the canopy of heaven; it mattered not; wherever an audience could be gathered there was heard the voice of the fearless United American, preaching the doctrines of American patriotism, and warning the people against the Jesuit and the demagogue.

But no *reporters* came to those assemblages;—the public press of the land passed them by with the silence of a feigned contempt, or noticed them only to revile. "The rich Irish brogue, and the sweet German accent," had supplanted the American idiom, and, while every press was muzzled, or turned against the American sentiment, every gathering of foreigners was gazetted with fulsome laudation. Even the popular sentiment, although confessing in its heart the soundness of the doctrines of the Order, lacked the moral courage to avow openly its convictions. Thousands of men have said to the orators of the Order, "Your principles are correct—your object is noble and patriotic, *but your cause is hopeless.*" They gave to the members of the Order a mingled meed of admiration and sympathy, but not their coöperation. They said, "It is too late—the foreign influence is already overwhelming, and the fangs of the Papacy are even now in our vitals!" And so they retired silently to their homes, hoping, doubtless, that they might possibly live out their span of life before the awful climax should arrive, yet conscious of the fact that their posterity must bow before the blast! They were willing to admit that the deadliest foe of our institutions —the arch-enemy of liberty, was at our doors—nay, actually within our household, yet refused to raise a hand to expel or disarm the invader, quieting their consciences with the puerile plea, "*it is too late!*" They said, in effect—"*Our forefathers have provided for us, let posterity provide for itself*," and under this selfish refuge, they shut themselves up, as the periwinkle in his shell, and thus sheltered themselves from the fury of the brewing storm.

These accumulated discouragements were not without their effects. Many a true heart became weary and faint, and stopped by the wayside for breath; and some even retreated from the unthankful and burdensome task which they had assumed. But there were enough left to carry on the work. Though few, they were resolute. They had resolved, like Caius Marius, to sacrifice themselves for the salvation of the people. Their highest hope was that they might inspire their countrymen with a renewed spirit of *nationality*, awakening in their minds a sense of the impending danger, and thus, in their own time, pave the way for an effective resistance of the Anti-American theories and influences which were rapidly usurping the place of our time-honoured customs, sentiments, laws, and constitutions.

It is undeniable that our people were becoming strangely

un-Americanized, both socially and politically, and the first step of the Order of United Americans was to bring back the train of popular thinking to something like the old-time standard of American Republicanism. Her orators made war upon *theories*, *influences*, and *innovations*, rather than upon men or classes. Their effort was to *conserve* what was in possession, and *restore* what had been squandered, not to tear down the old, and build up a new system. They presented no hypothesis; but the simple, demonstrative theory of self-preservation, and this they strove to present in its simplest aspect, to the people.

Against the current of obstacles presented, the Order made a steady though not a rapid progress. The expense of obtaining and holding membership in the Order was in itself a serious obstacle in the way of accumulating a large membership, yet, although slow, its course was never retrograde. It was established, as I have stated, at the close of the year 1844, in the city of New York: in that State it now numbers (1855) ninety Chapters, which are distributed in every portion of the State. On the 17th of June, 1846, it was organized in Massachusetts. In 1848 the order was first started in New Jersey. In Pennsylvania it was organized in 1848. On the 22d of August, 1849 the first Chapter was instituted in Connecticut. In California it was instituted in the year 1850, by Messrs. Robt. D. Hart, John W. Ackerman, Charles M. Yarwood, and a few gentlemen, who were then members of the order in the Eastern States. Mr. Hart was the projector and first Sachem of EUREKA CHAPTER, located at San Francisco. The undertaking was one involving, at that time, great pecuniary responsibility, a responsibility which nothing but an earnest and patriotic zeal could have induced its members to take upon themselves. The rent alone of the room in which the Chapter held its meetings was $150 per month, or $1800 per annum. Eureka Chapter is still in existence, and has been effective in both its beneficial and political character.

In 1854 the order was instituted in the States of Vermont, Maine, New Hampshire, and Michigan, and in 1855 it has been instituted in Missouri, Ohio, Virginia, District of Columbia, Indiana, Illinois, Wisconsin, Tennessee, Alabama, Louisiana, and Rhode Island.

The first organized political effort of the order occurred in 1846, and was directed against the adoption of the New Constitution of the State of New York. That Constitution, which had been prepared by a convention of partisans, and which was about to be submitted to the people for their approval, contained several provisions repulsive to the sentiment of the Order, and hostile to the interests of the State, and the purity of the franchise. From the day that the State of New York first became a State, its Constitution had sustained the principle set forth in the Constitution of the United States; viz., that the highest executive officer should be an American by birth. No naturalized citizen had been eligible to the office of Governor, or Lieutenant Governor. The new Constitution struck out that principle, and extended that time-honored, conservative prerogative of the native-born American to foreigners. It gave to foreigners the right to *govern* the American people, and to execute the laws of an American State.

The State had also, from its incipiency, recognized by its

Constitution the principle that ministers of religion, being devoted by their profession to the care of souls, ought not to interfere with affairs of State, and that, therefore, they should not be eligible to any political office whatever. The new Constitution struck out this principle also, and vested this class of citizens with the right to hold any political office within the gift of the people. By these two provisions of the new Constitution it will be seen that a foreign ecclesiastic was made eligible to the executive chair of the State. Ergo, a foreign Roman Catholic Bishop might, through the chicanery of parties, be made Governor of New York, and thus a perfect union of the Church and the State would be brought about. But, apart from this extreme view of the case, a feature so well calculated to bring the State into collusion with religion, was deemed anti-American in its whole bearing, and dangerous to civil and religious liberty. This was of course obnoxious to the sentiment of the Order, and therefore the Order opposed it.

A third objectionable feature was that the new Constitution provided for an *elective* JUDICIARY. It was apprehended that such a system would tend to bring the judiciary into collusion with partisan corruptions; and that judges who owed their honors and their emoluments to the vote of a party, might through the frailties of human nature, be brought to tear the bandage from the eyes of Justice, and stain the ermine of their office with partiality.

These features brought down upon the new Constitution the opposition of the United Americans. At this time the Order was yet in its infancy, and its membership extended scarcely beyond the limits of the city of New York. Its influence was, therefore, confined to that locality. It was not long, however, in creating a feeling of popular hostility towards the new Constitution, and although that instrument was ratified by the popular vote of the State, yet in the city of New York, where the Order brought its influence to bear in opposition to it, *a majority of over twenty thousand votes was given against its ratification!*

Again, in 1850, the whole country was agitated, and the Union itself shaken to its foundation by the rancorous debates then pending in both Houses of Congress. The subjects of discussion were certain territorial organizations, the Texas boundary, the admission of California, and the fugitive slave law, all involving the vexed and vexing question of slavery. The zealots of the North, and the zealots of the South had seized again upon this apple of discord and with flaming eloquence had ruptured and consumed all ties of harmony, and absorbed all interests save the geographical interests of opposing sections. Reason seemed for a time to have forsaken her throne partisan attachments were submerged in the frenzy of local factions—the North standing against the South, and the South against the North—until all fraternal sentiments had been discarded, and a dissolution of the Union seemed inevitable.

In this terrific crisis the Order of United Americans resolved to make an effort to stay the current of civil strife, and to bring back order out of chaos. The duty of conceiving and perfecting a plan for the accomplishment of so singular and delicate a trust was confided to a committee of nine members of the Chancery of New York. That committee set forth on its mission with the hypothesis that the entire public sentiment of the country, both North and South, was outraged by the course pursued by the national representatives, and eager for a cessation of the dangerous controversy. They determined to obtain, if possible, an unequivocal expression of that public sentiment. The most convenient way to obtain speedily such an expression was by public assemblages. Accordingly, at their individual suggestion, in less than ten days from the passage of the resolution in Chancery, there appeared in nearly every daily and weekly paper of the city of New York, editorial articles, denouncing the agitation then pending in Congress, and calling upon the people everywhere, to assemble in their primary capacity, and, with appropriate resolutions and proceedings, demand of their representatives a cessation of their hostile feud. The first result of this course was the spontaneous organization of a committee of respectable and well-known citizens of New York, disconnected with the order, and under the auspices of that committee there was gathered within and about the immense enclosure of Castle Garden the proudest and most numerous meeting of citizens ever congregated in the Empire city. *Men of every party* mingled there with a patriotic enthusiasm, the Native American, the Whig, and the Democrat; and from that assemblage went forth a voice which pierced the remotest portions of the Union.

Tammany Hall was next besieged in continuation of the good work, and for once at least in her (*modern*) history her time-honored walls rang with the notes of pure patriotism.

Broadway House followed immediately in the wake of Old Tammany, and sent forth her resolutions of condemnation. The flame once lighted spread like a fire on the prairies; Union meetings were held at Philadelphia, Boston, Detroit, New Haven, and in every quarter of the land, and from them went the united voice of an indignant sovereign people, rolling onward with increasing force, until it thundered against the doors of the capitol in tones not to be misunderstood or unheeded! The frantic legislators, startled by the sound, paused in their mad career. A lull in the storm of passion ensued; men were brought back to reflection—they saw the popular will suspended like the sword of Damocles, by a single hair above them, and they shrank from the threatening blade. A compromise, the celebrated compromise of 1850, was effected, and the hour of peril was past! *This was the work of the* ORDER OF UNITED AMERICANS.

During the same year, the Common School system of the State of New York was in danger of a total abrogation. During the last previous session of the legislature, Jesuitism, having failed to secure an open apportionment of the school fund for its own purposes, obtained the passage of an act, submitting the public school law a second time to the popular decision; the people having just before approved it by a majority of *more than one hundred thousand votes.* After the passage of this submissive act, the Romanists set every engine of their machinery at work, in order to secure a repeal of the school law, bishop, priest, Jesuit, and layman were active with sophistry among the people, and it was soon apparent that a mysterious change was taking place in the public mind towards the system. The friends of popular education, viewing those symptoms with alarm, called a convention to be holden at the city of Syracuse, for the purpose of devising means to prevent the overthrow of the public schools. To that convention the Order of United Americans sent a delegate—and to that convention the editor of the *Freeman's Journal,* that bitter and unscrupulous foe of our schools, was invited. Both were present in convention, the delegate and the editor. The latter gave as his opinion that the education of children should be entrusted only to the Church, and when he was asked "what Church?" he answered: "I know of but one Church—I mean, of course, the Roman Catholic Church." The delegate, on the other hand, related the course that had been pursued by the editor in opposition to the whole system of public education, and exposed the devices and efforts of the Romanists as a body to destroy the public schools. Thus a new view of the subject was presented to the public mind—a better feeling towards the system sprang up—men who had been opposed to the system as one imposing unequal and unjust taxation, became its friends, and the public schools were saved, though by a greatly reduced majority.

Thus the Order of United Americans have, in numerous instances, silently and unostentatiously put forth the arm of conservative influence, and always with effect. Assimilating with no political party, it has always occupied an attitude of independence—making no nominations peculiarly its own, it has afforded no inducements to personal ambition among its members, and in this posture it has operated as an *American* balance of power between rival factions, invariably striking down the candidate of either party whose antecedents were those of the demagogue or the pander to foreign or Romish influences. Regarding "the unity of government" which constitutes us one people, in the language of Washington, as "the main pillar in the edifice of our real independence," and as the "support of that very liberty which we so highly prize," it has been the firm and the steadfast advocate of the Union, and the sovereign rights of the States. Regarding "foreign influence" as "one of the most baneful foes of a republican government," it has unwaveringly resisted that influence in whatever form it may have been presented. Regarding popular intelligence, regulated by a sense of true religion and morality, as the palladium that must shield us from the inroads of ignorance and superstition, it has been the fearless champion of free schools and an open Bible. Regarding the popular suffrage as a freeman's heritage, to be exercised either *for* or *against* our institutions of civil liberty, it has steadfastly striven to maintain the purity of the ballot-box, and to withhold therefrom all deleterious and dangerous influences. In the language of the preamble to its constitution, its political action has been "adapted to the exigency of the crisis" that has arisen, and "its polar star has ever been the salvation of our country, and its institutions."

## CHAPTER XXII.

THE "KNOW NOTHINGS"—ORIGIN AND RISE OF THE ORDER—ITS MISSION.

THE vast organization which is at present so numerous and powerful in the United States, vulgarly denominated "Know Nothings," was originally conceived and planned by a gentleman of New York, who, singularly enough, had never been associated with any other American political organization, nor actively engaged with either of the political parties. As early as 1849 this gentleman prepared and systematized his plan for uniting the National sentiment of the American people, against the foreign and papal encroachments so frequently occurring and concentrating in the political atmosphere, and began, among his immediate friends, the work of recruiting members and co-workers. But after more than two years of persevering effort his associates numbered scarcely thirty, all told.

With most of men, this ill success would have proven a fatal source of discouragement, but the author of this movement was not the man to yield the palm of victory to any obstacle, so long as his own judgment remained true to his purpose. This was his case. He never lost confidence in the plan which he had laid out, and with a full conviction that his system was both feasible and just, he persevered. Although a man of fine intelligence and clear judgment, the founder of this association was not an orator. It was not his faculty to rise before an audience of his countrymen, and in glowing language depict either the construction of, or the necessities that called for the organization of which he was the progenitor, and to this circumstance, doubtless, may be attributed, in a great degree, the tardy propagation of his measure.

In 1852, a few active members of the Order of United Americans were induced to examine this new plan. They found a society consisting of *forty-three members*. The general objects of the association were the same as those of the O. U. A., but the qualifications necessary to obtain membership were far more restrictive, and the appurtenances of secrecy more specific and stringent, and although the plan was somewhat incomplete in detail, and unadapted to the government of an expanded organization, extending over and ramifying all the States and territories of the Union, it yet presented one peculiar feature calculated to promote a rapid, if not a healthy growth. *It cost nothing to acquire and hold membership.* Having no beneficial feature to demand funds for charitable purposes, it required no such fund, and as the plan did not seem to contemplate any systematic or stated meetings, or even the sub-division of the Order into "Councils," no provision had been made for room-rent. No fees or dues whatever were charged upon the members, the whole system relying on voluntary contributions for its pecuniary support. The groundwork had been laid out for an immense army, with a general and staff at the head, but without companies, regiments, or even a commissariat.

The first requisite was members, the next a more solid and consecutive system of organization. It was evident that the plan, once well organized, pruned, and adapted more strictly to the republican spirit of the people, would afford a powerful auxiliary in promoting and disseminating the theory and demands of the American policy. Its plan of political action, like that of the Order of United Americans, contemplated the *control* rather than the *making* of nominations, proper; hence in that respect there could be no clashing in their *modus* of procedure. As yet the new order had no stated time or place of meeting. It was called together whenever occasion required, by the president, either at a private house, or in some lodge-room, after the lodge had adjourned; and at each meeting small collections were taken to defray whatever slight expense might have been incurred. The giant that was destined to grind the corrupt parties of the country into powder, to appall the demagogue, and shake to pieces the political papal structure in the United States, was as yet but an *embryo*, a conception unborn!

Immediate measures were taken to increase the membership, and for that purpose the Chapters of the Order of United Americans were prolific of material. Meetings of the new Order were held at various places, almost every evening, and at each meeting many were added to its membership. Committees were soon formed, with proper dispensations to initiate members, and thus, nightly, two or three of these committees were engaged in the work of recruiting, and in less than four months the membership amounted to about *one thousand persons.* It was soon found necessary to obtain a place for general assemblages of the order, and a large hall was hired for that purpose on Broadway. There a series of weekly meetings were instituted, at which from six hundred to eight hundred members were regularly assembled. At those meetings the freedom of speech was unabridged—addresses were delivered, and an enthusiasm created on behalf of the American policy which could have been aroused by no other means.

Thus far the membership had been gathered in from all parts of the city indiscriminately, and no "councils" had been formed, except the one great council to which the members rallied in their weekly gatherings. The hive was overflowing, and for the want of the elements for an expanded action, it was inoperative To be effective, councils were needed in every ward of the city, every county in the State, and every State and territory of the Union.

The constitution was accordingly revised for that purpose. A system of national, State, and subordinate, or local councils was adopted, and several other amendments perfected in accordance with the necessities of a wide-spread and numerous organization. The effect was immediately visible. Like a vast body of pent up waters when the floodgates have burst asunder, the membership poured forth in torrents:—councils were founded in the several wards of the city, thence in the interior counties of the State. Soon after the order was planted in some of the adjoining States, and eventually in every State and territory under the jurisdiction of the United States.

The organization of the order in the several States occurred in the following order.

In New York, April 4, 1852. State Council formed, Dec. 7, 1853.

In New Jersey, April, 1853. State Council, November, 1853.

In Vermont, (Date unknown.)

In Maryland, May 22, 1853. State Council, October 14, 1853.

In Connecticut, July 1853. State Council, November, 1853.

In Massachusetts, September 6, 1853. State Council, October, 1853.

In Pennsylvania, December 10, 1853. State Council, in spring of 1854.

In Ohio, in the fall of 1853.

In Washington, D. C., January 23, 1854.

In New Hampshire, February 6, 1854. State Council, June, 1854.

In Indiana, State Council formed, February, 1854.

In Rhode Island, March, 1854. State Council, July 10, 1854.

In Maine, March, 1854. State Council, July, 1854.

In Alabama, State Council, April or May, 1854.

In Georgia, May, 1854. State Council same year.

In Illinois, May 25, 1854. State Council, June 18, 1854.

In Michigan, June 2, 1854. State Council same month.

In Iowa, July 26, 1854. State Council, October 5, 1854.

In Wisconsin, State Council, August 30, 1854.

In North Carolina, August or September, 1854.

In South Carolina, State Council, October 2, 1854.

In Kentucky, State Council, August, 1854.

In Missouri, State Council, Sept., 1854.

In Tennessee, State Council, October, 1854

In Virginia, (Date unknown.)

In Delaware, State Council, October, 1854.

In Mississippi, State Council, November, 1854.

In Texas, State Council, fall of 1854.

In Florida, State Council, December, 1854.

In Arkansas, State Council, December, 1854.

In California, State Council, formed fall of 1854.

In Louisiana. (In this State there are two organizations; The first was started early in 1854; this has been repudiated by the National Council as spurious. The second, which is recognized as legitimate, was organized in September, 1854.)

In Oregon, September, 1854.

In Minnesota, State Council, formed in May, 1855.

In New Mexico, Kansas, and Nebraska the order was established during the spring and summer of 1855.

Thus, in about three years from the organization of the first council in the city of New York, we find this extraordinary political society, not only established, but exerting a powerful influence in every State and territory of the whole Union, and numbering in its membership at least *one and a half million of legal voters!* And among its adherents—the open advocates and exponents of its principles, we find many of the brightest intelligences, the ablest statesmen, and the purest patriots of the land. It is plain to the commonest, as well as to the most acute understanding, that results so imposing could never have been achieved upon a "narrow-minded," "bigoted," or "proscriptive" proposition. None of the elements of coercion, or superstition, nor the authoritative force of intelligence over ignorance have been employed in their development. The whole work has been performed within *a nation of intelligences;* where every man is his own monitor; the master of his own opinions; free to approve or condemn by the test of his own conscience and his own judgment, and by that test this million and a half of freemen have recorded their verdict in favor of the American policy.

The principles which actuated the order were precisely the principles which actuated the American party in 1834 and 1844, and the objects sought to be obtained by the order were the objects sought to be obtained by that party. The success of the experiment has proven conclusively that when the popular mind is left untrammelled by partisan influences, and free to exercise its own proper functions, away from the corrupting sophistry of the demagogue, the patriotic sentiment will prevail, and a stern, inflexible spirit of *nationality* will preponderate over the mercenary or factional demands of a mere party.

The advent of this organization was most opportune for the peace of the country, and the maintenance of the Union of States. The old parties had already exhausted their legitimate resources of cohesion, and become *effete*, and their components were gradually dissolving into a sectional slime, whose stagnant and fetid odors would have been poisonous to the national health. Already the current of political fraternity had ceased to flow across the geographical line, dividing the

Northern from the Southern States, and as a natural result of estrangement, sectional hostilities were being engendered in their most noxious form. National parties had ceased to exist, except *pro forma*, and the whole political blood of the country was running in adverse directions, the one portion into a channel of aggression upon the sovereignty of the States, and the other into that of disunion. The advent of the American organization opened a new avenue to intersectional harmony. It broke down the imaginary line of Mason and Dixon, and re-established political inter-communication between the North and the South; it stoutly declared against both of the opposing factions, and fearlessly stood forth the advocate of State sovereignty, and the foe of the spirit of disunion.

## CHAPTER XXIII.

THE "KNOW NOTHINGS"—PROGRESS OF THE ORDER—ITS INFLUENCE—ITS ENEMIES—THE FREE SOIL INOCULATION AND EXPULSION—MASSACHUSETTS—THE PHILADELPHIA CONVENTION—PARASITES——THE MISSION FULFILLED.

IT was not in the nature of things that an organization, wielding so powerful a political influence as this has done, could long escape, even in its secret chambers, the hostility of startled demagogues.

Its mysterious successes first called the attention of political parties to its existence. Unseen and unknown, it wielded an overwhelming influence wherever it developed its power. Demagogues fell before the swing of its keen scythe like grass before the mower, and in dismay found themselves enveloped in defeat where victory seemed more certain. In many a district, where its existence was uususpected, it has, in an hour, like the unseen wind, swept the corruptionist from his power and placed in office the unsoliciting but honest and capable citizen.

The unscrupulous leaders of every faction and party, saw in the up-growing giant, a power which, if left to itself, would become the ruling spirit of the nation, and as its ingredients were found to be utterly uncongenial with their habits, and utterly foreign to their desire, it was plain that in the success of that organization their hopes of aggrandizement would be blasted for ever. No obstacle had ever been presented so formidable to their plans. Before they were well aware of its existence, it had risen to such magnitude as to set at defiance all the ordinary machinery of partisan hatred and hostility. It had already taken too deep a root in the public mind to be overthrown by an assault upon its avowed principles, and it was even then so numerous as to overwhelm any single faction that should have ventured to stand up as its opponent. It could not be strangled with defamation as the American party had twice been strangled; it could not be beaten in an honorable and open issue at the ballot-box; it could not be decoyed from its purpose by promises of patronage, nor coerced from it by persecution and proscription, both of which were (and still are) employed to destroy it, *by the General Government at Washington*, and as all these expedients failed, it was at length determined to try the plan of *subversion*. The fortress that could not be reduced either by storm or siege, might, it was thought, be *undermined*.

In the State of New York the followers of William H. Seward sent their emissaries into the councils of the order. They entered with a feigned admiration of its principles, and bound themselves by the strongest of moral obligations to sustain the measures of the organization. They went even so far as to create one or more councils in the rural districts, for which they obtained the requisite authority from the legal head of the order in the State, and continued to act with the order with the strongest assurances of fidelity. They chose delegates to the State and National Councils, and were in all respects in the full confidence of the fraternity at large.

The defective character of these organizations was first developed at a State convention, held at Syracuse, in the fall of 1854, for the nomination of candidates for a governor, lieutenant governor, and certain State officers. This convention had been called ostensibly as a whig convention, but in it the members of the order held a considerable majority. It soon became apparent, however, that the order was not so well represented in *spirit* as in numbers. Men professing its principles were opposed to its candidates, and although the Seward faction failed in the choice of their favorite, they succeeded in nominating Myron H. Clark for governor, under the plea that he was a member of a legitimate council of the order in full fellowship. It was soon discovered, however, that a fraud had been practised; Mr. Clark was found to be identified with the free-soil or Seward faction of what was *once* the whig party, and the order generally refused to support his nomination. Measures were taken for the nomination of another candidate on behalf of the order itself. This step was stoutly resisted by the council at Utica, and a few others in the interior of State, and by this and their subsequent action the true character of those councils was developed; they were shown to be no more than spies in the camp.

A meeting of the State Council was soon after held in the city of New York, at which Daniel Ullmann, Esq., was nominated as the American candidate for governor, and a full State ticket was prepared. Those nominations the Utica council with its associates refused to sustain, and they were subsequently expelled from the order. The shock occasioned by this *ruse* was but momentary. The order having purified itself by shaking off the excrescences that had been fastened upon it by the abolition interests and the followers of Mr. Seward, progressed as though nothing had occurred to interrupt the harmony of its proceedings, or the success of its aims.

At that time not more than one-fourth of the towns in the State had been reached by the organizations of the order, and its nominations were made rather with a view to concentrate the American vote of the State as a distinct element, than with any expectation of electing its candidate. Yet, their candidate for governor received *one hundred and twenty-two thousand votes*, a result, under all circumstances, at once gratifying and encouraging to the friends of the American policy. Since that election the order has largely increased its membership, and its organizations extend to every township in the State.*

In Massachusetts, although the same elements appeared, to distract the national spirit of the order, they were presented in a different form. In that State, free-soilism had long before become a popular sentiment, a sort of moral epidemic, from the influence of which few of its citizens escaped. The introduction of this sectional element into the order in that commonwealth, was therefore by a natural process. No subterfuge was necessary. The citizens entered the order with the true American spirit, and with a resolute, honest in-

* At the election held the year following; viz., in November, 1855, the American State candidates received *one hundred and forty-six thousand votes*, and were elected with a plurality of *more than ten thousand* over the candidates of the free soil combination. This conclusively shows that the policy of Mr. Seward is not sustained by the people of his own State.

tention to abide by its doctrines, and sustain its measures—but they carried with them *imperceptibly*, their free-soil proclivities. At the first election they secured to themselves the entire government of the State, and in all their public acts which involved directly the American doctrine, they exhibited an unwavering fidelity to the cause they had espoused. But the *inner* sentiment—the free-soil proclivity developed itself in the choice of United States Senator, in the passage of the "Personal Liberty Bill"—and subsequently in their attempted persecution of Judge Loring, for having, in his judicial character, sustained the fugitive slave law. When censured for these acts they sheltered themselves under the plea that they had acted in accordance with the conscience of their State, and in conformity with their own views on that subject—views which they had entertained from first to last, and on which they had never been questioned or qualified by any express requirement of the order. Governor Gardner, who had also been elected by the American party, exhibited his attachment to the compromises of the Constitution, and the laws of Congress, by refusing to give his assent to either the Personal Liberty Bill, or the removal of Judge Loring, and by thus interposing the Executive authority prevented the consummation of the latter, and saved the commonwealth from the stain which threatened her escutcheon.

The attitude thus assumed by the legislature of Massachusetts necessarily created much excitement throughout the order. It was evident that an organization entertaining views hostile to the sovereignty of a portion of the States, and entirely *sectional* in its nature, could not consistently form a component of a party whose whole predilections were *national*. She was, however, permitted to appear through her delegates in the National Convention of the order held at Philadelphia, in the month of June, 1855. At that convention, finding it impossible to engraft any portion of her free-soil doctrines upon the platform there adopted, her delegates withdrew, accompanied with those of two or three other of the free-soil States.

But the sentiment of Massachusetts, and of the order in that commonwealth, as it subsequently appeared, was not represented in the acts of her delegates in the convention, or by the men who spoke for her in the local legislature. The legislature, as I have shown, was not sustained by the Executive, and the delegates to the convention at Philadelphia were subsequently rebuked, and their sentiments repudiated by *the order* and *the people* of their own State. In fact, it would seem, that, as in New York, the free-soil agitators had surreptitiously entered the order for the purpose of advancing, through its influence, their own peculiar views, but their action in the legislature, and especially in the convention at Philadelphia, seems to have opened the eyes of the honest, conservative men of the State, to their true character and objects.

A division took place, and in the summer of 1855 two State conventions were held for the nomination of a governor and State officers. The first, *purporting* to be American and free-soil in its complexion, refused to tender a re-nomination to Governor Gardner, on account of his fidelity to the Constitution, and his hostility to the sectional movement of the free-soil party. The second convention was called by that portion of the American Order which approved of the national attitude assumed by the governor. This convention renominated Governor Gardner, and a full set of candidates for State officers, all of whom were opposed to that sectional spirit which had been characterized as "*the conscience* of the State of Massachusetts."

The result proved that the conscience of Massachusetts, like that of her illustrious son, DANIEL WEBSTER, is true to the Constitution and the Union. At the election held in the month of November following, the national course of Governer Gardner was sustained, and the real American candidates triumphantly elected.

After the Massachusetts delegation had withdrawn from the convention at Philadelphia, the convention adopted the following:

### PLATFORM AND PRINCIPLES OF THE ORGANIZATION.

I.—The acknowledgment of that Almighty Being, who rules over the Universe,—who presides over the Councils of Nations,—who conducts the affairs of men, and who, in every step by which we have advanced to the character of an independent nation, has distinguished us by some token of Providential agency.

II.—The cultivation and development of a sentiment of profoundly intense American feeling; of passionate attachment to our country, its history and its institutions; of admiration for the purer days of our national existence; of veneration, for the heroism that precipitated our Revolution; and of emulation of the virtue, wisdom, and patriotism that framed our Constitution and first successfully applied its provisions.

III.—The maintenance of the union of these United States as the paramount political good; or, to use the language of Washington, "the primary object of patriotic desire." And hence:—

1st. Opposition to all attempts to weaken or subvert it.

2d. Uncompromising antagonism to every principle of policy that endangers it.

3d. The advocacy of an equitable adjustment of all political differences which threaten its integrity or perpetuity.

4th. The suppression of all tendencies to political division, founded on "geographical discrimination, or on the belief that there is a real difference of interests and views between the various sections of the Union.

5th. The full recognition of the rights of the several States, as expressed and reserved in the Constitution, and a careful avoidance by the general government of all interference with their rights by legislative or executive action.

IV.—Obedience to the Constitution of the United States, as the supreme law of the land, sacredly obligatory upon all its parts and members; and steadfast resistance to the spirit of innovation upon its principles, however specious the pretexts. Avowing that in all doubtful or disputed points it may only be legally ascertained and expounded by the Judicial power of the United States.

And, as a corollary to the above:—

1. A habit of reverential obedience to the laws, whether National, State, or Municipal, until they are either repealed or declared unconstitutional by the proper authority.

2. A tender and sacred regard for those acts of statesmanship, which are to be contra-distinguished from acts of ordinary legislation, by the fact of their being of the nature of compacts and agreements; and so, to be considered a fixed and settled national policy.

V.—A radical revision and modification of the laws regulating immigration, and the settlement of immigrants. Offering to the honest immigration who from love of liberty, or hatred of oppression, seek an asylum in the United States, a friendly reception and protection. But unqualifiedly condemning the transmission to our shores of felons and paupers.

VI.—The essential modification of the Naturalization Laws.

The repeal by the legislatures of the respective States, of all State laws allowing foreigners not naturalized to vote.

The repeal without retroactive operation, of all acts of Congress making grants of land to unnaturalized foreigners, and allowing them to vote in the territories.

VII.—Hostility to the corrupt means by which the leaders of party have hitherto forced upon us our rulers and our political creeds.

Implacable enmity against the prevalent demoralizing system of rewards for political subserviency, and of punishments for political independence.

Disgust for the wild hunt after office which characterizes the age.

These on the one hand. On the other :—

Imitation of the practice of the purer days of the republic ; and admiration of the maxim that "office should seek the man, and not man the office," and of the rule that, the just mode of ascertaining fitness for office is the capability, the faithfulness, and the honesty of the incumbent or candidate.

VIII.—Resistance to the aggressive policy and corrupting tendencies of the Roman Catholic Church, in our country, by the advancement to all political stations—executive, legislative, judicial or diplomatic—of those only who do not hold civil allegiance, directly or indirectly, to any foreign power whether civil or ecclesiastical, and who are Americans by birth, education and training:—thus fulfilling the maxim, "AMERICANS ONLY SHALL GOVERN AMERICA."

The protection of all citizens in the legal and proper exercise of their civil and religious rights and privileges: the maintenance of the right of every man to the full, unrestrained and peaceful enjoyment of his own religious opinions and worship, and a jealous resistance of all attempts by any sect, denomination or church to obtain an ascendency over any other in the State, by means of any special privileges or exemption, by any political combination of its members, or by a division of their civil allegiance with any foreign power, potentate or ecclesiastic.

IX.—The reformation of the character of our National Legislature, by elevating to that dignified and responsible position men of higher qualifications, purer morals, and more unselfish patriotism.

X.—The restriction of executive patronage—especially in the matter of appointments to office—so far as it may be permitted by the Constitution, and consistent with the public good.

XI.—The education of the youth of our country in schools provided by the State; which schools shall be common to all, without distinction of creed or party, and free from any influence or direction of a denominational or partisan character.

And, inasmuch as Christianity by the constitutions of nearly all the States; by the decisions of the most eminent judicial authorities; and by the consent of the people of America, is considered an element of our political system; and as the Holy Bible is at once the source of Christianity, and the depository and fountain of all civil and religious freedom, we oppose every attempt to exclude it from the schools thus established in the States.

XII.—The American party having arisen upon the ruins and in spite of the opposition of the whig and democratic parties, cannot be held in any manner responsible for the obnoxious acts or violated pledges of either. And the systematic agitation of the Slavery question by those parties having elevated sectional hostility into a positive element of political power, and brought our institutions into peril, it has therefore become the imperative duty of the American party to interpose, for the purpose of giving peace to the country and perpetuity to the Union. And as experience has shown it impossible to reconcile opinions so extreme as those which separate the disputants, and as there can be no dishonor in submitting to the laws, the National Council has deemed it the best guarantee of common justice and of future peace, to abide by and maintain the existing laws upon the subject of slavery, as a final and conclusive settlement of that subject, in spirit and in substance.

And regarding it the highest duty to avow their opinions upon a subject so important, in distinct and unequivocal terms, it is hereby declared as the sense of this National Council, that Congress possesses no power, under the Constitution, to legislate upon the subject of slavery in the States where it does or may exist, or to exclude any State from admission into the Union, because its constitution does or does not recognize the institution of slavery as a part of its social system; and expressly pretermitting any expression of opinion upon the power of Congress to establish or prohibit slavery in any territory, it is the sense of the National Council that Congress ought not to legislate upon the subject of slavery within the territories of the United States and that any interference by Congress with slavery as it exists in the District of Columbia, would be a violation of the spirit and intention of the compact by which the State of Maryland ceded the District to the United States, and a breach of the National faith.

XIII.—The policy of the Government of the United States, in its relations with foreign governments, is to exact justice from the strongest, and do justice to the weakest; restraining, by all the power of the government, all its citizens from interference with the internal concerns of nations with whom we are at peace.

XIV.—This National Council declares that all the principles of the order shall be henceforward everywhere openly avowed; and that each member shall be at liberty to make known the existence of the order, and the act that he himself is a member; and it recommends that there be no concealment of the places of meeting of subordinate councils.

The order, in its primitive character and purpose, ignored entirely the sectional issue of free-soil and slavery. It took the Constitution of the United States as it found it, and it also took for granted that whatever domestic institution any State might choose to adopt, not inconsistent with Republicanism and Christianity, was guaranteed by the Constitution to that State, without question or cavil, and hence beyond the reach of argument or discussion. To reiterate that guarantee is, therefore, to admit indirectly that the subject is open to discussion.

The intention of this organization was the formation of a great national party, having as its cardinal object the maintenance of the institutions of American Republicanism. This is what I call the "American Policy." In forwarding this object it came necessarily in contact with every influence directly or indirectly hostile to those institutions; as, for example, the political and despotic power of the Romish hierarchy which was rapidly overshadowing the power of the American government; next, the ostentatious demands of foreigners who claimed the right to hold the public offices, and thus give direction to the government itself by moulding its several departments to their own imported notions; next, the American demagogues who encouraged these influences and yielded to their demands; and finally, it came in contact with those political matricides who, by engendering a sectional hostility, would have torn their own mother country limb from limb, and murdered her by dismemberment.

Here we have, in few words, the intrinsic purpose of the society, and the immediate objects of its political hostility. In this character alone it was sent forth upon its ennobling mission as an auxiliary of the Order of United Americans—a national, conservative, patriotic propaganda, and the introduction of an extraneous subject in its national and local councils must be an innovation, apart from the original purpose, and calculated to destroy its efficiency and power.

The history of this order presents, also, another emasculating ingredient, which now forms a component of its numerical strength. That very success which appalled and stupefied the corruptionist of the parties, operated as an allurement to many of their office-seeking adherents. Connected with all parties there are men who adapt their political views—as Napoleon is said to have adapted his religious sentiments—to the people among whom they are thrown, and as their aim is to be ever with the strongest, they can throw off and put on their principles with wonderful facility, and without the slightest drawbacks of conscience. They want office, and, to use a vulgar but trite expression, they "go in to win." As rats flee from a sinking ship, such men will hasten from a decaying party. Whatever their object may be, it is always against their principles to be found long on the weak side. The successes of the American Order and its rapid advances towards a complete preponderance in the nation, were so many signals of migration to these parasites, and in obedience to those signals they came in numbers and enlisted under the banners of the victorious army.

Carrying with them a mercurial zeal, the offspring of mercenary interest, these men are invariably among the most active and bustling of partisans. They are voluble, earnest, and, at times, seemingly ubiquitous, for they are seen everywhere, and heard of everywhere. By perseverance and seeming loyalty to the principles of the party, they secure confidence, are entrusted with responsible duties, and when nominations for public offices are to be made, either themselves or their friends are chosen as delegates to the conventions. Then come their claims for nominations, and it too often occurs that they are successful. They are nominated as the candidates of the party, and the party is called upon to support them. The Jeffersonian test has not been applied in their cases, and as they do not always occupy the highest places in public esteem, the judicious and the honest are frequently made to grieve over the discredit thus thrown upon their cause. These are the men who bring corruption into public life, and fling the stain of disgrace upon the parties who elect them.

Whatever the principles of a political party may be, its strongest bulwark will be found in a sterling integrity. This is especially the case in a popular republic, and the best evidence of an honest purpose that it can give to the people, is the unimpeachable character of its candidates for public offices.

These unprincipled parasites, as I said, hurried into the American organization, and they instinctively clamored for office. They base their claims upon the zeal they have exhibited, and the labors they have performed since their connection with the party, claiming precedence over men whose calmer judgment has been, from first to last, the stay and support of the organization and its principles. In some cases they have been successful, and after their election they have invariably cast discredit on the party, or at least left their constituents to regret the misplacement of their confidence. Others, again, who have failed to secure the nominations they sought, have returned to the parties they had deserted, and stood forth the bitterest antagonists of the American party and its candidates. A distinguished case of this kind is exhibited in the municipal government of the city of New York.

The elevation of bad men to office, apart from the evils

which it imposes upon the community, is an act the most impolitic, because it is certain to alienate the confidence of the public from the party that commits it. A dishonest or incompetent public officer is, indeed, an object of public contempt, but the party which recommended him for popular confidence must suffer the odium of popular indignation which his misconduct has aroused. It is held in the light of a *particeps criminis*, "an accessory before the fact," and is, therefore, deemed accountable before the bar of public sentiment, for all the evils resulting to the community from his misdeeds. Thus the party suffers through the acts of its agents. Let this maxim be written on the banner of the American organization, viz.: *That it is better to defeat a bad candidate than to elect him.* Its good effects will be two-fold. It will make nominating conventions prudent, and secure the confidence of the people.

The class of politicians to whom I have alluded, form a natural, if not a necessary appendage to a successful party. They rush to it as flies swarm about a sugar-cask—for what they can get—and since, in the very nature of things, they cannot be avoided, it is proper that, like all "necessary nuisances," they should be *regulated.*

The motive which actuated the two great American organizations in adopting the policy of secrecy in the details of their affairs, I have stated in a previous chapter. The machinery of the old parties was so complete and pervading, and the political influences of Romanism were so subtle, that every open effort to destroy their corrupting influences had been cut down or strangled in its very inception, and the popular sentiment—I mean that innate sentiment which lay deep in the popular heart, overlaid, it is true, by partisan affiliations *yet still there*—was suppressed, and its first instinctive efforts at emancipation were stifled and silenced by those overshadowing elements. To use a very common political expression, the public heart was in party "traces," and it dared not kick against them in the face of its drivers.

The power of their political and Romish engines is also witnessed in its effects upon every public journal that has ventured to advocate the American policy. The question has often been asked, "Why cannot an American paper be sustained?" The answer is plain. Every attempt to establish one, until recently, has been made odious through the Romish and partisan presses of the country. The most earnest and disinterested appeals to the patriotism of the people, though never combated, have been ridiculed, and the authors of them stigmatized with opprobrium. Thousands who in their hearts were conscious of the correctness of the theory, and who secretly coincided with the sentiments of the American policy, were deterred from giving their patronage to those journals, lest they should share in the general obloquy, or suffer in their business or private relations. Few, therefore, ventured to place upon their counter, or to exhibit at their houses, any publication that savored of Native Americanism, and an advertisement in them was regarded as a dangerous experiment. As a natural consequence, those publications were, one by one, discontinued from want of patronage, the publishers consoling themselves under their pecuniary losses, with the consciousness of having performed a patriotic duty.

In the year 1851, I undertook the publication of a monthly literary journal, devoted to the American policy. It was entitled "THE REPUBLIC." In that journal was maintained a temperate tone and a conservative policy. The *religion* of the Romanist was never assailed, nor the rights of the adopted citizen invaded. Notwithstanding this, but a few numbers had been issued, when I received an anonymous note, which ran as follows:

"SIR:—Your publication will struggle through an existence of about two years. At the end of that time, your cash-account will exhibit a balance of time and money lost.

"Signed, A ROMAN CATHOLIC."

There was a coolness and deliberate preciseness about this note which bore evident marks of the existence of an undercurrent of hostility—a secret enemy. It appeared that there had been a careful calculation made of every element on which the publication depended for success. Its resources had seemingly been measured to a farthing, and critically weighed against the elements that were to be brought to bear against it, and the result of the estimate was frankly, but tauntingly and *secretly* conveyed in the note.

The prophecy of the author was technically fulfilled. At the end of two years the publication terminated for want of patronage, yet, although pecuniarily a sufferer, and minus the time devoted to the journal, I never regarded either the one or the other as "lost." The "Republic" while it existed performed a patriotic mission, and created a wholesome national sentiment wherever it was read. In this I found a reward for my labors and sacrifices.

Under circumstances like these, while the minds of men were held in the vassalage of a mysterious fear, and with the subterranean influence of the papacy meeting them in a mask at every turn, any attempt to develop the public sentiment in relation to the American policy *must* have terminated in defeat. It became necessary to meet those influences in their own armor and on their own ground, and the successful result of such a plan is seen in the majestic, and almost miraculous growth of the American party.

When the necessity for secrecy is found to exist no longer, the secret policy of the organization will be abandoned. When the sentiment of the country is fully awakened to the necessity of the adoption of those measures of self-preservation which have been set forth—when it is no longer regarded as dishonorable to prefer, in a political view, our own country and our own people over every other country and every other people—when the natural-born citizens of the country shall freely express their patriotic sentiments, unawed by foreign or partisan influences, and the Protestant speak out everywhere, fearless of papal persecution—then may the close councils of the order be abandoned, and their proceedings be, as their principles ever have been, placed unreservedly before the world.

The mission of the secret organization will then be fulfilled, and it will remain for the American people to demand of their government the enactment of such measures as will, in all the future, guard our dear-bought and cherished institutions of freedom against all foreign influences, whether civil or ecclesiastical.

## CHAPTER XXIV.

THE UNITED AMERICAN MECHANICS—EFFECTS OF THE COMPETITION OF IMMIGRANT LABOR ON THE INDUSTRIAL INTERESTS OF THE UNITED STATES—THE REMEDY—THE UNITED SONS OF AMERICA.

THE Mechanics of America have heretofore occupied a position in society which has not been attained by their class in any other nation. In European countries, the word mechanic designates not only a class but a *caste* in society; and that too, of a low grade. The dignity of labor is not recognized in their *effete* social systems. But here it *has been* otherwise. The reasons of this difference are obvious. In all aristocratic systems, the sole protection of the aristocracy lies in distinctions of caste, and the broader those distinctions are made, the better for the aristocrats, and the worse for the producing classes. It is not because labor is disreputable in itself that aristocracy sneers at it, but because of this feigned distinction, which is essential to the very existence of a privileged class.

The effect of this distinction is threefold—moral, social, and financial. Its moral effect is to degrade the workingman in his own estimation, and render him easily subservient to the dominion, the whims, or the caprice of those who lord it over him. The social effect is to deprive him of his rights as a man; to place him in a position subordinate to others, and, by closing the doors of promotion against him, dampen his ambition, and confine his efforts to the bare necessities of the present. The financial effect is the natural result of his moral and social condition. Owing to that condition of hopeless passiveness, the spirit of noble emulation is stifled in his bosom, and he entertains no aspirations for a loftier position in life. His necessities alone are present to his view, and to supply them is the burden of his ambition and his energies. He is willing to work for them alone, and the competition of poverty, brought about by these influences, compels him to be content with a mere pittance.

In the United States the only castes intrinsically recognized are founded upon merit. This is the natural and imperative result of our system of government in its unadulterated form. The American mechanic is morally, socially, and politically on a par with his fellow-citizens of every calling, whether rich or poor, and his *right* to the highest executive office of the nation is as complete, perfect, and undisputed as that of any other living man.

This being his attitude in society, his self-respect is stimulated, and his ambition awakened. He has an inducement to emulate the best in the land, and he strives by mental culture to qualify himself for the highest intellectual pursuits and enjoyments. How many of our American mechanics have been elevated to positions of lofty honor and responsibility! How many have given lustre to the name of America!

The question before us at the present moment is this: Can the American mechanic retain his rights and high social position against the competition of immigrant labor? "Coming events cast their shadows before." The view that I have given of this class is a view of the primitive, *natural* position of the mechanic, under the unadulterated workings of our system of government. It is a view of his position where all things and all men are in that state of *social* as well as moral and political equilibrium which is contemplated by our institutions. If that equilibrium is destroyed by any unnatural or uncontemplated antagonism between capital and labor—if the interests of capital become from any cause opposed to the interests of labor, it follows that the rewards of labor must be reduced, and although the intrinsic *rights* of the mechanic remain, his means of acquiring and assuming those rights are proportionately lessened.

Before the unequal competition of immigrant labor cast its shadow over the industrial interests of our country, every American journeyman mechanic was enabled, by the force of his industry, to maintain a financial position equal to that of his social, moral, and political position. He was sure of employment, at wages adapted to the dignity of his franchise; to the necessities of the present, and the vicissitudes of the future. He could dwell in his own cottage, supply his family with comforts and luxuries, rear his children respectably, find time for his own mental improvement, and lay by a little of his earnings each week for a rainy day. Neatness and cleanliness pervaded his home, and the cheerful hearth was to him the ever-welcome refuge from toil. But with a superabundant immigration from Europe came a train of evils which are now rapidly developing themselves. Many an American mechanic still lives in the enjoyment of all his just privileges, but how great the proportion of those who, from want of employment, or reduced compensation, or both, have been alienated from their homes, their comforts, their ambition! How vast the number of those who have been driven from their employments to make room for the under-bidding competition of the foreign laborer! The American mechanic cannot live upon the pittance demanded by his European competitor. It is not his custom—it was not the custom of his fathers—it is degrading to his sense of self-respect.

I will relate two instances of the manner in which this disparaging competition is carried on.

A German cabinetmaker, who received work from storekeepers, occupied a spacious loft in Ann street, in the city of New York. In that loft was his workshop and his dwelling. He employed three *apprentices*, all Germans, and with them was constantly occupied in manufacturing furniture. This man, under a plea of destitution, *obtained all his winter fuel, with other necessaries, from the Alms-House department of the city!*

The other case is that of a tailor, also a German, who obtained a constant supply of work from clothiers. He employed from eight to ten hands, all of whom *boarded* with him. This man kept his two children constantly employed *in begging for broken victuals from door to door, by which means his table was supplied with provisions!*

Here are the elements of competition which the American mechanic is called upon, by excessive immigration, to withstand—*Imposture and pauperism!* The elements are too unequal. The odds are against him. He cannot contend with them. His moral sensibilities—his sense of self-respect forbid it. The alternative presented is poverty or disgrace. He chooses the former, and quits his shop, in hopes that something will "turn up" to his advantage. He seeks in vain for employment at remunerating prices. It is not to be had. He must work at the prices of the *foreign pauper*, or remain idle. He turns to the country, but even there the same spectacle is presented. Foreigners are working the farms. The teeming earth, which has till now sent forth its abundance from beneath the hand of the hardy American farmer, struggles on in a succession of short crops, under the cheap system of European tillage.

In his pressing necessities, the discharged workman bethinks him of the public service. He determines, as a last resort, to obtain some subordinate public office, from the emoluments of which he may support his family with respectability. He has done good service to his party in times past, and he is sure it will not deny him an appointment. For the first time in his life he looks into the public departments, and applies for a situation. He finds every post occupied—*occupied by foreigners!* There is *nothing* left to him but submission or beggary. In the workshop, on the farm, and in the public offices, the aspect is the same. In every department he encounters the drudging and importunate foreigner.

To turn from the home of childhood and the associations of early life, and seek subsistence on the broad prairies of the far West—to build his house in the wilderness, and endure the hardships of a pioneer life, becomes his final recourse. But even there he finds the same competition. The foreign squatter has staked out the best portions of the public domain.

Thus the personal interests of the American mechanic are submerged, his rights neutralized, and his hopes thwarted by excessive immigration of the poor of Europe. These are the *direct* effects. *Indirectly*, the effects assume a different phase. The introduction of this degraded element into the industrial arena of the country, is in itself calculated to promote *caste*, and stimulate a puerile aristocratic taste among the rich. In such hands, labor puts on a repulsive aspect—it is shorn of all dignity. With them, the instincts of refinement, heretofore shared by the working-men of America, in common with *all* their fellow-citizens, are unknown. They present the positive distinction between *intellectual* labor and mere drudgery, and thus they themselves draw the distinguishing line which forms the basis of caste, and encourages an aristocratic, anti-republican sentiment.

Again, the effect of excessive cheap labor is to aggrandize capital. And this affords another incentive to aristocracy—an aristocracy of wealth, which is the worst of all aristocracies. We may find some excuse, perhaps, for the peculiarities of one educated to pride of noble lineage, or personal intellectuality, when he claims superiority of caste; but the mere purse-proud claimant of distinction is but an object of disgust. Men who have made honest fortunes by cutting up their fathers' cabbage-gardens into city lots, should wear their honors wisely, if they know how, but at all events they should wear them meekly, and when dealing with a producer, remember that they, as well as their fathers, once belonged to that honorable class.

But this rational thesis, which is intrinsically susceptible of the most logical support, is met, and forcibly met, on mere circumstantial grounds. The answer given is, that " the producer of to-day is not, in any essential, the producer of *our* day, or the days of our fathers." " The class of laborers," they say, " is degenerated, and with them, labor itself." Such is the argument afforded by immigration in favor of an American aristocracy!

The respectable mechanics of our country have seen and felt these influences sorely. They have witnessed the gradual and ruinous absorption of their interests, their social position, and their political rights, through the channel of European pauper competition. The labor of years devoted to the acquirement of an honorable trade has been thrown away, because they could not compete with beggars and impostors. They have appealed in vain to their countrymen, to their employers, and their legislatures for relief, and, as a last resort —as the only means of self preservation left to them, they have, like their fathers of old, resolved to take the matter into their own hands, and by a combination of action and interest maintain the rights and the dignity of their class. From these causes sprung the Order of

UNITED AMERICAN MECHANICS.

The incipient meeting of this organization was held in the city of Philadelphia, Pa., on the evening of the 8th of July, 1845. At that meeting several trades were represented. The object of the meeting was stated by the President, to be the formation of a secret society for the protection of American

Mechanics, and a committee was appointed to draft resolutions expressive of this object.

At a subsequent meeting, held July 15th, that committee reported the following:

"That we form a society to be called 'The American Mechanics' Union,' whose object shall be,

"1st. To assist each other in obtaining employment.

"2d. To assist each other in business, by patronizing each other in preference to foreigners.

"3d. To assist the unfortunate in obtaining employment suitable to their afflictions.

"4th. To establish a cemetery for deceased members of the society.

"5th. To establish a funeral fund.

"6th. For the establishment of a fund for the relief of widows and orphans of deceased members."

This code, with the exception of the title, was adopted, and at the next meeting, held on the 22d of the same month, it was "resolved, that the title of the society be 'The United American Mechanics of the United States.' "

On this basis and with this title the society was formed, and an appropriate constitution subsequently adopted.

Whatever may appear to be partial in the 2d clause of this code, as relates to foreigners, is justified, first by the exigency which suggested its adoption, and especially by the precedent which had already been set by foreigners themselves. Secret societies, composed entirely of foreigners, and having for their objects the patronage and support of their own countrymen in preference to Americans, existed at that time in almost every city of large population in the United States.

Around this nucleus gathered a vast and wide-spread organization, extending its counsels in all directions, and exerting a happy influence over the interests of the mechanic in nearly every State in the Union.

The purpose of the order was entirely that of mutual aid and protection in the business callings of its members, and of benevolence towards their individual necessities and misfortunes, yet it is impossible that such an organization could long exist without discovering the necessity of a more radical plan of operations. They must have discovered that the first great cause of the evils which called the order into existence were to be found in *a system*, of which the pauper competition from Europe was but the natural fruit. The existing laws of naturalization, by which the meanest serf of Europe could be converted into a voter in five years, offered great inducements to the home demagogue to encourage or at least to wink at that class of immigration. Were it not for the fact that these men can be used as political instruments by the wire-pullers of the once great parties, the voice of the whole country would long since have been raised against the admission of that class of immigrants, and the two parties, instead of encouraging it would have vied with each other in the adoption of measures to prevent their admission.

It is impossible that a body of intelligent American mechanics could have failed to discover this fact, and having discovered it, it is impossible that they should fail to assist in applying the remedy. When the naturalization laws are so framed as to preclude the possibility of using the alien vote for nefarious purposes, we shall find little difficulty in preventing that ruinous competition which has heretefore grown out of the cheap labor of pauper immigrants.

The interests of the American mechanic lie in the adoption of measures that will check the tide, the overwhelming tide of European immigration, or, at least, of that class of immigration which, while it imparts nothing to the genius of the country, saps the fountains of honest industry, and brings the deserving to want. The ballot-box is his legitimate court of appeal, and the freeman's suffrage must be his advocate.

### THE UNITED SONS OF AMERICA.

This order originated in the City of Philadelphia, in the year 1845. It was one of the spontaneous results of the Kensington massacre of which I have spoken in a preceding chapter, and has been the mainspring of the Native American party in that city from that time to the present.

The object of this organization has been to sustain, against all obstacles, the principles of the native party as it existed in 1844, and its members have for years, like a band of Spartans, held the pass, and courted defeat rather than yield to the foreign legion or become the allies of corrupt partisans. Their organization, although not numerous, has been planted in many States, and wherever the American party has made a stand, the "Sons of America" have evinced their integrity and patriotism by sustaining it with energy and decision. In

Massachusetts it has been active in sustaining and concentrating the national sentiment against the sectional tendencies of local aspirants, thereby exhibiting, as on other occasions, its fidelity to the Union, and its unyielding hostility to the foes of State sovereignity.

## CHAPTER XXV.

### THE "ONE IDEA."

The American Party has been at all times opprobriously stigmatized by its enemies, as "a party with one idea"—*only* one idea. It may, perhaps, be difficult to determine precisely how many ideas are necessary to constitute the legitimate basis of a political party; or, in fact, whether any idea is absolutely requisite for such a purpose. That a political party *can* exist without a single fundamental idea, is demonstrated in the lives of the two great parties of this country during the last quarter of a century, and it would seem that the advent of a new party, *with* an idea, should be hailed as an event to be applauded rather than reviled. We can account for the opposite result only upon the hypothesis that in politics, ideas are useless incumbrances. Certain it is, the prevailing idea of American politicians, for several years past, has contemplated only what is facetiously expressed as "the loaves and fishes," or, in other words, the honors and emoluments of office.

But, in discussing this matter, we must treat the subject as it is presented to us. It is very plain that the opprobrious sneer is intended to imply the necessity of a plurality of ideas in the formation of a political party, or that a single idea is not alone sufficient for that purpose. It means plainly, that any attempt to form a party with but one object in view, is an absurdity deserving nothing better than the contempt and ridicule of the world. The wise men who set this notion afloat, if they have ever read history at all, have read it to little purpose; and we are constrained to inquire, *if one idea is not sufficient, how many are required?* When the people of the old thirteen colonies were oppressed by the crown of England, they conceived the "one idea," that, by declaring and maintaining an independent government, they would ensure to themselves and their posterity great social and political advantages. On this idea a great party was formed, and immediately another party arose, which entertained the "one idea" of loyalty to the crown—two great parties, each with a single idea. The one was called the "rebel party," and the other the "tory party," and they waged unrelenting warfare against each other, until at last the rebel party was successful, and the "one idea" of independence was maintained. The triumph of that idea gave to the people of the United States a distinct *nationality.* Doubtless many a wiseacre of the present day will be astonished that a single idea could accomplish so much.

But this was not all. The idea of independence having been consummated, another idea took possession of the people. That singular set of malcontents were no sooner in possession of their independence, than they conceived the idea that a Republic would be more conducive to popular happiness than their old form of government, the monarchy. George Washington favored this idea. He could have worn a crown; but being an American he was extremely jealous of foreign influence, foreign customs, and the forms of foreign governments. He stood firm to the "one idea" of a republic, and *that* was also consummated. Thus, "one idea" gave us *nationality*, and another "one idea" gave us *freedom*.

Wherever consistency reigns this principle is universal. There can be but a single fundamental idea to any consistent purpose, however numerous or diversified may be the means employed, or the measures necessary to carry out the purpose. These are but the agents of the idea—the cognate aids employed for the completion of the great plan. To carry out the idea of Independence, revolution with all its attendant consequences became a necessary measure; it was a second thought, which came naturally and necessarily to the support of the first. The creation of the earth we may suppose to have been a single idea of Omnipotence, and as the means of carrying out and consummating that idea, the elements of chemistry, gravitation, attraction, repulsion, rotation, &c., were employed, but they formed no part or component of the Divine original plan.

I know of but one political organization which rests, primarily, upon a plurality of ideas, and here the most glaring inconsistency is observable. The hierarchy of the Romish Church is founded upon two distinct purposes, viz.: temporal sovereignty and spiritual sovereignty in one and the same system of government. But even this is denied. The Romanist claims that the two sovereignties are but the means employed in consummating an idea more remote; being no less than *the establishment of an universal rule of faith.* This is claimed to be the great "one idea" of the church, and I should be willing to believe it were it not so distinctly contradicted in the every-day practice of those who constitute the hierarchy.

Christopher Columbus conceived the idea that there must be a western continent beyond the great waters of the Atlantic, and, on the strength of that one idea, he set forth on a voyage of discovery. Now, the ship in which he sailed, being *absolutely* necessary to the proof of his theory, was just as much a part of the original idea of an unknown continent as the American Revolution was a part of the original idea of Independence, and no more.

A single idea has hitherto been found sufficient as a basis for any single purpose, whether that purpose has been the creation of a world, the discovery of a continent, or the freedom and independence of a great nation, and he who sneers at this truth subjects himself to the suspicion that his own ideas would not suffer by a contact with Paley.

The American party did set forth with a single purpose—with one idea. The purpose of the party was THE PRESERVATION OF OUR NATIONAL UNION, AND ITS GLORIOUS INSTITUTIONS OF CIVIL AND RELIGIOUS LIBERTY, under the "one idea," that, in order to accomplish this purpose, AMERICANS OUGHT TO BE, AND MUST BE, THE RULERS IN THEIR OWN LAND. The idea is rational; the purpose is noble and patriotic. They who deny the broad principle herein embodied, assume a position at once untenable and unnatural. They are proscriptionists of the worst stamp. They would proscribe their own countrymen. They would elevate the foreigner at the expense of the native-born, and they virtually ignore their own nationality. They concede to the alien, *as a right*, that which Reason and the Law of Nations recognize only *as a privilege*, to be granted or withheld at the option of the government.

But this is not the only repulsive feature contemplated in this denial of the American idea. It is virtually an admission that aliens, reared under monarchical institutions, are as well qualified to enact and execute laws for the government of the American republic as the Americans themselves. This is simply an insult to our national intelligence and character. It is an insult which, if applied to an individual in the ordinary affairs of life, would be resented on the instant. If we should tell a watchmaker to his face, that a horse-shoer, who had never seen the interior of a watch, was as well qualified to repair that delicate instrument as the watchmaker himself, we should most certainly incur the risk of an assault and battery. Yet we do not commit assault and battery upon the man who tells us that the most illiterate and immoral of the surplusage of European population are as competent to govern us as we are to govern ourselves—we only deny the proposition, and say to them, *you are not* competent to govern us, and therefore you shall not be chosen our governors.

This is the voice of the American *party*. It *should be* the voice of the American *people*. This proposition is plain—this conclusion is logical. No honest American, with a clear understanding of the subject, and possessing a becoming self-respect, will attempt to gainsay or combat it. The policy of the American party, in this aspect, presents an appeal not only to the patriotism, but also to the *individuality* of every American man and woman who glories in the achievements of his or her ancestors. What native American can look back through the glorious vista of the past, and contemplate the success of our arms and the wisdom of our statesmen, without experiencing a glow of national pride? Who can remember a Washington, a Warren, an Adams, a Jefferson, or a Franklin, without identifying himself with them, and claiming fellowship in the proud and dignified character of *countryman?* Where is the individual who can survey the vast field of our national greatness, and contemplate the ennobling and happy results of our free institutions, without recognizing with pride the link of national consanguinity which binds him to them, bone of their bone and flesh of their flesh?

Recognizing this individuality—this oneness, this unity of man and country, and realizing the stupendous benefits which have emanated from the very source of American nationality, and from no other, who is there, of all our countrymen, that can—without impeachment of his own reason and intelligence—who is there that can acknowledge superiority in any other race, or in any other government? Such an acknowledgment cannot be made. This is asserted, not in the boastful spirit of the egotist, but as a simple, logical, common sense conclusion, deduced from the tangible and irrefragible proofs of history. The race of the founders of our nation was that of the progressive and unconquerable Anglo-Saxon—and the government which they created is admitted by *the peoples* of all Christendom to have been better adapted to the social happiness and prosperity of man than any other at any time in existence.

We may safely conclude that the "one idea," which constitutes the basis of the American policy, is both sufficient for its purpose and sound in its theory. The party that opposes it is essentially anti-American. There is an adage extant, which says, "It is a vile bird that fouls its own nest." I think this adage is directly applicable, in its moral, to those American politicians who decry their own countrymen and eulogize the foreigner. Their motive is transparent—and the corruption of that motive is distinctly visible. If the foreigner had less political power, those eulogies would be less cheap in the market, and the American ONE IDEA more popular.

# CHAPTER XXVI.

## CONCLUSION.

In drawing these pages to a close it is not impertinent to say that my object has been to defend a principle which appears to me to be vital to the consummation of the great experiment of American republicanism. One important feature of that experiment is already wrought out to a solution, viz.: that, as affording the elements of social happiness and national power, the American system stands pre-eminent. It has also demonstrated the feasibility of popular government, beyond question or dispute. These comprise all that is sought for in social government, and the only question remaining is the question of permanence—or whether such a system can be made perpetual.

Reasoning *a priori*, we might assert that this question is also settled. But unfortunately we are not permitted in this instance to guess at the future by the circumstances of the past. The fact that American republicanism has existed three-quarters of a century does not convey the proof that it will exist three-quarters of a century longer. It is only a proof that it would exist *provided* the same circumstances which have favored the past shall continue in the future.

But how different are the circumstances of the present from those under which our Republic has been reared! Those changes of circumstances I have hastily portrayed in the pages of this work, and it is impossible to contemplate them without awakening the liveliest apprehensions in every patriotic mind. They prove that we have wandered from the path of safety, and they admonish us to return. They prove also that a course of policy adapted to the circumstances of one era is not always appropriate to the circumstances of a succeeding era, and they suggest such alterations as shall make them conformable to the new state of things.

Religion, patriotism, and morality, have been the foundation-stones of our success as a nation, and our happiness and prosperity as a people. These foundation-stones were laid upon the rock of a stern Protestant faith, and their fruits have been all that our institutions promised—civil and religious liberty. So long as the foundation and sub-structure remained firm and unshaken, so long we retained the assurance of a permanent government, and the guarantee of continued freedom.

But the foundation is being removed, and the rock upon which it was laid is in danger of being undermined. Imported infidelity is supplanting the religion of our fathers. It rears its unabashed visage, and boldly demands the abolition of all laws for the observance of the Sabbath. Patriotism is giving way to fanaticism and party spirit. A sectional war of opinion is now raging, which demands the disruption of our nation—the North from the South. The moral element of our success is diluted by the influence of imported vices and irreligion—and Romanism already begins to assert her supremacy over the Protestant basis of the Republic.

While these corroding changes are going on, it is impossible to hope that another quarter of a century will find our Union of States in existence, or our boasted and cherished institutions still shedding their invigorating and cheering example upon the nations of the earth.

My desire has been to present this subject in its true light to *the people* at large—to appeal to the patriotism of the native born, and to the hopes and judgment of the naturalized citizen.

The question involved in the American policy is a question of *humanity* in the true sense of that word. It looks not to the physical emancipation of a few blacks, but to the political and moral freedom of the whole human race. The solution of it involves the very existence of popular sovereignty. Its platform is universal, and the European who would drink from the fountain of liberty should give it his countenance and support—because in so doing he will sustain the republican experiment, and give a lift to the on-rolling car of popular freedom. The way for him to do this is to leave American politics to Americans. By such a course he will sacrifice nothing of his personal right, or of his expectations when he quit the fatherland and took up his abode in America. The policy of the American party would protect him in his religion, and in all his personal necessities, and he would escape those jealousies and prejudices which are naturally engendered when he assumes to force upon us his own peculiar notions and customs, or ventures officiously to dictate our policy, and demand public office.

The people of the United States, although they have thrown open their doors in the spirit of generous hospitality to the foot-sore traveller, are not yet willing to admit that their country "*belongs* to the whole world," or that those who feast upon their generosity are better able to arrange and manage their household than themselves. The stranger knocks at our door, saying: "I am weary and faint under the burden of despotism, and I thirst for the cooling waters of freedom." We bid him enter, rest, and partake with us—we remove the burden from his toiling shoulders—we refresh his frame, we assuage his thirst—we give him of our bread and wine, and protect him from every foe. Under our kind care he becomes strong, happy, FREE! He is no longer grovelling in the dust of servility—the heel of the oppressor is not upon his neck. Under the protecting ægis of the stripes and stars, he stands erect and looks despotism square in the face. He is as proud as an emperor, and twice as happy.

But this state of things does not satisfy him. His appetite "grows with what it feeds on." He wants *more* liberty! Our laws don't suit him. He *demands* a change. He asserts as *rights* what we have granted as privileges. He begins to assume prerogatives in the household, and to dictate the form of our bounty—and finally, he aspires to take into his own hands the management of our affairs. When in reply to his officiousness we claim to understand the peculiarities of our republican institutions better than he, and insist on our natural right, he pours upon us a flood of vituperation. He denounces us as "bigots," "proscriptionists," "cowards, and sons of cowards," with a further array of vile epithet and abuse.

Now all this, as I said, engenders jealousies and prejudices between the American and the foreigner which might well be avoided. Apart from the indelicacy of such a course, it involves equally the sin of ingratitude. It savors, also, so strongly of deliberate impertinence that few persons, possessing the least self-respect, would tamely submit to it, and it would be surprising, indeed, did not the American people resist it.

Where is the rational foreigner who does not recognize this truth?

The papal interest we cannot hope to reason with. The hierarchy is not content with civil and religious freedom—*it aspires to the government itself!* It thirsts for political authority that it may rule in the United States as it now rules in Tuscany and elsewhere. What would have been the result of these aspirations, had the Church exercised its usual prudence, is only to be conjectured. But the Archbishop of New York is a bad manager. He is ambitious. Eager to witness the triumph of Romanism in his own time, he shook the tree before the fruit was ripe. He cast off the mask of humility too soon, and entered the political arena with a fictitious force. His power fell short of his own estimate, and far short of his necessities. He failed, and the fruit of his rashness has been an awakened protestant republican sentiment that will assuredly hold a jealous watch over the future.

To the laity of the Romish religion we can only appeal as to *men*, and point out the way to make them *free*-men—free in their consciences; free in their temporal affairs. Without this freedom, they can never realize the full nature and scope of their intelligences, or lay claim to the prerogatives of perfect manliness. The individual who places his conscience in the keeping of another, divests himself of all individuality, and becomes the creature, the very slave of his conscience-keeper. In every sense, moral, social, and religious, he becomes a mere instrument, and as a natural consequence his whole being, his happiness or misery, his successes and defeats, his condition and circumstances, all are made dependent on the will or caprice of another.

This is not the case with him who devotes his conscience to a *faith*, instead of placing it under the dictation of a mere man. The difference is as broad as that between mutability and immutability—or between principle itself and mere profession. Principle is unchangeable—profession is changeable. Faith is reliance in a principle, and although faith may change under the dictates of the judgment, the principle remains. He, therefore, who gives his conscience through faith to a principle may retain and exercise his judgment; whereas he who gives his conscience to a human being creates a visible and present master over his judgment. In a matter of this nature the individual must choose for himself, taking the conseqences of good or evil as the fruits of his choice.

What can we say to the respectable foreign mechanic? Precisely the same that we say to the American mechanic. Your labor is cheapened and your talent undermined by the ruinous competition of those uneducated charlatans who come to us professing everything and knowing nothing. They work for a pittance that would starve out decency, and drive comfort from your firesides, and through the cupidity and avarice of employers, they find employment at your expense.

The proposed amendment of the laws of naturalization does not strike at the rights or privileges of any man. The attitude of the aliens who may be in the country at the time of enacting that amendment will not be changed one iota by its adoption. The act cannot be otherwise than *prospective* in its intent and effects. It is desirable, nay, imperatively necessary, as a conservative element in the future, and its benefits will be shared alike by the adopted and the native born citizen. It is a measure demanded by an exigency that was not contemplated at the time of the adoption of the existing law. All that is valuable, all that is precious, all that is desirable in rational freedom, demand it. It is due to ourselves, our posterity; to those from abroad who cast their lot with us, and to their posterity. It is due to the millions who now *hope* for liberty, and whose eyes are turned to our example as the cynosure of their anticipations.

If from any cause the institutions which are based upon American republicanism should pass away, the hopes of all men who thirst for freedom will pass away with them; because, in the destruction of those institutions, the great impetus which they have given to the development of the principle of popular sovereignty and human rights, will cease. In such an event, the rule of "legitimacy" would be reëstablished with tenfold force, not only in Europe, but in America also.

Society would retrograde, and the inert or terrified and disorganized masses, seeking in present submission the gracious meed of personal safety, would relax into the ignoble condition of subjects and serfs. Every element, therefore, that is calculated in the remotest degree to weaken those institutions, or to jeopardize the great experiment of popular liberty, should be met, by all men who are the partakers or the disciples of freedom, with stern and resolute resistance.

It is the constant dropping of water that wears away a stone, and it is the gradual but steady introduction of corrosive elements that endanger the institutions of freedom in America. In the result, it matters not whether those elements are introduced by secret enemies or by misguided friends. Regrets will not make whole the broken vase; and if the visionary theories of radical Europeans in America are to be carried out, the spirit of Liberty may well exclaim, "Save me from my friends!"

American republicanism has nothing to fear from its open foes—it is invulnerable against the world in arms. At the first signal of assault, a million of bayonets would bristle in its defence, and twenty millions of hearts would be offered as willing sacrifices upon the altar of its safety! No, American republicanism will yield to no warlike conqueror. If it falls, it will fall by the hands of those who have sought it as their ægis—it will fall as fell Rome—by the hands of those who flew to it for shelter.

"The history of Rome," says Samuel Whelpley, "furnishes a striking instance of the deplorable effects of an influx of strangers into a country. After the Romans had conquered

Carthage, Greece, Asia, and Gaul, Italy presently filled with emigrants from all quarters. Though they came, as it were, singly, and as humble suppliants, yet they, in effect, conquered the conquerors. They inundated all Italy. The majesty of the ancient Romans was obscured, overwhelmed, and utterly lost in an innumerable swarm of foreigners. *The evil came on by slow and imperceptible degrees*, but was at last irresistible and fatal. These," he adds, "were the persons generally employed in the civil wars. A multitude made up of such people is always fickle, inflammatory, outrageous, ungrateful, vindictive, and burning with ambition to level all distinctions."

Samuel Whelpley lived, wrote, and died when the American Republic was in its early infancy. Yet, even at that day, he delineated the foregoing picture of the circumstances of the present time—and as the *summum bonum* to our liberties, in view of these circumstances, he affixed the following maxim:

"No person should hereafter become a citizen but by being born in the United States."

"Let foreigners find in this country an asylum from oppression. Here let them buy, and build, and plant: let them spread and flourish, pursuing happiness in every mode of life which enterprise can suggest or reason justify: but let them be exonerated from the toils of government. We do not need their hands to steady the ark."

# APPENDIX.

The following pages are appended to this work with a view of introducing such matter as is essential to a complete illustration of certain statements made in the work, without encumbering the recital with lengthy "notes." The attention of the reader is especially invited to the subjects presented in this Appendix, as containing *matters of fact*, necessary, perhaps, to bring about conviction in the minds of those who doubt the existence of a necessity for adopting the policy of the American Organization.

Speech of Henry Clay, in reply to Governor Louis Kossuth, on the subject of American Intervention in the affairs of Europe.

I owe you, sir, an apology for not having acceded before to the desire you were kind enough to intimate more than once to see me; but really my health has been so feeble that I did not dare to hazard the excitement of so interesting an interview. Besides, sir (he added with some pleasantry), your wonderful and fascinating eloquence has mesmerized so large a portion of our people wherever you have gone, and even some of our members of Congress (waving his hand toward the two or three gentlemen who were present), that I feared to come under its influence lest you might shake my faith in some principles in regard to the foreign policy of this government, which I have long and constantly cherished.

And in regard to this matter, you will allow me, I hope, to speak with that sincerity and candor which becomes the interest the subject has for you and for myself, and which is due to us both, as the votaries of freedom.

I trust you will believe me, too, when I tell you that I entertain ever the liveliest sympathies in every struggle for liberty in Hungary and in every country; and in this I believe I express the universal sentiment of my countrymen. But, sir, for the sake of my country, you must allow me to protest against the policy you propose to her. Waive the grave and momentous question of the right of one nation to assume the executive power among nations for the enforcement of international law, or of the right of the United States to dictate to Russia the character of her relations with the nations around her, and let us come at once to the practical consideration of the matter.

You tell us yourself, with great truth and propriety, that mere sympathy, or the expression of sympathy, cannot advance your purposes. You require "material aid." And, indeed, it is manifest that the mere declarations of the sympathy of Congress, or of the President, or of the public, would be of little avail, unless we were prepared to enforce those declarations by a resort to arms, and unless other nations could see that preparation and determination upon our part.

Well, sir, suppose that war should be the issue of the course you propose to us, could we then effect anything for you, ourselves, or the cause of liberty? To transport men and arms across the ocean in sufficient numbers and quantities to be effective against Russia and Austria, would be impossible. It is a fact which perhaps may not be generally known, that the most imperative reason with Great Britain for the close of her last war with us, was the immense cost of the transportation and maintenance of forces and munitions of war in such a distant theatre, and yet, she had not, perhaps, more than 30,000 men upon this continent at any time. Upon land, Russia is invulnerable to us as we are to her. Upon the ocean, a war between Russia and this country would result in the mutual annoyance to commerce, but probably in little else. I learn recently, that her war marine is superior to that of any nation in Europe, except perhaps Great Britain. Her ports are few, her commerce limited, while we, on our part, would offer as a prey to her cruisers, a rich and extensive commerce.

Thus, sir, after effecting nothing in such a war, after abandoning our ancient policy of amity and non-intervention in the affairs of other nations, and thus justifying them in abandoning the terms of forbearance and non-interference which they have hitherto preserved towards us, after the downfall perhaps of the friends of liberal institutions in Europe, her despots, imitating and provoked by our fatal example, may turn upon us in the hour of weakness and exhaustion; and with an almost equally irresistible force of reason and of arms, they may say to us, you have set us the example. You have quit your own to stand on foreign ground; you have abandoned the policy you professed in the day of your weakness, to interfere in the affairs of the people upon this continent, in behalf of those principles the supremacy of which you say is necessary to your prosperity—to your existence. We, in our own turn, believing that your anarchical principles are inimical to the peace, security, and happiness of our subjects, will obliterate the bed which has nourished such noxious weeds; we will crush you as the propagandists of doctrines so destructive of the peace and good order of the world.

The indomitable spirit of our people might, and would be equal to the emergency, and we might remain unsubdued, even by so tremendous a combination; but the consequences to us would be terrible enough. You must allow me, sir, to speak thus freely, as I feel deeply, though my opinion may be of but little importance—as the expression of a dying man.

Sir, the recent melancholy subversion of the republican government of France, and that enlightened nation voluntarily placing its neck under the yoke of despotism, teach us to despair of any present success for liberal institutions in Europe. It gives us an impressive warning not to rely upon others for the vindication of our principles, but to look to ourselves, and to cherish, with more care than ever, the security of our institutions and the preservation of our policy and principles.

By the policy to which we have adhered since the days of Washington, we have prospered beyond precedent; we have done more for the cause of liberty in the world than arms could effect. We have shown to other nations the way to greatness and happiness, and if we but continue united, as one people, and persevere in the policy which our experience has so clearly and triumphantly vindicated, we may, in another quarter of a century, furnish an example which the reason of the world cannot resist. But if we should involve ourselves in the tangled web of European politics, in a war in which we could effect nothing, and if in that struggle Hungary should go down, and we should go down with her, where then would be the last hope of the friends of freedom throughout the world? Far better is it for ourselves, for Hungary, and for the cause of liberty, that, adhering to our wise, pacific system, and avoiding the distant wars of Europe, we should keep our lamp burning brightly on this western shore, as a light to all nations, than to hazard its utter extinction among the ruins of fallen or falling republics in Europe.

## OPINION OF THOMAS H. BENTON.

THE following remarks on this subject of Intervention were made by the Hon. Thomas H. Benton, while addressing a meeting of the citizens of Missouri.

"I am opposed to intervening; and under all its forms; and, as much as any, in the form of 'protest' to be unsupported by acts, if the protest should be disregarded. Of the eminent public men of our country, who have accosted this question most to my satisfaction, Mr. Fillmore and Mr. Clay are the two foremost; they have given it a prompt and unqualified opposition in all its forms. This, in my opinion, is the American position. Others have spoken well against the new doctrine; but I have not seen any argument which, in my opinion, went to the beginning—to the argument number one in the case, namely, the want of constitutional power in Congress to engage in any such scheme.

"I eschew this new doctrine of interfering in the affairs of Europe, mystified as it is in the cautious phrase—where caution itself betrays the danger of the idea by veiling its nakedness in a confusion of words—'intervene to prevent intervention;' I stand upon the ancient ways, *antiquas vias*, of our fathers—peace and friendship with all nations, entangling alliances with none; good wishes to all people struggling for freedom; acknowledgment of their independence if successful, without inquiry into the right or wrong of the revolt; asylum to the vanquished from the moment he touched the soil, or trod the deck of an American vessel; with the rights of person and property, from the instant of his arrival among us."

## KOSSUTH'S APPEAL TO THE GERMANS IN AMERICA.

We copy from a German paper, called the *New York Staats Zeitung*, the following report of Kossuth's interview with a committee of Germans in the city of New York, on the 14th of June, 1852.

"About ten o'clock on Saturday morning, about twelve German citizens visited Kossuth. They were presented to the Governor by Col. Ihazi, when Mr. Jacekel made a short address, referring to the sacredness of their cause, and their valor in upholding the same."

Kossuth replied as follows:

"German Citizens.—*You are strong enough to effect the election of that candidate for the Presidency who gives the most attention to the European cause.* I find that quite natural, because between both parties there is no difference as regards the internal policy, and because only by the inanity of the German citizens of this country, the election will be such that, by and by, the administration will turn their attention to other countries, and give every nation free scope. No tree, my German friends, falls with the first stroke; *it is therefore necessary, that inasmuch as you are citizens, and can command your votes, you support the candidate who will pursue the external policy in our sense*, and endeavor to effect that all nations become free and independent, such as is the case in happy America."

As early as February, 1852, Kossuth addressed the Germans at Louisville, Ky., at which time he appealed to them in the same strain, urging them, by the force of their votes, to *compel* the United States government to adopt his scheme of intervention.

On the 23d of June, 1852, Kossuth again addressed a large assemblage of Germans, on the same subject, at the Broadway Tabernacle, in New York, and when the address was ended, the meeting adopted the following incendiary resolutions. These resolutions exhibit an utter forgetfulness of the sworn duties of naturalized citizens to their adopted country, and the prostitution of an American suffrage to the miserable uses of European revolutionists.

"*Whereas*, The whig party, in their platform recently adopted in Baltimore, which has been adopted by their candidate, have declared themselves against participating in the fate of Europe; and whereas, furthermore, the democratic party in America, which, at least in their fundamental principles, cherishes progress, have not declared themselves against partaking of the European struggle for liberty; and the policy of intervention may be expected to be adopted by the democratic party as well as by their candidate; therefore,

"*Resolved*, That as American citizens, we will attach ourselves to the democratic party, *and will devote our strength to having a policy of intervention in America carried out.*

"*Resolved*, That, *we expect that the candidate of the democratic party will adopt the principles of this policy*, which has been sanctioned by all distinguished statesmen of his party.

"*Resolved*, That *we protest* against the manner in which, heretofore, the government of the United States has interpreted and applied the policy of neutrality, *which is in violation of the spirit of the Constitution of the United States.*

"*Resolved*, that we ask that every American citizen, *not being attached to the soil*, may support the strength of any other people in the sense as the juries have interpreted the principles of the American Constitution, and especially of the policy of neutrality.

"*Resolved*, That we ask that the United States be officially represented by an ambassador to each nation which is battling against monarchism, and has framed its own constitution.

"*Resolved*, That we will unite, hand in hand, with all German-Americans *in the revolutionary union of Europe* for the advancement of the real progressive policy in America and Europe, and that we desire the Committee of Arrangements of this meeting to frame statutes for the said end, and to do everything necessary for the promotion of the said revolutionary union.

"*Resolved*, That we confidently hope that all nations of Europe struggling for liberty, as well as their leaders, according to the principles of solidarity, will consider their end a common one, without interfering with the independence of each nation, and that they rest united in the days of peace and war.

"*Resolved*, That we express our thanks and sympathy to Governor Kossuth, and to the German agitators, for their noble efforts; that we promise them results, and that *the Germans* of New York and environs will continue to work for the great end of a universal liberation of nations."

These resolutions give evidence alike of the influence of Kossuth over the German population, and of the fact that those who passed the resolutions were imbued solely with the spirit of European revolutionists.

Kossuth had by this time abandoned all hope of enlisting the sympathies and coöperation of the American government to his plans. He had discovered, also, that the American people would listen no longer (even by courtesy), to his inharmonious and visionary theories; and, so, he did not hesitate to step from his lofty position, and stoop to seditious measures. He strove to arouse the foreign population in the United States against the peace of the country—advising and urging them to use their united political privileges and powers in the selection of men and the adoption of measures which would disturb the harmonious relations of the country, violate the national honor, and set at naught the treaty obligations of the government.

Finding that his public harangues on this subject were met with public indignation, and subject to the censures of the American press, and that, with these obstacles of popular sentiment against him, his progress would be one of great difficulty and delay, he ventured to stoop to a still lower depth, and endeavored to accomplish, by secret communication with the German societies, that consummation of his wishes, which he could not reach by a frank, open, and manly course. With this view, immediately after his speech at the Tabernacle, he prepared and sent forth a secret circular, of which the following is a verbatim copy :—

### KOSSUTH'S SECRET CIRCULAR TO THE GERMANS.

NEW YORK, June 28, 1852.

SIR :—I hope you have read already my German farewell speech, delivered June 23d, in the Tabernacle at New York, and also the resolutions of the meeting, which were passed consequently.

I hope further, that the impression which this matter has made *upon both political parties* has not escaped your attention.

Indeed, it is not easy to be mistaken that the German citizens of America will have *the casting vote* in the coming election, if they are united in a joint direction upon the platform of the principles set forth in the speech afore mentioned.

They may *decide* upon the exterior policy of the next administration of the United States, and with that upon the triumph or the fall of liberty in Europe.

Never yet were the German citizens of America in this decided position.

The leaders of the political parties have arrived at the acknowledgment of this power, and they are alarmed, for they know that in the most unfavorable case, the Germans are able to make unsafe, at least, any combination or calculation of the parties.

Will the German citizens concede this important position, which will not come back in a century?

I hope God, the almighty protector of liberty, may prevent it. They are neglecting the moment. Won't they esteem principles higher than names and denominations of parties?

I hope they will. The position of America is a power—the liberty of Europe, of Germany, of Hungary, of Italy—depends upon them.

For God's sake do your best, that your German fellow-citizens occupy this position and ratify the principles put up in said speech, by meetings and resolutions, and declaring the intimated direction as theirs.

Act quickly. Keep the power of the position uncompromised in your hand, until the one or the other party offer substantial guarantees. This is now of the utmost importance. If I should be so happy as to induce the German citizens in different parts of the United States publicly to approve of my principles and of the intimated direction, thereby furnishing the argument that they would support this policy, this would put me in a position *to carry on efficient negotiations with the parties* and would enable me to offer such guarantees to them as will answer the principles and sympathies of German hearts.

God sees my most secret thoughts. He knows it is not mere vanity which agitates my heart. No; the consciousness that European liberty depends upon the unanimous support of the German citizens of America, stimulates me in making this communication.

My requests are as follows:

1.—Cause a German meeting to be called without delay. The object of it should be to consult which way the German citizens of America should take in the pending Presidential question.

2.—A committee of influential men—if possible of both parties—should prepare resolutions, among which, the following:

*a.*—That the German citizens of —— who are entitled to vote, approve of the principles laid down in my New York speech, of June 23, and sustain the means and policy which were recommended there, because they acknowledge them as such that are only and solely fit to promote the true interests of the United States, and of freedom in Europe. On that reason they should govern the conduct of all German citizens.

*b.*—That they request me publicly not to leave the United States without having communicated before to the German citizens of —— *which party* have given the most acceptable assurances, or rather guarantees, of being resolved to act on this basis in the Presidential question.

*c.*—That they consider, especially the repeal, or at least an interpretation of the neutrality laws of 1818, conformable to the principles of the individual rights, guaranteed by the Constitution to the citizens of the United States, as a specially desirable issue.

*d.*—That they request their fellow-citizens of other races to unite with them on that high basis of universal liberty, and of the honor and welfare of the United States.

These proceedings would be of immense importance. Open actions and secret intrigues are at work to annihilate this success.

But the Germans *have become a power*. Woe to them if they should neglect this hint of Providence! The movement must be crystallized, that it may not waste its strength. The more it is manifest that I and my policy may rely upon the support of the German citizens, the more I can do for that matter which is so dear also to your hearts.

In the name of the veneration I entertain for America, in the name of the suppressed nations of Europe, I conjure you to lend us your aid in the direction intimated.

Let us soon hear of an activity so ardently longed for.

With high esteem, fraternal respects, and shaking of hands, your most obedient,

(Signed) L. Kossuth.

N. B.—So far is this confidential that the letter is not to be given to the public, but is to be used only for private communications.

## THE REVOLUTIONARY LEAGUE.

THE plan of operations proposed by this "League" of foreigners, as published below, and as indicated in the resolutions passed by Germans at the Tabernacle, exhibits the outline of a system which contemplates the employment of every element which our liberal institutions place in the hands of the naturalized citizen, for the purposes of European revolution. The right of suffrage; the right to bear arms; the right to speak, write, and publish opinions; the right of protest; the right of peaceable assembly; the right to hold office in the militia of the several States; in a word, every function of the American citizen, is employed and rendered subservient to the one absorbing idea—EUROPEAN REVOLUTION. Are the American people *justified* in granting those precious rights, those delicate powers, to persons who thus employ them?

### ADDRESS

#### OF THE AMERICAN REVOLUTIONARY LEAGUE FOR EUROPE.

*Adopted at the Revolutionary Congress, held at Philadelphia, from January 29th to February 1st,* 1852.

ADDRESS TO THE AMERICAN PEOPLE.

FELLOW-CITIZENS:—The Congress of the "American Revolutionary League for Europe," herewith submit the result of their deliberations to the judgment of the people, all parties of which were represented in that body.

Earnestly resolved to find the means of terminating the desperate condition of the liberty-thirsting people of Europe, firmly convinced that the first great step to the attainment of this goal, is the cordial coöperation of all who seek it, it was for us to explore the middle ground upon which all parties could honorably and cheerfully unite their forces.

The Revolutionary Directory will not fail to detect that the objects of the League, as stated in the second article of the Constitution, were adopted in view of the difficulties arising from the distinction between the ideas of *Union* and *Platform*. We hold, that to have solved the problem at the expense of the just claims of any section of the party, thus confounding union with subjection, would have been to entirely misconceive our duty. We hold the strife of party, of opinion, of mind, as beneficial, necessary, and eternal. Freedom of mind is the first source of political aspirations, the most legitimate method of their pursuit, and the last goal of their attainment. It is the principal sphere of a revolution to protect the free contest of mind from the disturbing intervention of material forces. The points specified in that article are, therefore, not to be looked upon as a treaty of peace, but as the terms of a cessation of hostilities, under which we leave our separate camps to form a solid phalanx for the destruction of the common foe. When the common foe shall be crushed, not in appearance alone, but in reality, then the allied victors may contend for the spoils; although we entertain the confident expectation that the second struggle will be of a character vastly different from the first.

The conscious determination to achieve a revolution thorough and complete, was the warrant for our actions; and of you, sovereign people, we ask the ratification of this warrant, in the readiness with which you shall erect upon the foundation we have laid, the superstructure of an extensive, yea, a universal fusion of all revolutionary elements.

Let us then be up and doing! Our cause is noble: is sacred. The barriers that cramp the growth of active, intelligent, and high-souled nations, are to be stricken down; mankind to be restored to its humanity. Let the motto for the strife be, Union in the American Revolutionary League.

N. SCHMITT, President.

P. WAGNER, of Boston,<br>
J. R. FUERST, of Baltimore, } Vice-Presidents.

C. GOEPP, of Philadelphia,<br>
C. KING, do.<br>
LEWIS MEYER, of Boston, } Secretaries.

Willimann, of Baltimore; A. Faller, of Bridesburg; J. Fickler, A. Gregg, of London; C. Hollinger, Newark, N. J.; E. F. Loewenthal, N. Y.; H. Tiedemann, W. Rosenthal, A. H. Rosenheim, J. Eckhard, G. Leidensticker, J. Dotter, A. Pohleg, G. Kerrlein, C. F. Elwert, Nefflen, Louis Schwartzwaelder, of Philadelphia; C. Meœ?, of Philadelphia, for Lancaster; Gloss, of Richmond, Va.; S. Buchsweiler, of Brooklyn; C. A. Knoderer, of Reading; the Revolutionary Association of Easton, Pa., by the officers of the Congress.

Philadelphia, Feb. 1, 1852.

## CONSTITUTION

### OF THE AMERICAN REVOLUTIONARY LEAGUE OF EUROPE.

The American Democrats, desirous of furthering the cause of European Revolution, do hereby adopt the following organization :

ART. I.—NAME OF THE ORGANIZATION.

The name of the organization shall be "The American Revolutionary League for Europe."

ART. II.—OBJECT OF THE LEAGUE.

The object of the League shall be the radical liberalization of the European continent, for which are required

1. The overthrow of monarchy and the establishment of the Republic; because in the Republic alone can all the horrors of tyranny be prevented.

2. Direct and universal suffrage, and the recall of representatives by the majority of their constituents; because this alone secures the supremacy of the popular will in the working of popular institutions.

3. The abolition of standing armies, and inviolability of the right of the people to bear arms; because the last resource of forcible resistance is the only protection against the last device of forcible usurpation.

4. The union, for these ends, of all persons, associations, parties, and nations, for the annihilation of oppression; because, without such concerted efforts, the organized power of the tyrants is invincible.

ART. III.—MEANS.

Section 1. Agitation as well in Europe as in America.

Section 2. Accumulation of a Revolutionary fund.

Section 3. Formation of *armed organizations* desirous of entering personally into the struggle, and of preparing for it by *military exercises.*

ART. IV.—INTERNAL ORGANIZATION.

Section 1. Formation of auxiliary associations *and military corps in every city and county of the Union* where materials are found. Every revolutionary association is at liberty to prefer its own organization, and adopt its own constitution and by-laws, provided they contain the following provisions :—

I. Every member, upon his admission, must promise to assist in attaining the objects of the league, and is required to sign the constitution as well of the auxiliary association as of the league, thus binding himself to observe the behests of both. In case of withdrawal or expulsion, he shall forfeit all claim upon the property of the league.

II. Every association is at liberty to exact and collect contributions to be expended for the purposes of the association. Over and above this, every member is required to contribute to the Revolutionary fund not less than one cent per week, to be paid into a separate purse set apart for the purpose.

III. Every association upon joining the league is to report itself to the Executive Board, transmitting the constitution and by-laws, and a list of members. They are also required to submit quarter-yearly reports of their condition and prospects, the number of members, alterations in their organization, &c., and to make quarter-yearly remittances to all ordinary and extraordinary contributions to the Revolutionary fund.

IV. The executive board of the league is empowered to instruct every association to appoint emissaries, who must be commissioned by the central board, for the purpose of collecting contributions out of the associations, and of organizing new associations.

V. Every association must elect a President, Secretary, and Treasurer, who are to represent the associations in all communications with other associations, and with the central board. The Treasurers must give security for the moneys entrusted to them.

Section 2. Centralization.—For the purpose of concerted action, all revolutionary associations will unite under the management of the supreme authority of the league, and abide by their decisions as the supreme laws of the league. This supreme authority is a congress of all the revolutionary associations.

ART. V.—ORGANIZATION OF THE CONGRESS.

Section 1. Every association numbering not less than ten, and not more than fifty members, is entitled to one representative.

Section 2. Associations numbering more than fifty members are entitled to an additional representative for every additional 100 members, and for every fraction remaining over.

Section 3. Two or more associations, each numbering under fifty members, are at liberty to unite in sending a delegate.

Section 4. Every delegate must be furnished with credentials in writing, stating the number of his constituents.

Section 5. A majority of Congress is competent to decide upon the admission of a delegate.

Section 6. No compensation for loss of time is to be allowed any delegate. Every association is left to adjust all questions of mileage with its delegate.

Section 7. Every Congress is to fix the time and place of meeting of the next succeeding Congress.

Section 8. They shall transact business in the following order.

I. Reading and adoption of the minutes.

II. Reception and reference of memorials, letters, &c.

III. Reports of Committees.

IV. Order of the day.

V. Designation of the order of the day for the succeeding sessions.

Section 9. The jurisdiction of Congress extends over all the affairs of the League, and all amendments or alterations of this Constitution.

### ART. VI.—ORGANIZATION OF THE EXECUTIVE BOARD.

Section 1. The Board.

I. In the recess between one session of Congress and another, the business of the League shall be entrusted to an Executive Board.

II. The Board consists of seven members.

III. They are elected by Congress.

IV. The residence of the Board is to be determined by Congress.

Section 2. Method of activity of the Board.

I. In the principal town of every State there shall be established a State Committee, to consist of the Executive Board of the Revolutionary Association there located. If there are several Revolutionary Associations in such principal town, they elect the State Committee between them.

II. The duty of the State Committee shall be to receive the communications of the Board, and transmit them to the several Associations, and to transmit the proposals of Associations to the Board, to establish new Associations, and generally to make all possible exertions in furtherance of the cause in the State assigned to its care.

Section 3. The Revolutionary Fund.

I. The Revolutionary Fund is under the management of the Board.

II. It consists of contributions of individuals and associations.

III. The Treasurer of the Board must give security for the moneys entrusted to his keeping.

IV. When the funds collected exceed $100 in amount, they are to be invested in good security, bearing interest.

Section 4. Jurisdiction of the Board.

I. The functions of the Board are administrative and executive. Its duties are to execute the objects stated in Art. II, by the means specified in Art. III. of this Constitution.

II. During the session of Congress, its authority is confined to the execution of the resolutions of that body.

III. As soon as Congress has assembled and organized, the Board are to transmit a message, containing a report of all events of importance that have taken place in the League since the last session of Congress; a general review of the condition of the various associations, and the number of their members; of the accounts and of the funds in hand. If required, it is also the duty of the Board to submit to the inspection of Congress all documents in its possession, and to call for information, so far as is in their power.

Section 5. The Political Committee.

I. The Board is to maintain the most intimate relations with a Political Committee.

II. The Political Committee consists of three members, to be elected by the next Congress.

III. The Committee has unrestricted powers, in connection with the revolutionary representatives of other nationalities, to take all necessary steps in support of the European revolution.

IV. The Committee is represented by a headman, in a central European Committee, to consist of the Chiefs of all the revolutionary national Committees.

V. The Political Committee is responsible to Congress.

At the close of the congressional sittings, Messrs. Goegg and Fickler, the delegates and plenipotentiaries of the Agitation Society in London, publicly declared—"That the Agitation Society is from henceforth dissolved, and that its members join the League now established on the free-soil of America."

Congress resolved to publish this declaration; and, further to convoke the next Congress of the American Revolutionary League at New York, on Monday, the 17th of May, 1852, when the attendance, by representation, of all the friends of the cause is invited.

Whether the session of *Congress* convoked in the last paragraph was held or not, is unknown. If held, it was held in *secret*. The numerous *military organizations* and *secret political societies*, composed entirely of foreigners, which have been created in various parts of the country during the last few years, afford strong evidence of the fact that this seditious league is, and has been, in active operation. No military organizations of foreigners should be permitted in the United States.

## GOVERNOR RAYMOND AND THE IRISH LEAGUE.

One of the surest evidences of the correctness of a principle is to be found in the involuntary or accidental approval of that principle by men who profess to be its opponents. Thus we find many of the leading journalists of the country, men who oppose, on political grounds, as partisans, the whole American movement, at times inadvertently preaching its doctrines, sustaining its position and measures, and acknowledging the existence of those grievances and evils which it is striving to eradicate.

As a case in point, the *New York Times* may be cited. The *Times* is edited by the Hon. Henry J. Raymond, Lieut.-Governor of the State of New York, a gentleman of youth and talent, and a warm supporter of the policy of Mr. Seward. Mr. Raymond was a *whig* in his politics during the palmy days of that party, but as the great lights of the party, one by one, went out, and the gloom of night seemed to be settling over its history, Mr. Raymond fell into the ranks of those who seized upon the northern wing, and by holding aloft the old banner, attempted to lead it *en masse*, name and all, into a sectional organization. The new party struggled a long time in its efforts to retain the whig name and *prestige*; long enough, indeed, to win over many into its net, but being hard pressed by the true men of the old whig party, and finally compelled to lay down the stolen standard, it seized upon and usurped another, equally inappropriate, and adopted the name of "Republican."

Mr. Raymond is a leader in this mis-called *Republican* party, and a decided opponent of the American policy. Yet we find the following article, showing distinctly the necessity of that policy, and admitting, in part, the causes which led to its adoption, in the columns of his paper. When the "Irish League," which had been formed for the purpose of wresting Ireland "from the grasp of England," by invasion and revolution, held its convention in the city of New York, during the autumn of 1855, the *Times* frankly deprecated and ridiculed the whole movement. This brought forth a letter to the editor complaining of the course pursued by his paper in the matter. To that letter Mr. Raymond replied through the columns of the *Times*, and from that reply we make the following extract :—

"The *people* of Ireland have a perfect right to rebel against the government which they think oppresses them, and to ovethrow it if they are able; but the Irish *in America* are not the people of Ireland. They have no right to a voice in its government, nor are they sufferers from its oppression. If they desired to reform it they should have stayed there. As subjects of the British rule in Ireland they would have had a right to rebel against it; but as American citizens they have simply nothing at all to do with it. If a revolution should be started in Ireland they would have a right to sympathize with it, and divesting themselves of their American citizenship, to go there and take a part in it; but if they did so they would forfeit all claims to American protection, and would subject themselves to all the hazards of the enterprise.

"But the Irish who come to live in America, who become citizens of the United States, and thus clothed with the power of self-government which all American citizens possess, are bound to discharge all the duties and conform to all the obligations of American citizenship; and, as they have renounced allegiance to every other Government, they have no more right to interfere with any other than have the native citizens of the United States. Every citizen has the right of expatriation; but, while the Irish remain in America, they have no right to set on foot hostile operations against any Government with which we are at peace. Their duty is to *become Americans*, to study the institutions of the country, to fit themselves for the discharge of the duties which American citizenship imposes. If they had done this more generally; *if they had acted here more uniformly as Americans and not as Irishmen; if they had been less clannish, less anxious to perpetuate here their foreign habits and feelings, and more ready to adapt their conduct to their new relations, they would have given no occasion for the political movements which are now so rife and so strong against them.*

"We submit that our correspondent would do his countrymen in America a much better service by urging them to become more thorough *Americans*, in spirit and in conduct, than by feeding their resentments against the Government from whose authority they have escaped, and perpetuating the passions which made them so wretched and so helpless at home."

In this article Governor Raymond sunk the politician, and stood forth *himself*. There is nothing meretricious or equivocal in his position. He admits, to a given extent, the causes which brought the American Party into existence, and in deprecating those causes, he admits virtually the necessity of measures to abate them.

At Cincinnati, Ohio, a branch of this organization of Irish *fillibusters* was so unfortunate as to fall into the hands of the authorities; some of the leading parties in the movement were arrested and brought to trial on a charge of violating the neutrality laws of the United States, and on that trial the council for the prosecution produced the following address, which he said was issued by the society of which the prisoners were members.

ADDRESS OF THE ROBERT EMMETT BRANCH OF THE IRISH EMIGRANT AID SOCIETY OF OHIO, TO THE IRISHMEN OF THE BUCKEYE STATE.

FELLOW EXILES: The sun of Ireland's independence, so long obscured by the clouds of adversity, is bursting through the darkness of centuries, and may soon shine in splendor over a liberated nation! For ages our fathers fought and bled in vain—for centuries they suffered the penalties of subjection to the stranger, and died in the confident hope that the men of succeeding ages would avenge their wrongs and liberate the nation from the oppression of the Anglo-Norman robber.

The day for which they sighed and prayed has come, and the spirits of our martyred dead call on us from above, to blot out the shame of centuries, and lift our dear old nation up to happiness and freedom. The voice of the exiled Celt has gone forth from the bay of Boston, to cheer the drooping, to stimulate the slothful, and unite all Irishmen in one grand rally for the freedom of Ireland! Shall we, then, the Irish inhabitants of the West, hold back in such an hour, and in such a cause? Shall the opportune moment be lost, and the day that God gives us for vengeance be spent in doubt and fear?

No! by the faith of our race, by the bones of our insulted dead! by the memory of Clintarf! by the massacre of Mullaghmart and Tara! by the recollection of the starved millions of '46 and '47! by the glorious deeds of Wexford and Vinegar Hill!

by the ruthless perfidy of the Saxon! by the untimely death of Tone and Fitzgerald! and the uninscribed tomb of Emmett, vengeance is ours, and we shall repay!

Awake, then, Irishmen of Ohio! and to the rescue. The day of England's tribulation is now—the withering breath of an angry God is upon her, scourging her for the robberies, the murders, the massacres of ages, and dissolving her power like snow before the warm sun! With the opportunity presented, and freedom before us, shall we, the exiled sons of a crushed and lacerated mother, remain for ever helots of every people who wish to put the yoke upon our necks, toil through reproach and opprobrium, in the rags of servitude, and die with slavery's fetters on our limbs, without an effort to efface the black and bitter memory of the past? Ireland speaks to us through the Massachusetts convention. Shall we not heed her call, and organize as she directs? Cincinnati has already adopted the Massachusetts platform and plan of action, and is duly authorized to organize the State of Ohio! The Robert Emmett Club of Cincinnati, therefore, calls on you, Irishmen, to organize clubs in every city, town, and village in the State, on the above plan, and every necessary information will be furnished you here, on application to our secretary. When the State is thus organized into clubs, a State convention will be called, and a State directory elected, who shall manage the funds and other business of the society.

Irishmen, let no man fail and falter now. The work is light if action be united, and every man do his duty.

Oh! how long have we wept over the tale of sorrow, that weekly comes to us from our own Innisfail, and how ardently we watched for any movement that would cast a ray of hope across the polluted waters of Irish politics; but never, in our most ardent imaginings, and loftiest dreaming, did we hope for such a grand opportunity as the God of nations gives this day to the land of our love. Let us, then, if we are men, prepare to accept the boon, and grasp the liberty of Ireland with a strong and armed hand. The man who now holds back, was made for a slave, and deserves the coward's fate.

The men of Massachusetts have set a noble example, one worthy of imitation by every State in the Union, and be assured that nothing will give the true friends of the cause such buoyant hopes as to find that Ohio is firm in the ranks of Irish patriotism.

Let each man's motto be, to cultivate the friendship of his neighbor, to be sober, prudent, and hopeful, and we cannot fail

"To win the fight that must be won,
The freedom of our land, which they so well begun."

Signed in behalf of the Club.

Daniel Conahan, *President.*
Edward Kenifeck, *Secretary.*

Cincinnati, *Sept.* 27, 1855.

The following was also read by the learned counsel as the oath taken by the members at the time of their initiation into the Society.

THE OATH.

"In the awful presence of God, I do voluntarily declare and promise that I shall use my endeavors to form a brotherhood amongst Irishmen of all persuasions for to uproot and overthrow English government in Ireland; and I furthermore declare that neither hopes, fears, rewards nor punishments, shall ever induce me to make known any of the secrets of this Order. To all this I most solemnly pledge my most sacred honor."

## FOREIGN PAUPERS AND CRIMINALS

### SENT TO THE UNITED STATES BY THEIR GOVERNMENTS.

The immense aggregate of European paupers and criminals found in the United States, is readily traced to a system by which many of the communities, and even some of the States of Europe have relieved themselves of those incumbrances at the expense of the American people. In proof of this it is only necessary to call the reader's attention to the following correspondence. The communications were made to the United States Consul at Leipsic, in reply to certain inquiries addressed by him to the several emigration societies, and by the Consul forwarded to the Mayor of New York. It will be seen also that the agitation of the subject has extorted a promise to refrain from such practices hereafter.

*To the Consul of the United States of North America, Dr. J. G. Flügel, at Leipsic.*

LEIPSIC, June 4, 1855.

We feel honored in giving you the following answer to various questions which you put to us, in relation to the emigration from the Kingdom of Saxony.

*It cannot be denied that for some time the Governments of some States, and also the authorities of several communities have deemed it convenient to free themselves from their paupers by shipping them to the United States. It is also notorious that criminals, after having suffered punishment, have, in the same manner, been transported to the United States, with a view to free the community of them forever.* In consequence of this a system of economy was adopted productive of unavoidable evils, as they (the emigrants) were supplied with merely money sufficient for the payment of their passages, and hence on their arrival at distant ports, being destitute of all means of support, they were compelled immediately to apply for aid and were therefore regarded as very unwelcome visitors.

The practices are certainly as inhuman as they are impudent, but the Government of Saxony has not at any time had recourse to this system of economy. We have been thoroughly acquainted with the emigration affairs of Germany for the last eight years, during which time not a single case which could implicate the Kingdom of Saxony in such action has ever come within our knowledge. On the contrary it is a subject of regret to us that with very few exceptions the greater part of those who emigrate from Saxony, are composed chiefly of the wealthier class of our people, and our best mechanics. We, therefore, instead of gaining, are put to a loss of millions of dollars, and of the best portion of our honest and most valuable citizens.

As it appears the German emigration to the United States is becoming too powerful and troublesome, you may assure the American authorities that a speedy change in this respect is unavoidable. The decrease of emigration in general, and to North America in particular, during the last year, has become so apparent that we are warranted in asserting that the emigration of this year will not be half so numerous as that of last year. The seaports present quite a destitute appearance at the usual time of emigration; but the accounts which we receive, from all the interior parts of Germany, of the great change in emigration, is still more remarkable. Hundreds of thousands who intended to emigrate have entirely abandoned the notion. Most respectfully, the Directors of the National Society of German Emigration.

A. Schultze.

*To the Consul of the United States, Dr. Flügel.*

Leipsic, June 9, 1855.

I beg leave to add a few remarks to the subject of our verbal conversation. It cannot be denied that European Governments and Principalities have been in the practice of freeing themselves from their paupers and even of their more or less guilty criminals by sending them to America and paying the cost of their voyage to the seaports and the passage from thence to America, without making provision for the wants of this unhappy class of people to enable them to commence an honest trade.

Without any means of support they become a burden to the authorities abroad, and it is to be wondered at that measures have not ere this been taken to put a stop to this practice.

But I am happy to state that our Fatherland, Saxony, is free from such an imputation. The Emigrants from here were all powerful, healthy, and industrious people, supplied with means, yes, even wealthy, such as I could see leave here only with a feeling of sadness, and such as America will receive with open arms.

For myself I have never taken part in the above-numbered affairs, and would not give my sanction to them. Accept the assurance of my highest esteem.

Yours,

GEORGE SCHOERIBERG,

General Agent for the German Emigration Society.

This frank official acknowledgment that the governments, principalities, and communes of certain portions of Europe have used the United States as a receptacle for the dregs and offscourings of their societies, and that they have systematically relieved themselves of the burden of pauperism and crime by transferring those ingredients unceremoniously upon our shores, will doubtless bring conviction to the minds of those who have been skeptical, and produce a more general concert in the adoption of measures to prevent in the future so flagrant an abuse of American hospitality.

But this exposition, startling as it may be, has been excelled in effrontery by the new position assumed by the Government of Wurtemberg. It will be seen by the following preamble and resolution adopted by that Government (a copy of which was transmitted to the German Emigration Society of New York, in the month of November, 1855), that the government not only claims the right to impose its refuse population upon us, but *actually denies the right of the United States* to relieve themselves by sending the objectionable persons home again.

The following exhibits the position taken by the Kingdom of Wurtemberg in this matter.

"*Whereas*, It has repeatedly occurred that German emigrants to America, and among them natives of Wurtemberg who desired to return home on account of sickness, or incapacity to labor, have been forwarded to this country by the German Emigration Society of New York, and

"*Whereas*, It is desirable that those who have once emigrated to America, *and especially those who have been transported thither at the expense of the State or the Communes*, and are unable, whether or not it be from any fault of their own, to earn their subsistence, should not return here, to be a burden to the State or the Commune (*which in that case will have defrayed the expenses of their journey in vain*): and

"*Whereas*, The American authorities *are scarcely authorized* to send back those who, having once been admitted to the country, cannot earn their subsistence in America, and

"*Whereas*, It is much less the business of the German Emigration Society of New York to promote the return of such individuals; therefore

"*Resolved*, That necessary steps are to be taken to prevent their transportation back to this country.

While we may but smile at the ludicrous and imbecile threat implied in this laconic resolve, we may nevertheless learn from it something of the tone of sentiment prevailing in Germany on this subject. The petty State Governments of the Germanic confederation have so long practised this species of imposture with impunity, that it has at length come to be regarded as a legitimate prerogative, and *measures are to be taken to enforce it!* This movement on the part of the Government of Wurtemberg is rendered the more racy and interesting from the fact that at the time of its occurrence the Commissioners of Emigration for the city of New York alone, were in debt in the sum of *sixty-three thousand, and thirty-one dollars and seven cents*, incurred in the maintenance of *European paupers!*—See the report of the Commissioners for the year ending December 31st, 1855.

## DESECRATION OF THE SABBATH.

In the chapter appropriated to the subject of "Immigration," allusion is made to that class of immigrants which may be denominated infidels, or irreligionists—men who, having no God of their own, cannot endure that others should worship theirs—men who look upon every religious ceremony as a senseless, unmeaning formula—who regard the time set apart for religious worship as a restraint upon their licentious desires, and who, consequently, demand the total abrogation of the Sabbath, and the repeal of all religious observances.

The manner in which these men spend their time, and inoculate their moral poison in the youthful minds of Sabbath-observing, Christian communities in the United States, cannot be realized by those who reside in localities remote from the cities or villages where they congregate. Their disregard of all religious observance may be seen, it is true, in individual cases, wherever one or more of them are to be found; but for that audacious disregard of all the decencies of religion and morality which is certain to follow in the wake of infidelity, we must turn our eyes to those localities where accumulative numbers give encouragement to their excesses, and where their *political* influence is sufficient to overawe the venal authorities.

Therefore I deem it appropriate to introduce here the description of a single Sabbath scene in the city of New York. I do so in order that our countrymen in the peaceful rural districts, those who are yet away from the jargon of many tongues, may see the encroachment already made upon our moral and religious habits and customs, and be able to realize the deleterious influences of this class of immigrants upon our national character and morals. In doing this I do not intend to place myself in a position to be doubted or misrepresented. I will not give even my own impression, but state simply the facts as related by one of these very people—the editor of a German paper in the city of New York. The account is given in a translation from the columns of the "STAATS-ZEITUNG," a newspaper, published by a German, in the *German language*, and for the German people in the United States. The translation was made for the *New York Express*, and first published in the columns of that paper. The occasion, it is true, was an unusual one, being the anniversary of what is called the German *Sängerfest*, but the scenes depicted are enacted weekly, in miniature, of a Sunday evening, in the *lager-bier* saloons of a great city. The following is the account as translated from German authority, and is to be found in the *Staats-Zeitung* of June 25th, 1855.

### THE SÆNGERFEST.

Yesterday (Sunday) was the scene of great hilarity—though the sky was dull and morose, and annoyed us from time to time with rain. But the German quarters were full of life and gaiety. The singers adorned with ribbons loitered in the streets, and recalled in the heart of every German the most joyous emotions. Friends and acquaintances of olden times met unexpectedly together—greeting each other, and talking of "auld lang syne," (our version,)—the Present and the Future,—the sorrows which have befallen them, and the hopes which they cherish, all *over lager-bier*. In the morning they looked over their cups of coffee, with anxiety to the sky—and to its wrinkle-covered forehead, as all now were afraid of losing any of the enjoyments of this occasion, devoted to social amusement. In the evening the Germans passed into the German quarters, from the streets, and in them, they were very much amused. *From divers lager-bier-saloons, issued the noise of hilarity, songs, sounds of the harp, &c.*, and the girls peeped through the doors to see the handsome singers that were there. In one word *Gotham had a holiday.*

At 9 o'clock the rehearsal began, and the singers were numerous. We admired Mr. Bergmann's tact in conducting at Head Quarters, who has not an equal in the United States. * * * * On Sunday evening, too, the Singing Societies amused themselves in the circles of their friends, at different places. We went first to the Quarter of the "Arion,"—at 5 o'clock (at Winken's) to which we were invited, where we found every thing *in dulce jubilo* (in sweet hilarity). In the saloon of the Brewery (House) sat the Arions (der Tòne Meister), and up stairs, in the second story, the Turners amused themselves with their friends. After a short, sober conversation, we found among the Philadelphia guests, many good people, among whom we became acquainted with two Natives (Americans)—and we went, adorned with Red Republican Turner badges, up to the higher regions, and we were amused with oration, song, declamation, *and lager-bier*. Among the orators, we must mention Mr. Schlüter (who seems to have made quite a speech). In consideration that our conversation was exhausted, and that down-town higher duties commanded, for the next two days, all the strength of our craft, the joyous assembly of the Upper and Lower House dispersed, at sunset.

### TURTLE BAY BREWERY PARK.

The Teutonia Männerchor had for guests here the Baltimore Liederkranz, and the "Virginia" from Richmond, and *all devoted to hilarity and mirth*.—The German National Songs were sung in choir, and all were enraptured who witnessed these scenes.

### TO HOBOKEN,

—there was a march in the afternoon of the Societies "Sängerrunde," the "Orpheus," with the "Sicilians" from Philadelphia, and the "Quartette Club" from Albany.

They went to Vauxhall Garden, and here commenced, IN SPITE OF THE *Sunday Law, joyous life, loud song*, and the ringing *of the glasses*.—The different Societies alternated their songs, but the "Sängerrunde" was the best of them. "The Confession," "Up Comrades," "The world is so beautiful," were sung. * * We heard from the stranger singers, Mendelssohn's beautiful composition, "Who has built for thee this beautiful wood," admirably executed. * * After a delightful afternoon, the Society broke up at 8 o'clock. Herr Hartung contributed to the enjoyment *by his excellent lager-bier*.

### STATEN ISLAND.

After the "Liederkranz" with its guests from Boston and Hartford, had partaken in Pythagoras Hall, an excellent dinner, they all proceeded about 3 o'clock to the Staten Island Ferry—to go to Pythagoras Garden on that Island. In consequence of the bad weather only half of the 1500 tickets, which the Society had kept for friends and guests, were used. * * When the singers sang the first song on the boat, there was immediate quiet among the Americans, and when the last echo died on the waves, every countenance expressed a deep emotion. * * An American assured the reporter he had never known before what an infinite magic there was in a Mannerchoir. On the boat many songs were sang in spite of the unfavorable weather—*and the greatest hilarity prevailed.* * * The singers went to the garden where they spent the afternoon in social entertainment, and in singing. The presence of the singers had attracted *a great many natives*, and the tender feeling of the *American ladies* could not comprehend how these lager-beer drinking foreigners could sing so excellent, and such high poetic songs—and many whispered, that "*Pop goes the Weasel*," and "*O carry me back to old Virginia*, were inferior to these *Dutch songs*. A German, who thus spent the afternoon, in this hilarity of singers, may in his own breast, have well felt, that he was once more at home. * * The singers remained till 8 o'clock. In consequence of the great crowd on the boat, no songs were sung on their return, &c., &c.

It will be perceived that the German editor felicitates himself upon the influence which these infidel practices had upon *the natives*, and the *American ladies* who were present on board the Staten Island boat. Certainly such practices are seductive with the youthful or indifferent mind. It requires the strongest convictions of religious and moral duty to resist them, and hence the danger of their wicked example upon our country, our customs, and our institutions. Imported infidelity, if not the greatest, is certainly not the least of the foreign influences against which the friends of rational liberty should be forewarned and fore-armed.

## THE KENSINGTON MASSACRE.

### PHILADELPHIA.

From the accounts of this event, published at the time, we learn the following facts—

A meeting of Americans was called on the 3d of May 1844 for the purpose of considering the expediency of amending the Naturalization laws. This meeting was broken up, and dispersed by a band of Irishmen who assailed it with stones and bludgeons.

An adjourned meeting was held on the 6th of May at the same place. Upon this meeting was opened a fire "with fowling-pieces, rifles, and muskets, from roofs, windows, loop-holes, yards, and alleys of the houses in front, which was kept up without intermission until the ground was vacated by the American Republican party." During this fire young Shiffler was killed, and eleven others wounded.

This outrage called forth a spontaneous meeting of the citizens, which was held on the 7th in the State House yard, where appropriate resolutions were passed, after which it was determined to adjourn to Kensington (the scene of the former outrages) with the view to re-assert the constitutional right of the people, peaceably to assemble for the discussion of any subject of public interest. The assembly immediately proceeded to the spot of the former day's proceedings, and while in the act of raising the American flag, the American Republicans were again fired at from the direction of the Hibernian hose-house. A rush was then made toward the house, when a volley of musketry was poured into the meeting. John Wesley Rhinedollar, a young man, was shot through the back and killed upon the spot, and at least a half dozen others were wounded. A destructive fire was now kept up without intermission from the houses adjoining and the rear of the hose-house, from persons who were entirely concealed from view.

During the dreadful fire of their assailants, eight Native Americans were killed and about forty wounded.

The following extracts from the charge of Judge King, to the Jury, on the trial of one of the murderers, presents a brief and impartial view of the whole subject.

EXTRACTS FROM JUDGE KING'S CHARGE, IN THE CASE OF JOHN DALY,

*Convicted of Riot and Murder.*

OYER AND TERMINER, SEPTEMBER 18, 1844.

Before Judges King, Jones, and Parsons.

The meeting of the 3d of May, 1844, was called for the purpose of considering the expediency of a proposed alteration of the laws of the United States, in reference to the naturalization of foreigners, and promoting the ends and objects of the association known as the Native American Party. The meeting was organized, and the officers being placed on a platform erected for the purpose, Mr. S. R. Kramer commenced an address, but was interrupted by a large number of persons opposed to the objects of the meeting, among whom this defendant was particularly prominent. A scene of confusion arose, and shortly after the opponents of this meeting rushed forward, pulled down the platform, and dispersed the meeting. To this violence the meeting offered no resistance, preferring to submit to the aggression rather than resort to a forcible maintenance of their rights. It was, however, agreed to by some that an adjourned meeting for the same purpose should be held on Monday, the 6th of May, at 4 o'clock in the afternoon, at the same place.

If the call of the meeting of the 3d of May was addressed exclusively to persons favorable to its objects, the interference of individuals hostile to its proceedings, and the breaking up and dispersion of the meeting by them, was a great outrage on the rights of those who called it. It was a riot of a flagrant kind. A body of citizens, having in view a constitutional, a legal purpose, have the right, peaceably and quietly to assemble together, for its consideration and discussion. Any attempt by another body of citizens opposed to the objects of the assembly, to interrupt and disperse it, is not to be tolerated. In this instance it has led to the long train of riots, murders, and arson, which have disgraced our city, and shaken the foundation of social order.

* * * * * * * * *

The Attorney General insists, that the whole case shows an original and formed design, in the defendant and his associates, to disperse any meeting having for its object that contemplated by the meeting of Friday, the 3d of May, and to destroy and kill those concerned in it, if their object could be accomplished in no other way. He insists that the whole conduct of Daly and his associates manifest that such was their intention, and that the affair of the hose-house was a mere pretext to cover a deeper and deadlier design. If you should believe that the arming and array in the vicinity of the market was really with this diabolical motive, and that the slaying of the deceased and all others who fell on that day, was the product of such a design, and done in consummation of it, then all those concerned in this deed, principals, aiders, and abettors, are guilty of murder in the first degree.

## PAUPERISM AND CRIME.

By the United States census of 1850, we find the free populatiou of the country, to be as follows:

| | |
|---|---|
| Native | 17,737,578 |
| Foreign | 2,210,839 |
| Unknown | 039,154 |
| Total | 19,987,571 |

The following table, copied from the census returns, shows the total number of paupers supported by each State during the year ending June 1st, 1850.

| States. | Native. | Foreign. | Total. |
|---|---|---|---|
| Maine | 4,553 | 950 | 5,503 |
| New Hampshire | 2,853 | 747 | 3,600 |
| Vermont | 2,043 | 1,611 | 3,654 |
| Massachusetts | 6,530 | 9,247 | 15,777 |
| Rhode Island | 1,115 | 1,445 | 2,560 |
| Connecticut | 1,872 | 465 | 2,337 |
| New York | 19,275 | 40,580 | 59,855 |
| New Jersey | 1,016 | 576 | 2,092 |
| Pennsylvania | 5,898 | 5,653 | 11,551 |
| Delaware | 569 | 128 | 697 |
| Maryland | 2,591 | 1,903 | 4,494 |
| Virginia | 4,933 | 185 | 5,118 |
| North Carolina | 1,913 | 18 | 1,931 |
| South Carolina | 1,313 | 329 | 1,642 |
| Georgia | 978 | 58 | 1,036 |
| Florida | 64 | 12 | 76 |
| Alabama | 352 | 11 | 363 |
| Mississippi | 248 | 12 | 260 |
| Louisiana | 133 | 290 | 423 |
| Texas | 7 | .... | 7 |
| Arkansas | 97 | 8 | 105 |
| Tennessee | 994 | 11 | 1,005 |
| Kentucky | 971 | 155 | 1,126 |
| Ohio | 1,904 | 609 | 2,513 |
| Michigan | 649 | 541 | 1,190 |
| Indiana | 860 | 322 | 1,182 |
| Illinois | 386 | 411 | 797 |
| Missouri | 1,248 | 1,729 | 2,977 |
| Iowa | 100 | 35 | 135 |
| Wisconsin | 169 | 497 | 666 |
| Aggregate | 66,434 | 68,538 | 134,972 |

By the above table, we find that the proportion of foreign paupers in the United States, during the year ending June 1st, 1850, was *over three per cent* of the foreign population; whereas that of the native paupers (including colored persons) was less than *one-third of one per cent* of the native population. The proportion being about *ten foreigners* to *one American*, according to their respective populations.

The following statistics of crime are also reported in the United States census of the same year.

"CRIME.—The statistics of crime form a subject of our investigation. From the returns, it appears that the whole number of persons convicted of crime in the United States, for the year ending the first day of June 1850, was about 27,000: of these, 13,000 were native, and 14,000 foreign born."

The Report adds,

"It will be borne in mind that the native prisoners include colored convicts, the number of whom it is impossible to state, as time has not sufficed to admit of the more particular separation into classes other than native and foreign. Our criminal statistics, when fully understood, will present many subjects for reflection, and open a wide and interesting field for the study of the Christian, moralist, and statesman."

## NEW PLATFORM OF THE AMERICAN PARTY.

Owing to the discontent manifested in the Northern States, in consequence of the adoption of the 12th section of the platform of the American Party, at the Convention in June, 1855 (as published in the body of this work); and also in consequence of a like discontent manifested in some portions of the South respecting the 8th section of the same platform—it was deemed proper that a special National Convention should be held, with a view of making such alterations as should render the platform more generally acceptable, and thereby effect a harmonious action of the Party throughout the Union.

This Convention assembled on the 18th of February, 1856, at Philadelphia, and the result of its deliberations was the adoption of the following, in lieu of the platform adopted in June, 1855. Our work being in press, we have barely time to drop the new platform into the last page of the Appendix, without a word of note or comment.

### PLATFORM OF THE AMERICAN PARTY, ADOPTED AT THE SESSION OF THE NATIONAL COUNCIL, FEBRUARY 21st, 1856.

1st. An humble acknowledgment to the Supreme Being, for His protecting care vouchsafed to our fathers in their successful Revolutionary struggle, and hitherto manifested to us, their descendants, in the preservation of the liberties, the independence, and the Union of these States.

2d. The perpetuation of the Federal Union, as the palladium of our civil and religious liberties, and the only sure bulwark of American Independence.

3d. *Americans must rule America*, and to this end, *native*-born citizens should be selected for all State, Federal, and municipal offices or government employment, in preference to all others: nevertheless,

4th. Persons born of American parents residing temporarily abroad, should be entitled to all the rights of native-born citizens; but

5th. No person should be selected for political station (whether of native or foreign birth), who recognizes any allegiance or obligation of any description to any foreign prince, potentate, or power, or who refuses to recognize the Federal and State constitutions (each within its sphere) as paramount to all other laws, as rules to political action.

6th. The unqualified recognition and maintenance of the reserved rights of the several States, and the cultivation of harmony and fraternal good-will between the citizens of the several States, and to this end, non-interference by Congress with questions appertaining solely to the individual States, and non-intervention by each State with the affairs of any other State.

7th. The recognition of the right of the native-born and naturalized citizens of the United States, permanently residing in any Territory thereof, to frame their constitution and laws, and to regulate their domestic and social affairs in their own mode, subject only to the provisions of the Federal Constitution, with the privilege of admission into the Union, whenever they have the requisite population for one Representative in Congress. *Provided always*, that none but those who are citizens of the United States, under the Constitution and laws thereof, and who have a fixed residence in any such Territory, ought to participate in the formation of the constitution, or in the enactment of laws for said Territory or State.

8th. An enforcement of the principle that no State or Territory ought to admit others than citizens of the United States to the right of suffrage, or of holding political office.

9th. A change in the laws of naturalization, making a continued residence of twenty-one years, of all not hereinbefore provided for, an indispensable requisite for citizenship hereafter, and excluding all paupers, and persons convicted of crime, from landing upon our shores; but no interference with the vested rights of foreigners.

10th. Opposition to any union between Church and State; no interference with religious faith or worship, and no test oaths for office.

11th. Free and thorough investigation into any and all alleged abuses of public functionaries, and a strict economy in public expenditures.

12th. The maintenance and enforcement of all laws constitutionally enacted, until said laws shall be repealed, or shall be declared null and void by competent judicial authority.

13th. Opposition to the reckless and unwise policy of the present administration in the general management of our national affairs, and more especially as shown in removing "Americans" (by designation) and conservatives in principle, from office, and placing foreigners and ultraists in their places; as shown in a truckling subserviency to the stronger, and an insolent and cowardly bravado towards the weaker powers; as shown in re-opening sectional agitation, by the repeal of the Missouri Compromise; as shown in granting to unnaturalized foreigners the right of suffrage in Kansas and Nebraska; as shown in its vacillating course on the Kansas and Nebraska question; as shown in the corruptions which pervade some of the departments of the government; as shown in disgracing meritorious naval officers through prejudice or caprice; and as shown in the blundering mismanagement of our foreign relations.

14th. Therefore, to remedy existing evils, and prevent the disastrous consequences otherwise resulting therefrom, we would build up the "American Party" upon the principles hereinbefore stated.

15th. That each State Council shall have authority to amend their several constitutions, so as to abolish the several degrees, and institute a pledge of honor, instead of other obligations, for fellowship and admission into the party.

16th. A free and open discussion of all political principles embraced in our platform.

THE END.

W. H. TINSON, Printer and Stereotyper, 24 Beekman Street, N. Y.